THE NEW

CLARENDON SHAKESPEARE

Under the general editorship of

R. E. C. HOUGHTON, M.A.

Fellow and Tutor of St. Peter's Hall
Lecturer in English Literature, Oriel College, Oxford

Edited by

Antony and Cleopatra	R. E. C. HOUGHTON
As You Like It	ISABEL J. BISSON
Coriolanus	B. H. KEMBALL-COOK
Hamlet	GEORGE RYLANDS
Henry IV, Part I	F. A. B. NEWMAN
Henry IV, Part II	WILLIAM R. RUTLAND
Henry V	R. F. W. FLETCHER
Julius Caesar	R. E. C. HOUGHTON
King Lear	R. E. C. HOUGHTON
Macbeth	BERNARD GROOM
Merchant of Venice	R. F. W. FLETCHER
Midsummer Night's Dream	F. C. HORWOOD
Much Ado about Nothing	PHILIP WAYNE
Richard II	J. M. LOTHIAN
Romeo and Juliet	R. E. C. HOUGHTON
The Tempest	J. R. SUTHERLAND
Twelfth Night	J. C. DENT
The Winter's Tale	S. L. BETHELL

THE NEW CLARENDON SHAKESPEARE

KING LEAR

Edited by

RALPH E. C. HOUGHTON, M.A.

Fellow and Tutor of St. Peter's Hall
sometime Lecturer of Oriel College, Oxford

OXFORD
AT THE CLARENDON PRESS

Oxford University Press, Amen House, London E.C.4

GLASGOW NEW YORK TORONTO MELBOURNE WELLINGTON
BOMBAY CALCUTTA MADRAS KARACHI LAHORE DACCA
CAPE TOWN SALISBURY NAIROBI IBADAN ACCRA
KUALA LUMPUR HONG KONG

FIRST PUBLISHED 1957
REPRINTED WITH CORRECTIONS 1959, 1960, 1963

PRINTED IN GREAT BRITAIN
AT THE UNIVERSITY PRESS, OXFORD
BY VIVIAN RIDLER
PRINTER TO THE UNIVERSITY

PREFACE

THE *New Clarendon Shakespeare* aims primarily at presenting the text in such a way that it can be easily read and understood. The language of Shakespeare presents considerable difficulties to the beginner, difficulties which are constantly overlooked by readers familiar with the plays. But the answers of examination candidates, even at the university stage, often reveal unexpected ignorance of common Elizabethan usage and vocabulary. In this edition, therefore, the main emphasis has been placed on the interpretation of words and phrases, rather than on such linguistic matter as received much space in the old Clarendon Press editions of Clark and Wright. The notes have been divided, short glosses being placed below the text, while the more difficult passages are reserved for the commentary at the end. The latter, in the introductions to each scene and in the notes on individual lines, also gives full attention to points of literary and dramatic interest which have rightly come to the fore in modern teaching of English literature. Discussion of the true text and a few other more difficult notes are printed in smaller type within square brackets. The commentary and the introduction are supplemented by a substantial selection from the best criticism of the play, both old and new: it is the belief of the General Editor that students can best be taught to criticize by the provision of material which they can use as a starting-point as well as a model.

It may be assumed that students approaching *King Lear* have already read one or more plays of Shakespeare. In this edition, therefore, appendixes dealing with the life of Shakespeare, the language of Shakespeare, and with Shakespearean blank verse have been omitted to make way for other matter: they will be found in most other volumes of the *New Clarendon Shakespeare*. Many of the end-notes in this volume also assume that the users will be of sixth form or university status; but care has been taken to paraphrase all possible difficulties in the footnotes.

ACKNOWLEDGEMENTS

The editor wishes to thank Mr. A. L. P. Norrington, President of Trinity College, Oxford, and former Secretary to the Delegates of the Oxford University Press, in which capacity he was 'nursing father' of this series, for his kindness in reading the first draft and making a number of suggestions. He is not responsible for anything in the final form of this book.

Some of the material in the Select Literary Criticism is copyright, and thanks are due to the following owners of copyright for permission to reproduce it: Messrs. George Allen & Unwin, Ltd., and the *Contemporary Review* (M. Maeterlinck: 'King Lear in Paris', translated by A. T. de Mattos); Mr. D. A. Traversi and *Scrutiny* (D. A. Traversi: 'King Lear'); Messrs. Macmillan & Co. Ltd. (Sir Walter Raleigh: *Shakespeare* and A. C. Bradley: *Shakespearean Tragedy*); Messrs. Sidgwick & Jackson, Ltd., and the Executors of the Estate of H. Granville Barker (H. Granville Barker: *Preface to Shakespeare*); The Macmillan Company, New York (T. Spencer: *Shakespeare and the Nature of Man*, 1942); Louisiana State University Press (R. B. Heilman: *This Great Stage*); Messrs. Methuen & Co. Ltd. (G. Wilson Knight: *The Wheel of Fire* and W. H. Clemen: *The Development of Shakespeare's Imagery*); The Clarendon Press (D. G. James: *The Dream of Learning*, J. W. Mackail: *The Approach to Shakespeare*, and A. Sewell: *Character and Society in Shakespeare*); Messrs. Basil Blackwell & Mott, Ltd. (J. S. H. Bransom: *The Tragedy of King Lear*); Messrs. Clarke, Irwin & Co. Ltd., Toronto (J. M. Lothian: *King Lear—A Tragic Reading of Life*); The Executors of the Estate of C. F. E. Spurgeon (C. F. E. Spurgeon: 'Leading Motives in the Imagery of Shakespeare's Tragedies'); Penguin Books, Ltd. (L. C. Knights: *The Pelican Guide to English Literature*); Messrs. Faber & Faber, Ltd. (J. F. Danby: *Shakespeare's Doctrine of Nature*); Messrs. William Heinemann, Ltd. (A. C. Swinburne: *A Study of Shakespeare*); Messrs. Routledge & Kegan Paul, Ltd. (Edward Dowden: *Shakspere*).

CONTENTS

LIST OF ILLUSTRATIONS

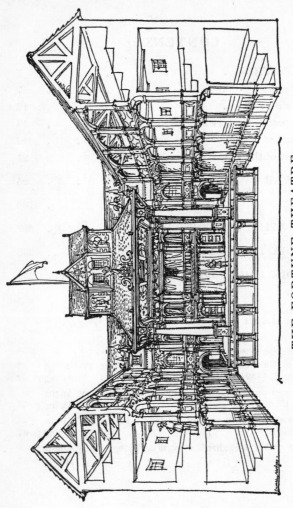

THE FORTUNE THEATRE

A reconstruction by Mr. C. Walter Hodges. The theatre was built in 1600, one year later than the Globe, at which most of Shakespeare's plays were performed, and burnt down in 1621

INTRODUCTION

IT is the plan of the series of which this volume forms part
that the main help to the interpretation of the play should be
provided by the Select Criticism. What follows in this short
Introduction should be taken in conjunction with, and as
supplementing, the material there provided.

King Lear has often been regarded as the greatest work of
Shakespeare, or indeed of any dramatist. It may not have
the splendour of the *Agamemnon*, or the relentless concentra-
tion of the *Oedipus Tyrannus* or *Phèdre*, but the variety of
character and incident prevents Elizabethan drama from
being strictly comparable with Aeschylus, Sophocles, or
Racine. Among Shakespeare's tragedies *Lear* has not quite
the popular fame of *Hamlet*, partly because it is less full of
'quotations', partly because the character of the protagonist is less enigmatic. *Othello*, usually regarded as preceding
Lear, may arouse our pity even more keenly, while *Macbeth*,
probably successor to *Lear*, has even more splendid poetry;
but *Lear* may be regarded as more universal in its scope than
either *Othello* or *Macbeth*. For the king here is no murderer,
nor is he the victim of an almost incredible malice and extreme credulity, but rather a hero of inherent largeness of
soul, who, partly by his own errors of judgement, suffers exceptional calamity. Because the suffering of Lear is not
unconnected with his character it is tragic and not melo-
dramatic, but because it is out of proportion to his fault
(and this is still more true of Cordelia) it raises the whole
problem of evil. The perennial appeal of tragedy to the
human mind lies in its presentation in artistic form of the
eternal question of evil and suffering. 'Is there any cause in
nature that makes these hard hearts?' (III. vi. 75). Is there
justice in the world, or in the heavens? It is mainly because
questions like this are kept more persistently before us in

Lear than in the other tragedies that the drama may be spoken of as more universal. For the problem is one which faces most adults at some time, and some nearly all the time. *Lear* goes farther than the other tragedies of Shakespeare in answering the problem by insisting on the value of endurance, and by showing us the hero purged through suffering. If *King Lear* is a *tragic* reading of life, it is not a *cynical* one; for it goes as far as tragedy can go, without ceasing to be tragedy by passing beyond the purview of this mortal life, to provide a solution of the mystery. But apart from the hint which some may find (with Bradley, see p. 237) of something beyond death, all sensitive readers are left with the feeling that it is quality not quantity of life that matters, that we would rather our lot was that of Kent or Cordelia than that of Edmund or Goneril, even if their prosperity had lasted longer than it did. The same answer is given by a recent critic who asks: 'On what in the world as we know it can a man take his stand?' and finds the answer, embodied in Cordelia, to be 'Love'.

Thus the play of *Lear*, though not a religious work, is compatible with religion. In one way, too, it is more 'theological' than any other tragedy of Shakespeare—in the continual reference to 'the gods' and 'heaven' or 'heavens'. It is true that Shakespeare has dropped the overt references of the old play, *King Leir*, to the Christian religion (where, for example, Cordelia says on one occasion, 'No, no, it is the pleasure of my God') and introduced references to 'the gods' generally or even by name ('Apollo', 'Jove', 'Juno' 'Hecate'); but this superficial paganism, which ceases with the storm scenes, seems the mask for a consciousness of divine overruling much more noticeable than in the other tragedies. The extent to which we subscribe to this feeling will no doubt depend a good deal on the presuppositions with which we come to the play. Some may only be able to agree with Lothian (cf. p. 227) that 'in this tragedy, man braces himself to walk precariously, as it were, to the edge of the universe, and hurl his reiterated question into the void'. Others may go a step farther and say with Fluchère: 'The very extravagance of evil, in its most hateful form, exhausts the possibility of the reign of chaos.'[1] Those who agree with D. G. James (cf. p. 216) that 'Shakespeare writes without a philosophy, and we cannot say his writings are Christian writings' must admit his continuation: 'And yet he conducted a dramatic exploration of human experience which is without parallel for depth and range in the world's history.' And the result was not to blur but to make clear the differences in human character and human values. For the *dramatis personae* of this play fall more markedly into opposing groups than do those of most plays. On the one side stand Cordelia, Edgar, Albany, Kent, and the servant who loses his life in opposing Cornwall's brutality; on the other Goneril, Regan, Edmund, Cornwall, and Oswald—one group as much the embodiment of instinctive and selfless goodness and loyalty, as the other of hard-hearted and deliberate evil and self-seeking. It is of the injustice of man, not of the gods, that Lear speaks. It may be that Edmund and the sisters at least reflect the new paganism of the Renaissance, a Machiavellism less crude than that of Richard III in Shakespeare's early play, but at the same time such invocations of Nature as Edmund's are common enough in the twentieth century to make the play as topical as it is universal.

'For all those who cannot go beyond the moral interpretation of life to the religious interpretation, it might easily be held that Shakespeare is the most precious of thinkers' (Stauffer). And nowhere in Shakespeare are 'integrity, loyalty, patience, love, forgiveness, humility' more powerfully presented than in *Lear*. 'Love bears it out even to the edge of doom' is true of Cordelia, Kent, and Edgar. But a dramatist is neither preacher nor moralist: and what we can

[1] *Shakespeare*, trans. by G. Hamilton, 1953.

draw from the play of Shakespeare's judgements of value are important to us just because he is a supreme dramatist and a supreme poet. He is a supreme dramatist because he surpasses his fellows in the insight and sympathy with which he can present a vast variety of characters of every age and condition of life, a range which makes the work of other Elizabethans like Marlowe, Jonson, Webster, or Ford look narrow and stilted. Indeed, there is little likelihood of Shakespeare's strictly dramatic power being neglected at the present time. It is rather the mastery of word and phrase that the young student of drama is likely to undervalue. For this appreciation depends on a trained susceptibility to poetry, and on a long and intimate acquaintance with the language of Shakespeare himself. First a reader must grasp Elizabethan phraseology enough to be sure of the logical meaning of the word and phrase, and that is why this edition devotes so much space to paraphrase; then there must come slowly, and in different degrees to different readers, the realization of the superiority of Shakespeare's language to the mere meaning of the words; till finally we may hope to feel something of the supreme felicity of Shakespeare's language. In the end we no longer distinguish poet from dramatist, and even the meaning or thought of a line or speech is inseparable from, in fact derives half its force from, the form of expression.

The criticism of the nineteenth century was seldom deficient in appreciation of Shakespeare's poetry, any more than of his character-drawing. It was more often inclined to isolate both the characters and the poetry from their dramatic context. Our century reminds us that the poetry is not an outcome of the characters so much as the means by which the characters are created; and that ideas and atmosphere are as important as character. 'As always in *Lear*' writes a modern critic, of Edmund, 'situation precedes character in significance.' So that perhaps the most valuable constructive work, on the literary as opposed to the textual side, done in our time has been the study of language in its dramatic context. Much of this comes under the heading of *imagery*, i.e. the metaphors and similes in which a poet is, as Aristotle once said, richest of all men, and Shakespeare richest of our poets. But to get a true picture we must not exclude the direct reference to a subject. (For example, we must take into account the direct references to darkness in *Macbeth* as much as a metaphor like 'the blanket of the dark'.) Where the two are taken together it is found that certain plays, certain characters, or even certain scenes, are marked by the recurrence of fixed groups of words or ideas, and it is from their repetition or recurrence that much of the powerful effect is unconsciously derived. In particular such irony as every reader or spectator of *Othello* would notice in the application of the word 'honest' can be found more subtly present in other places. In *King Lear* the most marked patterns are concerned with sight, clothes, animals, sex, and 'nature', and attention will be drawn to some of these recurrences in the commentary.

The writer would like to conclude his Introduction by assuring his reader that all the material added to the text of Shakespeare in footnotes, commentary, and appendixes is only intended to increase that reader's appreciation of the text. An exact understanding of the text, including Elizabethan idiom (which is by no means every Englishman's inheritance, even if it be his birthright!), is an essential preliminary to any worthwhile criticism; and that is mainly dealt with in the footnotes. But even then there is a great deal in a play like this which we shall not see for ourselves at the first or even the tenth reading; and this it is the main purpose of the commentary to point out. It is in the end 'all for your delight'. The editor began to study *Lear* carefully when he bought the (old) Arden edition forty years ago. In that the notes are almost entirely confined to illustrating the meaning of the words. The difference between that edition and the new (revised) Arden well illustrates the change of approach over half a century. And something of the same movement of emphasis can be found between this edition and the older Clarendon Press edition of W. Aldis Wright. The present writer is conscious of deep obligation to three writers whose work appeared at intervals of roughly twenty years: Bradley's *Shakespearean Tragedy* (1904), H. Granville-Barker's *Prefaces to Shakespeare*, first series (1927), and R. B. Heilman's *This Great Stage* (1948). Modern trends in Shakespearean criticism are represented by quotations from this last work and from Traversi. If Bradley and Granville-Barker still loom largest in *Select Criticism* it is due to the quality of their writing. The *New Variorum* edition of this play appeared as long ago as 1880 and has proved of little value except for its conspectus of eighteenth-century editors. The Select Criticism here given is, with the exception of extracts from Johnson and Hazlitt, all subsequent to that date. On the other hand, the recent revision of the Arden edition (1952) has been a most useful check on the editor's own collections of more recent material. He is glad both to find that he is so often in agreement with the views of Professor Muir, and also that his own volume is removed by its scope and price from direct competition with so excellent a piece of work.

The task of an editor of a work so famous as this must be largely one of selection; only occasionally can he hope to have contributed his mite of interpretation, as in the notes to i. i. 268; i. ii. 110, and iii. iv. 27 and 82–97.

DATE

It will suffice most readers to know that the date at which Shakespeare wrote *King Lear* is about 1605, the year of Gunpowder Plot, the second–third of the reign of James I.

The evidence for this will be given briefly below. The plays of Shakespeare cover a period from about 1590 to 1612, and the great tragedies begin at the turn of the century with *Hamlet*, followed four or five years later by *Othello* and then in rapid succession by *King Lear* and *Macbeth*, though there is not complete agreement as to the order of the last two. As *Hamlet* had been preceded by the first Roman play *Julius Caesar*, so *Lear* and *Macbeth* are followed by *Antony and Cleopatra* and *Coriolanus*, the former of which has passages of unsurpassed genius, but both of which show a slackening of the tragic tension, which (ignoring *Timon of Athens*) is even more marked in the so-called romances that followed. *King Lear* then belongs to the full maturity of Shakespeare's powers employed upon what is, with the possible exception of the epic, the greatest work a poet can attempt—tragedy. Nowhere has he plumbed more fully the depths of evil.

The earliest possible date for *Lear* is fixed by the appearance of a book which he undoubtedly used, Harsnett's *Declaration of Egregious Popish Impostures* of March 1603 (see Commentary at III. iv. 52–53, &c.). The latest date is fixed by the acting of the play on 26 December 1606. For the first Quarto edition, known from the shop where it was published as the Pied Bull Q, contains on its title-page the words 'As it was played before the Kings Maiestie at Whitehall upon S. Stephans night in Christmas Hollidayes', and, although this was not published till 1608, we know from an earlier entry in the Stationers' Register that it refers to a performance of 1606. Since Shakespeare was in a position to have his plays acted almost as soon as he could write them, it has usually been held that he wrote *King Lear* in 1605–6, especially as the old play was not available in print till 1605. Recently it has been argued that Shakespeare knew the old play before it was printed, that some of the language in the storm scenes influenced a sonnet written in late 1604, and that Shakespeare was too busy on *Macbeth* in 1605–6 to have been writing *Lear* then. The editor of the New Arden edition therefore dates *Lear* 1604–5, before *Macbeth*. It can be seen that the difference is very slight, and perhaps not very important.

SHAKESPEARE'S SOURCES AND HIS USE OF THEM

The basis of *King Lear* is a very old and widespread story. One of the folk-tales which R. M. Dawkins found current in modern Greece and translated begins thus:

'Once upon a time there was a king with three daughters; he sent for them all and asked them how much they loved him. The eldest said that she loved him like honey; the second like sugar; and the third like salt. The king was angry with the youngest princess, she who had told him that she loved him like salt. Then still angry he went and stood at the gate of the palace: he saw an old man passing by and declared that he would make him his son-in-law. "My king and many be your years! shall I who am a poor man, marry the princess?" "That is my wish," and the king gave him his youngest daughter to be his wife.'

Here the parallel extends only to the first act—that a king has three daughters, two of whom express their love acceptably, while the third does not, and is punished accordingly.

In England the first account of Lear comes in the largely fabulous *History of the Kings of Britain* written in Latin by Geoffrey of Monmouth about 1135. Leir is supposed to be king fairly soon after the founder Brut (i.e. Brutus, great grandson of Aeneas) had come from Rome. His story is, in outline, that of our play except that Leir is restored to his throne and there is no tragedy. Some names are already recognizable—Gonorilla, Regau, and Cordeilla, but the dukes of Cornwall and Albania have different personal names. It is by no means certain that Shakespeare ever saw this work, since it was repeated, in more or less the same form, by poets and chroniclers down to the sixteenth century, some forty to fifty versions being known. Whether or not Shakespeare read any of these earlier accounts, he certainly came across the story in the book he had used for so many of his plays from English history written during the nineties of the sixteenth century. That was Holinshed's *Chronicles*, first printed in 1577 but read by Shakespeare in the second edition of ten years later. Some points in which the story there differs from Shakespeare are that Leir seems to have intended to hand over the whole kingdom to his favourite daughter, but when he was disappointed by her answer he then married his two other daughters to the dukes of Cornwall and Albania, promising them his kingdom after his death, but they both revolted against him till his other son-in-law, Aganippus, one of the twelve kings of Gallia, restored him to the throne of Britain. After his death Cordeilla became queen, but after five years her nephews, sons of the dukes, revolted against her and imprisoned her, whereat she committed suicide (contrast her *murder* in the tragedy).

Besides Holinshed, Shakespeare knew two re-tellings of the story in verse. The earlier was poor poetry, a work by various authors published in successively enlarged editions from 1559 called *The Mirror for Magistrates*, giving the tragic history of twenty princes. The Lear portion was done by Higgins in 1574, and he puts the tale into the mouth of Cordell. He makes Gonorell (a form somewhat nearer Shakespeare's) reduce her father's guard from three score to half that amount, gives her Albany (instead of Albania) as husband (whereas she had in earlier versions been the wife of Cornwall) and possibly suggests a few phrases to Shakespeare, such as Edmund's about Cordelia's supposed despair in v. iii. 254–5.

In the *Faerie Queene*, on the other hand, Shakespeare was reading the work of the greatest Elizabethan poet before himself. Spenser tells the story of Lear in six stanzas of canto 10 of Book II of *The Faerie Queene*, published in 1590. Here first occurs the musical form of the name Cordelia which Shakespeare adopted. The king had already divided his realm into three portions, in order to give one to each daughter. Spenser also makes Cordelia die by hanging (where in earlier versions she had stabbed herself), but it is still suicide, and this is where Shakespeare made the important change. Spenser's treatment is on a small scale and not a very memorable part of his poem, and by no means so important as the two that remain.

For his sub-plot—here in a close relation to the main plot unequalled elsewhere—Shakespeare took a story from Sidney's *Arcadia*, a romance published in 1590. Although the story of the king of Paphlagonia and his two sons is only an episode in the *Arcadia*, the charm of Sidney's style and the nobility of his mind probably made a deeper appeal to Shakespeare than any of his sources for the main plot, and for that reason the episode is printed in an appendix to this edition (see pp. 242-6). I believe that the chivalry of Edgar and his unselfish love in this play, as also the chivalry with which women are treated in many of the comedies (as opposed to that usual in comedy before Lyly), owes not a little to Sidney. Many parallels to the Gloucester story will be noted (and the influence of Sidney is occasionally discernible in the main plot too; e.g. in Lear's death), but these do not detract from the genius shown by Shakespeare in taking for his sub-plot a story which so powerfully enforced the tragic aspects of his main plot, and in so skilfully interweaving the two.

Lastly we come to the old play—*The True Chronicle History of King Leir, and his three daughters, Gonorill, Ragan, and Cordella* . . . published in 1605 and quite probably to be

identified with a play acted in 1594. Shakespeare might
have seen the early play, or even acted in it, and its publica-
tion (if indeed it was before his own play and not prompted
by it) might have spurred him on to do something better.
For his own tragedy bears something of the same relation to
the other play as it does to his own early chronicle histories.
Some editors have doubted Shakespeare's knowledge of the
old play and R. W. Chambers belittled it because of the
supreme difference of Shakespeare's tragic ending; but
anyone who reads it quickly through would probably be
struck by general resemblances, while W. W. Greg after a
recent full examination was convinced that 'ideas, phrases,
cadences from the old play floated in his memory below the
level of conscious thought' and also that he had read *King
Leir* carefully before writing his own play.

The belief that Shakespeare knew the old play does not
mean that one rates it very highly. It is prosaic and didactic,
the verse mostly end-stopped and the imagery conventional.
In some ways the probability is greater than in Shakespeare.
Lear does not divide his kingdom till after Cordelia has
failed him. We do not have the mixture of medieval France
with pure paganism, for the atmosphere is full of references
to Christianity, particularly on the lips of Lear and Cordelia.
There is a fair amount of comedy intermingled, mostly
from Mumford, who speaks somewhat after the fashion of
the Bastard in *King John*, e.g.:

> I long to see the gallant British dames,
> And feed my eyes upon their rare perfections.

The King is tame, compared to the awful figure we know,
and is soon penitent for his treatment of Cordelia. The
recognition scene where Lear and Perillus (who corresponds
to Kent) meet France and Cordelia on the shore without at
first recognizing them has some merit (Tolstoy found it more
moving than Shakespeare!), but the comedy of the drunken

watchmen who let in the French army shows for what trivialities this tragi-comedy found room. In fact the play becomes less and less like Shakespeare as it proceeds, and it is chiefly worth reading in order that we may contrast it with the depth of Shakespearean tragedy (see Appendix I).

Apart from that supreme thing, the quality of the poetry, we owe to Shakespeare most of the character of Kent, all of the Fool, the madness of Lear, the murder of Cordelia, and the whole of the interweaving of plot and sub-plot, including the intrigue of Edmund with Goneril.

THE TEXT OF THE PLAY

The text of Shakespeare's plays does not depend on his own handwriting (of which, apart from signatures, we have only one possible fragment in the play *Sir Thomas More*), but on the early printed editions. These consist of single plays, called *quartos* from their size, in which form about half of Shakespeare's plays made their first appearance, and of the collected edition published in a large *folio* volume after his death, in 1623. Where, as is the case with *Lear*, we have both Quarto and Folio, the main problem consists in deciding which to prefer where they differ. Sometimes there is the additional complication of the existence of more than one Q with different readings, or even of different readings in copies of the same edition on account of changes made while the printing was in process. All these difficulties present themselves in the case of the play before us, but the most difficult is the relation of F and Q.

Speaking generally the nineteenth century tended to attach more authority to the F, and this century increasingly to prefer the Quartos, partly because the skill of bibliographers has enabled them to distinguish between 'good' and 'bad' Quartos. This preference for Q has probably been carried farthest in the *New Temple Shakespeare*, and in some cases results in a text which few of us could accept (e.g. 'Look on the tragic lodging of this bed', instead of 'loading' in the last speech in *Othello*). But even those editors who most strongly proclaim that the right policy is to choose what seems the most authentic text and then follow it unless it is manifestly corrupt, have not followed this out in *Lear*. For here the Q has nearly three hundred lines not in the F, while the F gives some hundred lines not found in Q; but, apart from exact reprints, no one has put forth a text of the play omitting either set of additions as if they were not Shakespeare's work (cf. note to III. i. 22–42). So also, to anyone who works through the chief variations between F and Q in *Lear* or *Othello* with an open mind, it appears fairly certain that sometimes the one and sometimes the other preserves a reading more likely to represent Shakespeare's intention, or at least his final intention. What Bradley says of the last sixty lines of the play seems more widely applicable: 'All good modern texts are eclectic.'

Since Bradley wrote the above words bibliography has become a more elaborate and a more exact science, and it has become the aim of its exponents to deliver us from choosing our text on literary grounds by setting up a theory as to the source of the F and Q text for each play and then attempting to show from the nature of Elizabethan hand-writing and printing a likely source for the differences. For *Lear* the chief work on these lines has been done by Sir Walter Greg and Professor Duthie, the latter of whom produced in 1949 the most elaborate critical edition of the text. Duthie thinks that Q was constructed by a company on tour which had lost its text, each actor contributing his own part as well as he could remember it, and that F was printed from a copy of Q revised from the playhouse manuscript in London. He then attempts to account for the readings of Q on his theory of its origin, and prefers them to those of F on more occasions than do most editors. But it must be observed that his account of its origin is a very elaborate hypothesis.

The study of the variations between F and Q is a fascinating game, but the present editor had not gone far in his work before it became apparent that the length and difficulty of *King Lear* would make it impossible to find room for a discussion, or even the mention, of most of them. Only a few of the more interesting variants are given in the commentary (usually in square brackets), and students who wish to know more should consult the *apparatus criticus* below the text in either the old or the new *Arden* edition. The text printed here is, as in the other volumes of this series, substantially that of the *Oxford Shakespeare* (which is almost identical with that of the older *Arden* edition of this play, also edited by W. J. Craig), except in the following places where the change is usually that of most modern editors:

   I. i. 20: 'something' for 'somewhat'.*
      34: s.d. 'Exit [Gloucester]' for 'Exeunt Gloucester and Edmund'.
      61: 'speak' (F) for 'do' (Q).
      227: 'murder or' for 'nor other'.*
      238: 'Love's' (F) for 'Love is' (Q).
      iv. 2: 'defuse' for 'diffuse'.
   II. i. 15–16: s.d. instead of after 19.
      iv. 187: s.d. instead of after 189.*
   III. iv. 107: s.d. (F) instead of after 110 (Q).
      113: 'squinies' for 'squints'.
      vii. 77: change of ascription.
   IV. ii. 57: 'state begins to threat' for 'slayer begins threats'.
      vi. 22: 'pebble' for 'pebbles'.*
      42: s.d. moved forward.
      162: 'lusts' for 'lust'st'.*
   v. iii. 18: 'sects' for 'sets',* (probably a misprint).
      24: 'good years' for 'goujeres'.
      44: 'I' (F) for 'We' (Q).

84: 'attaint' (Q) for 'arrest' (F).
157–8: s.d. omitted.*
160: attribution changed (Q instead of F).
323: attribution changed (F instead of Q).

An asterisk denotes the restoration of the reading of *both* F *and* Q (i.e. F 1 and Q 1).

A few changes of punctuation have also been made.

There are no expurgations in this edition.

THE PLOT OF THE PLAY

(This analysis is chiefly intended to serve the student for finding any desired passage)

I. i. Lear, King of Britain, now ageing, has decided on a threefold division of his kingdom; but first asks for an expression of love from his three daughters. The youngest, Cordelia, fails to come up to the expectations which his preference for her aroused, and, in anger, Lear divided her share between Goneril and Regan with their husbands, Albany and Cornwall. The Earl of Kent, the king's faithful follower, protests at the injustice, but is banished for his pains. The King of France accepts Cordelia as his wife without her dowry.

I. ii. Edmund, the illegitimate son of the Earl of Gloucester, causes his father to suspect his true son, Edgar, of plotting against his life.

I. iii. Goneril complains to Oswald, her steward, about Lear's conduct, and encourages him to allow the servants to be negligent in their service to him.

I. iv. The disguised Kent gets himself engaged in Lear's service, and attacks Oswald. The Fool mingles with his jests shrewd comments on his master's folly. Goneril reproaches her father to his face, receives his solemn curse, and sends Oswald with a letter about him to her sister, Regan.

I. v. Amid the Fool's patter Lear prepares for departure to Gloucester, sending Kent ahead with a letter to Regan.

II. i. Edmund pretends to Gloucester that he has been attacked and wounded by Edgar for refusing to join a plot against his father. Regan has received letters from her father and sister, and, preferring not to be at home when her father arrived, has come with her husband to Gloucester's castle.

II. ii. Kent renews the quarrel he had picked with Oswald, is punished by Cornwall, and receives the sympathy of Gloucester.

II. iii. Edgar, in danger of his life, decides to disguise himself as a mad beggar.

II. iv. Lear, indignant at finding Kent in the stocks, receives no more consideration from Regan than from Goneril. The latter arrives, and the two sisters support one another in refusing to receive any of Lear's followers into their houses. Lear goes out into the storm.

III. i. Kent, searching the heath for Lear, meets a gentleman who informs him of the growing split between Albany and Cornwall, and of the landing of an army from France.

III. ii. Kent finds Lear and his Fool out in the storm, and guides them to the shelter of a hovel.

III. iii. Gloucester, who has heard what Kent was told, betrays to Edmund where his sympathies lie.

III. iv. Lear, outside the hovel, displays the pity he has now learnt to feel for others. He meets the disguised Edgar feigning madness and they are joined by Gloucester.

III. v. Edmund betrays his father to Cornwall, and receives the promise of his earldom.

III. vi. Gloucester has got the victims of the storm into shelter, where the mad king stages a mock trial. Gloucester arranges to send Lear to Dover for safety.

III. vii. Gloucester has been captured and brought before Cornwall, who, as a punishment for his services to Lear, puts out his eyes; but himself receives a fatal wound from an outraged servant.

iv. i. Edgar in disguise meets his father, now humbled, and offers to lead him to Dover.

iv. ii. Goneril reveals to Edmund her partiality for him, and openly quarrels with her husband.

iv. iii. Kent hears from a Gentleman how Cordelia received the news of her father's state.

iv. iv. Cordelia causes search to be made for Lear.

iv. v. Regan reveals to Oswald her design to marry Edmund, and solicits his help to persuade his mistress to relinquish him.

iv. vi. Gloucester is saved from suicide by Edgar and becomes a witness of Lear's 'reason in madness'. Edgar rescues his father from Oswald and finds on the dead body of the latter evidence of Goneril's intrigue with Edmund.

iv. vii. Cordelia, Kent, and a Doctor witness the awakening of Lear and his partial recovery of his wits.

v. i. Regan and Goneril become more open rivals for the love of Edmund, who himself is cynically impartial. Edgar leaves a letter with Albany.

v. ii. Edgar leaves his father in shelter while he goes to the battle, and returns to report the defeat of Lear and Cordelia.

v. iii. Edmund orders the murder of Lear and Cordelia, who themselves are full of their delight in recovering one another. Edgar appears to support his challenge to Edmund, and gives him a fatal wound. Goneril poisons Regan, but, her intrigue with Edmund having been exposed by Albany, kills herself. Lear brings in the strangled Cordelia, and, thinking for the moment that she still lives, dies. Kent will soon follow his master, and Albany and Edgar are left to carry on the state.

DRAMATIS PERSONÆ

LEAR, King of Britain.
KING OF FRANCE.
DUKE OF BURGUNDY.
DUKE OF CORNWALL.
DUKE OF ALBANY.
EARL OF KENT.
EARL OF GLOUCESTER.
EDGAR, Son to Gloucester.
EDMUND, Bastard Son to Gloucester.
CURAN, a Courtier.
OSWALD, Steward to Goneril.
Old Man, Tenant to Gloucester.
Doctor.
Fool.
An Officer, employed by Edmund.
A Gentleman, attendant on Cordelia.
A Herald.
Servants to Cornwall.

GONERIL,
REGAN,   } Daughters to Lear.
CORDELIA,

Knights of Lear's Train, Officers, Messengers, Soldiers, and Attendants.
SCENE—Britain.

KING LEAR

ACT I

Scene I. A ROOM OF STATE IN KING LEAR'S PALACE

Enter KENT, GLOUCESTER, *and* EDMUND.

Kent. I thought the king had more affected the Duke of
Albany than Cornwall.

Gloucester. It did always seem so to us; but now, in the
division of the kingdom, it appears not which of the dukes
he values most; for equalities are so weighed that curiosity
in neither can make choice of either's moiety.   6

Kent. Is not this your son, my lord?

Gloucester. His breeding, sir, hath been at my charge: I
have so often blushed to acknowledge him, that now I am
brazed to it.   10

Kent. I cannot conceive you.

Gloucester. Sir, this young fellow's mother could; where-
upon she grew round-wombed, and had, indeed, sir, a son
for her cradle ere she had a husband for her bed. Do you
smell a fault?   15

Kent. I cannot wish the fault undone, the issue of it being
so proper.

---

*The sign [N] in these footnotes indicates that further remarks on the
same line, not necessarily on the same difficulty, will be found in the
End Notes.*

1 had more affected: was more partial to, preferred.   **5 equalities
. . . weighed:** shares are so carefully equalized.   5–6: i.e.
neither duke can find ground for preferring the other's share to his
own. **curiosity:** careful examination. **moiety:** part, share
(not necessarily half).   **8 breeding:** upbringing.   **10 brazed:**
hardened (as in one slang sense of 'brass'). **11 conceive:**
understand.   **16 issue:** *both* (1) result *and* (2) offspring.
17 proper: handsome.

Gloucester. But I have a son, sir, by order of law, some year elder than this, who yet is no dearer in my account: though this knave came something saucily   20 into the world before he was sent for, yet was his mother fair; there was good sport at his making, and the whoreson must be acknowledged. Do you know this noble gentleman, Edmund?

Edmund. No, my lord.   25

Gloucester. My Lord of Kent: remember him here-after as my honourable friend.

Edmund. My services to your lordship.

Kent. I must love you, and sue to know you better.

Edmund. Sir, I shall study deserving.   30

Gloucester. He hath been out nine years, and away he shall again. The king is coming.

Sennet. Enter LEAR, CORNWALL, ALBANY, GONERIL, REGAN, CORDELIA, *and* Attendants.

Lear. Attend the Lords of France and Burgundy, Gloucester.

Gloucester. I shall, my liege.

                                 [*Exit.* GLOUCESTER.

Lear. Meantime we shall express our darker purpose. 35
Give me the map here. Know that we have divided
In three our kingdom; and 'tis our fast intent
To shake all cares and business from our age,

---

18 **son by order of law**: legitimate, born in wedlock [*N*].
19 **some year**: about a year.   20 **account**: reckoning.
something: somewhat.   23 **whoreson**: rascal (literally 'son of a whore' but often used playfully, like 'knave' above).   29 **sue**: beg.   30 **study deserving**: try to be worth (the effort you make).
31 **out**: away from home, abroad.   s.d. *Sennet*: a set of notes on a trumpet heralding a procession.   33 **attend**: wait upon (and bring in, cf. l. 188).   35 **express**: expound, show.   **darker**: hitherto unrevealed (i.e. the details of the division) [*N*].   37 **fast**: firm, fixed.

Conferring them on younger strengths, while we
Unburden'd crawl toward death. Our son of Cornwall, 40
And you, our no less loving son of Albany,
We have this hour a constant will to publish
Our daughters' several dowers, that future strife
May be prevented now. The princes, France and Bur-
    gundy,
Great rivals in our youngest daughter's love,   45
Long in our court have made their amorous sojourn,
And here are to be answer'd. Tell me, my daughters,—
Since now we will divest us both of rule,
Interest of territory, cares of state,—
Which of you shall we say doth love us most?   50
That we our largest bounty may extend
Where nature doth with merit challenge. Goneril,
Our eldest-born, speak first.
    Goneril. Sir, I love you more than words can wield the
        matter;
Dearer than eye-sight, space, and liberty;   55
Beyond what can be valu'd, rich or rare;
No less than life, with grace, health, beauty, honour;
As much as child e'er lov'd, or father found;
A love that makes breath poor and speech unable;
Beyond all manner of so much I love you.   60
    Cordelia. [*Aside.*] What shall Cordelia speak? Love, and
        be silent.
    Lear. Of all these bounds, even from this line to this,

40 **son**: in law, Duke of Cornwall.   42 **constant**: firm.   43
several dowers: respective dowries.   46 **amorous sojourn**:
stay for purposes of love (to woo Cordelia).   47 **are** . . .
answer'd: await a decision.   49 **interest**: right, title to (and
so possession of).   52 **nature**: affection.   **challenge**: claim
(it) [*N*].   55 **space**: the world (unless the word simply expands
the notion of 'liberty').   57 **with**: combined with.   58
found: experienced (love).   59 **unable**: unequal to expressing
it.   60 **all . . . so much**: all degree of such comparisons.

With shadowy forests and with champains rich'd,
With plenteous rivers and wide-skirted meads,
We make thee lady: to thine and Albany's issue   65
Be this perpetual. What says our second daughter,
Our dearest Regan, wife to Cornwall? Speak.

   Regan. I am made of that self metal as my sister,
And prize me at her worth. In my true heart
I find she names my very deed of love;   70
Only she comes too short: that I profess
Myself an enemy to all other joys
Which the most precious square of sense possesses
And find I am alone felicitate
In your dear highness' love.

   Cordelia. [*Aside.*]   Then, poor Cordelia!   75
And yet not so; since, I am sure, my love's
More richer than my tongue.

   Lear. To thee and thine, hereditary ever,
Remain this ample third of our fair kingdom,
No less in space, validity, and pleasure,   80
Than that conferr'd on Goneril. Now, our joy,
Although our last, not least; to whose young love
The vines of France and milk of Burgundy
Strive to be interess'd; what can you say to draw
A third more opulent than your sisters? Speak.   85

   Cordelia. Nothing, my lord.

   Lear. Nothing?

---

63 **shadowy**: shady.   **champains**: meadows, open country.
68 **self**: same.   **metal**: (1) material, (2) temperament (in this
sense now spelt *mettle*). [*N*].   69 **prize . . . worth**: I count
myself equal to her (in my affection for you).   **In my true heart**:
in all sincerity.   70 **names . . . love**: exactly describes my
love.   71 **that**: in that.   73 **most precious square of
sense**: most delicate sense [*N*].   74 **felicitate**: made happy.
78 **hereditary ever**: and to your heirs for ever.   80 **validity**:
value.   83 i.e. the King of F., rich in vineyards, and the Duke
of B., rich in pastures.   84 **interess'd**: concerned, bound up
with ('interess is an old form of interest, Lat. *interesse*) [*N*].

Cordelia. Nothing.

Lear. Nothing will come of nothing: speak again.

Cordelia. Unhappy that I am, I cannot heave   90
My heart into my mouth: I love your majesty
According to my bond; nor more nor less.

Lear. How, how, Cordelia! mend your speech a little,
Lest you may mar your fortunes.

Cordelia.   Good my lord,
You have begot me, bred me, lov'd me: I   95
Return those duties back as are right fit,
Obey you, love you, and most honour you.
Why have my sisters husbands, if they say
They love you all? Haply, when I shall wed,
That lord whose hand must take my plight shall carry 100
Half my love with him, half my care and duty:
Sure I shall never marry like my sisters,
To love my father all.

Lear. But goes thy heart with this?

Cordelia.   Ay, good my lord.

Lear. So young, and so untender?   105

Cordelia. So young, my lord, and true.

Lear. Let it be so; thy truth then be thy dower:
For, by the sacred radiance of the sun,
The mysteries of Hecate and the night,
By all the operation of the orbs   110
From whom we do exist and cease to be,
Here I disclaim all my paternal care,
Propinquity and property of blood,

---

92 **bond**: obligation (cf. 'bounden duty and service' of *Prayer Book*).
[*N*].   96 **right fit**: duties right and fit to be returned.   99 **all**:
entirely.   100 **plight**: plighted troth, vows.   107 **dower**:
dowry.   109 **Hecate**: Hécate (here two syllables) [*N*]   110
operation: work, influence.   **orbs**: heavenly bodies.   113 **propinquity**: *lit.* nearness, so kinship.   **property of blood**: ownership
of your blood.

And as a stranger to my heart and me
Hold thee from this for ever. The barbarous Scythian, 115
Or he that makes his generation messes
To gorge his appetite, shall to my bosom
Be as well neighbour'd, pitied, and reliev'd,
As thou my sometime daughter.

   Kent.   Good my liege,—

   Lear. Peace, Kent!   120
Come not between the dragon and his wrath.
I lov'd her most, and thought to set my rest
On her kind nursery. Hence, and avoid my sight!
So be my grave my peace, as here I give
Her father's heart from her! Call France. Who stirs? 125
Call Burgundy. Cornwall and Albany,
With my two daughters' dowers digest the third;
Let pride, which she calls plainness, marry her.
I do invest you jointly with my power,
Pre-eminence, and all the large effects   130
That troop with majesty. Ourself by monthly course,
With reservation of a hundred knights,
By you to be sustain'd, shall our abode
Make with you by due turn. Only we shall retain
The name and all the addition to a king;   135
The sway, revenue, execution of the rest,
Beloved sons, be yours: which to confirm,

---

116 **generation**: children. **messes**: dishes [*N*].   118 **as
well neighbour'd**: held as near.   121 i.e. don't try, to stop my
(natural) wrath (cf. 171 below).   122 **set my rest**: stake my all
(a gaming metaphor, but also involving the ordinary sense of 'rest').
123 **nursery**: nursing.   125 **from**: away from. **Who stirs?**
make haste.   128 **Let pride . . . her**: let her pride find her a
husband, i.e. let her find one for herself without a dowry.   130
large effects: manifestations of splendour.   131 **troop with**:
accompany. **by monthly course**: for a month in turn.   132
With reservation of: i.e. reserving to ourselves (properly a legal
word for an *exception*).   135 **addition**: title [*N*].

This coronet part between you.

Kent.   Royal Lear,
Whom I have ever honour'd as my king,
Lov'd as my father, as my master follow'd,   140
As my great patron thought on in my prayers,—
Lear. The bow is bent and drawn; make from the shaft.
Kent. Let it fall rather, though the fork invade
The region of my heart: be Kent unmannerly
When Lear is mad. What wouldst thou do, old man? 145
Think'st thou that duty shall have dread to speak
When power to flattery bows? To plainness honour's
    bound
When majesty falls to folly. Reserve thy state;
And, in thy best consideration, check
This hideous rashness: answer my life my judgment,   150
Thy youngest daughter does not love thee least;
Nor are those empty-hearted whose low sound
Reverbs no hollowness.
Lear.   Kent, on thy life, no more.
Kent. My life I never held but as a pawn
To wage against thine enemies; nor fear to lose it,   155
Thy safety being the motive.
Lear.   Out of my sight!
Kent. See better, Lear; and let me still remain
The true blank of thine eye.
Lear. Now, by Apollo,—
Kent.   Now, by Apollo, king,

142 **make from:** avoid.   143 **fork:** head, barb.   147
plainness: plain-speaking.   148 **state:** regal power.   149
best consideration: considering the matter more carefully.   150
answer ... judgment: let my life answer for (the correctness of)
my judg(e)ment.   153 **reverbs:** echoes back [N].   **on thy life:**
as you value your life.   154 **held:** accounted.   154-5 **pawn
to wage:** stake to wager, risk.   157-8 **let me ... eye:** keep
me always in view, always with you (**blank** = *white* centre of a
target).

Thou swear'st thy gods in vain.

    Lear.   O vassal! miscreant! 160

                             [*Laying his hand on his sword.*

    Albany. ⎫
            ⎬ Dear sir, forbear.
    Cornwall. ⎭

    Kent. Do;

Kill thy physician, and the fee bestow
Upon the foul disease. Revoke thy gift;
Or, whilst I can vent clamour from my throat, 165
I'll tell thee thou dost evil.

    Lear.   Hear me, recreant!

On thine allegiance, hear me!
Since thou hast sought to make us break our vow,—
Which we durst never yet,—and, with strain'd pride
To come betwixt our sentence and our power,— 170
Which nor our nature nor our place can bear,—
Our potency made good, take thy reward.
Five days we do allot thee for provision
To shield thee from diseases of the world;
And, on the sixth, to turn thy hated back 175
Upon our kingdom: if, on the tenth day following
Thy banish'd trunk be found in our dominions,
The moment is thy death. Away! By Jupiter,
This shall not be revok'd.

    Kent. Fare thee well, king; sith thus thou wilt appear,
Freedom lives hence, and banishment is here. 181

[*To* CORDELIA.] The gods to their dear shelter take thee, maid,

---

    160 vassal! miscreant! and **recreant!** (166): all used loosely as terms of abuse, 'villain'.   **162 Do:** execute your will.   **163–4 the fee . . . disease:** i.e. make things worse for yourself.   **gift:** i.e. of Cordelia's share.   **169 strain'd:** exaggerated.   **170 our power:** the execution of it.   **172 potency made good:** power shown to be (still) valid.   **174 diseases:** discomforts (consequent on lack of preparation for exile).   **175 to turn:** we sentence thee to turn.   **177 trunk:** body.   **180 sith:** since   **appear:** show thyself.

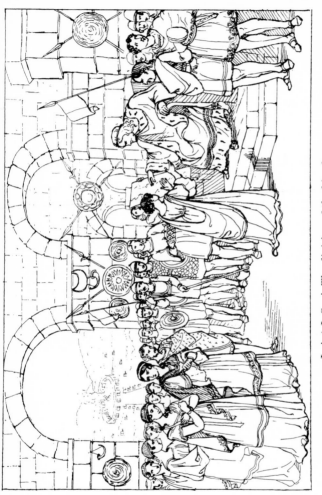

I. Act I, Sc. i. The division of the kingdom

(A contemporary drawing of Macready's production at Covent Garden Theatre, 25 January 1838)

II. Act I, Sc. iv. 'Are you our daughter?'

(Marius Goring as the Fool, Michael Redgrave as Lear, and Joan Sanderson as Goneril,

That justly think'st, and hast most rightly said!
[*To* REGAN *and* GONERIL.] And your large speeches may
    your deeds approve,
That good effects may spring from words of love.   185
Thus Kent, O princes! bids you all adieu;
He'll shape his old course in a country new.   [*Exit.*

Flourish. Re-enter GLOUCESTER, *with* FRANCE, BURGUNDY,
       and Attendants.

  Gloucester. Here's France and Burgundy, my noble lord.
  Lear. My Lord of Burgundy,
We first address toward you, who with this king   190
Hath rivall'd for our daughter. What, in the least,
Will you require in present dower with her,
Or cease your quest of love?
  Burgundy.   Most royal majesty,
I crave no more than hath your highness offer'd,
Nor will you tender less.
  Lear.   Right noble Burgundy,   195
When she was dear to us we did hold her so,
But now her price is fall'n. Sir, there she stands:
If aught within that little-seeming substance,
Or all of it, with our displeasure piec'd,
And nothing more, may fitly like your Grace,   200
She's there, and she is yours.
  Burgundy.   I know no answer.
  Lear. Will you, with those infirmities she owes,

184 **large:** grand.   **approve:** make good.   187 **shape ...
course:** make his way, old as he is, *or* continues his old habits
(of plain-speaking etc.).   187–8 s.d. *Flourish:* a blast of
trumpets or horns.   190 **address** (ourselves) **toward:** speak to.
191 **rivall'd for:** entered into rivalry for.   195 **tender:** offer.
196 **so:** dear (in value), worth a good dowry.   198 **little-
seeming substance:** person of few pretensions (sarcastic) [N]
199 **piec'd:** pieced out (with), added (to it).   200 **like:** please.
202 **owes:** owns.

Unfriended, new-adopted to our hate,
Dower'd with our curse, and stranger'd with our oath,
Take her, or leave her?

  Burgundy.   Pardon me, royal sir;   205
Election makes not up on such conditions.

  Lear. Then leave her, sir; for, by the power that made
    me,
I tell you all her wealth.—[*To* FRANCE.] For you, great
    king,
I would not from your love make such a stray
To match you where I hate; therefore, beseech you   210
To avert your liking a more worthier way
Than on a wretch whom nature is asham'd
Almost to acknowledge hers.

  France.   This is most strange,
That she, who even but now was your best object,
The argument of your praise, balm of your age,   215
The best, the dearest, should in this trice of time
Commit a thing so monstrous, to dismantle
So many folds of favour. Sure, her offence
Must be of such unnatural degree
That monsters it, or your fore-vouch'd affection   220
Fall into taint; which to believe of her,
Must be a faith that reason without miracle
Could never plant in me.

  Cordelia.   I yet beseech your majesty—

---

  204 **stranger'd with**: made a stranger (to us) by (cf. 114).
206 **Election . . . up**: choice does not decide, will not choose.
208 **For you**: as for you.   209 **make . . . stray**: depart from,
i.e. offend against.   210 **to**: as to.   211 **avert**: turn
aside. **a more worthier way**: in a worthier direction.   214
best: favourite.   215 **argument**: subject. **balm . . . age**:
see 122–3.   216 **trice**: moment (Spanish).   217 **dismantle**:
shed off.   220 **monsters**: makes it monstrous.   220–1 **your
fore-vouch'd . . . taint**: your previously affirmed affection must
be discredited [*N*].

If for I want that glib and oily art
To speak and purpose not; since what I well intend,
I'll do 't before I speak—that you make known   226
It is no vicious blot murder, or foulness,
No unchaste action, or dishonour'd step,
That hath depriv'd me of your grace and favour,
But even for want of that for which I am richer,   230
A still-soliciting eye, and such a tongue
That I am glad I have not, though not to have it
Hath lost me in your liking.

  Lear.   Better thou
Hadst not been born than not to have pleas'd me better.

  France. Is it but this? a tardiness in nature   235
Which often leaves the history unspoke
That it intends to do? My Lord of Burgundy,
What say you to the lady? Love's not love
When it is mingled with regards that stand
Aloof from the entire point. Will you have her?   240
She is herself a dowry.

  Burgundy.   Royal Lear,
Give but that portion which yourself propos'd,
And here I take Cordelia by the hand,
Duchess of Burgundy.

  Lear. Nothing: I have sworn; I am firm.   245

  Burgundy. I am sorry, then, you have so lost a father
That you must lose a husband.

  Cordelia.   Peace be with Burgundy!

---

  224 **If for**: If (you are disowning me) because.   225 **purpose
not**: not intend to carry out.   227 i.e. no wickedness, such as
murder or fornication.   228 **dishonour'd**: dishonourable.
230 **even for want of**: it is just because I lack.   231 **still-
soliciting**: always begging (for something).   235 **tardiness in
nature**: natural slowness (to speak).   236 **history**: verbal
record.   238 **What say . . . lady?** How do you like the lady?
[*N*].   239 **regards**: considerations (so **respects** 248).   240
entire: whole [*N*].   247 **Peace be with**: good-bye to.

Since that respects of fortune are his love,
I shall not be his wife.

France. Fairest Cordelia, that art most rich, being poor;
Most choice, forsaken; and most lov'd, despis'd!   251
Thee and thy virtues here I seize upon:
Be it lawful I take up what's cast away.
Gods, gods! 'tis strange that from their cold'st neglect
My love should kindle to inflam'd respect.   255
Thy dowerless daughter, king, thrown to my chance,
Is queen of us, of ours, and our fair France:
Not all the dukes of waterish Burgundy
Shall buy this unpriz'd precious maid of me.
Bid them farewell, Cordelia, though unkind: 260
Thou losest here, a better where to find.

Lear. Thou hast her, France; let her be thine, for we
Have no such daughter, nor shall ever see
That face of hers again, therefore be gone
Without our grace, our love, our benison.   265
Come, noble Burgundy.

>   [*Flourish. Exeunt* LEAR, BURGUNDY, CORNWALL,
>   ALBANY, GLOUCESTER, EDMUND, *and* Attendants.

France. Bid farewell to your sisters.

Cordelia. The jewels of our father, with wash'd eyes
Cordelia leaves you: I know you what you are;
And like a sister am most loath to call   270
Your faults as they are nam'd. Use well our father:
To your professed bosoms I commit him:

---

255 **inflam'd respect:** ardent esteem.   256 **chance:** lot.
258 **waterish:** perhaps literally 'well-watered', but certainly
implying that the man is as thin-blooded as his country is inferior
in wines to France (cf. 83).   259 **unpriz'd:** *either* not (properly)
valued *or* priceless.   260 **unkind:** see III. iv. 61.   261 **where:**
place (to parallel 'here').   265 **benison:** blessing.   268 **The
jewels:** vocative case [*N*].   271 **as they are nam'd:** by their
true names.   272 **bosoms:** love.

But yet, alas! stood I within his grace,
I would prefer him to a better place.
So farewell to you both. 275

Regan. Prescribe not us our duties.

Goneril. Let your study
Be to content your lord, who hath receiv'd you
At fortune's alms; you have obedience scanted,
And well are worth the want that you have wanted.

Cordelia. Time shall unfold what plighted cunning hides;
Who covers faults, at last shame them derides. 281
Well may you prosper!

France. Come, my fair Cordelia.

[*Exeunt* FRANCE *and* CORDELIA.

Goneril. Sister, it is not little I have to say of what most
nearly appertains to us both. I think our father will hence
to-night. 285

Regan. That's most certain, and with you; next month
with us.

Goneril. You see how full of changes his age is; the
observation we have made of it hath not been little: he
always loved our sister most; and with what poor judgment he hath now cast her off appears too grossly. 291

Regan. 'Tis the infirmity of his age; yet he hath ever but
slenderly known himself.

Goneril. The best and soundest of his time hath been but
rash; then, must we look to receive from his age, not alone
the imperfections of long-engraffed condition, but, there-

---

274 **prefer**: advance, recommend. 278 **At fortune's alms**:
as a humble gift of fortune; cf. 256. 279 **are worth . . .
wanted**: deserve the destitution that has befallen you [N]. 280
plighted: folded [N]. 281 **Who**: those who (antecedent to
them). 284 **will go hence.** 288 **full . . . age is**: changeable he is now he is old. 291 **grossly**: obviously. 295 **rash**:
hot-headed. 296 **long-engraffed condition**: a temperament
that has become firmly fixed (ingrafted) by habit.

withal the unruly waywardness that infirm and choleric
years bring with them.   298

Regan. Such unconstant starts are we like to have from
him as this of Kent's banishment.   300

Goneril. There is further compliment of leave-taking
between France and him. Pray you, let us hit together: if
our father carry authority with such dispositions as he
bears, this last surrender of his will but offend us.

Regan. We shall further think on 't.   305

Goneril. We must do something, and i' the heat.

[*Exeunt.*

Scene II. A HALL IN THE EARL OF GLOUCESTER'S CASTLE

Enter EDMUND, *with a letter.*

Edmund. Thou, Nature, art my goddess; to thy law
My services are bound. Wherefore should I
Stand in the plague of custom, and permit
The curiosity of nations to deprive me,
For that I am some twelve or fourteen moonshines   5
Lag of a brother? Why bastard? wherefore base?
When my dimensions are as well compact,
My mind as generous, and my shape as true,

297–8 **infirm . . . years:** years of physical weakness and prone-
ness to anger.   299 **unconstant starts:** fits of waywardness.
like: likely.   301 **compliment:** formal civility.   302 **hit
together:** strike a bargain, i.e. make joint plans.   303 **carry:**
i.e. still wields. **dispositions:** moods.   304 **offend:** harm
(stronger than nowadays). **surrender:** i.e. of the crown.   306
i' the heat: at once (cf. 'strike while the iron is hot').   3 **stand
in the plague of custom:** suffer from the inferior position custom
assigns to bastards [*N*].   4 **curiosity:** scrupulousness, squeamish-
ness.   **deprive me:** keep me out of my rights.   6 **lag of:**
behind (in coming into the world) [*N*].   7 **my dimensions:**
the proportions of my body. **compact:** made.   8 **generous:**
high-spirited.

As honest madam's issue? Why brand they us
With base? with baseness? bastardy? base, base?   10
Who in the lusty stealth of nature take
More composition and fierce quality
Than doth, within a dull, stale, tired bed,
Go to the creating a whole tribe of fops,
Got 'tween asleep and wake? Well then,   15
Legitimate Edgar, I must have your land:
Our father's love is to the bastard Edmund
As to the legitimate. Fine word, 'legitimate!'
Well, my legitimate, if this letter speed,
And my invention thrive, Edmund the base   20
Shall top the legitimate:—I grow, I prosper;
Now, gods, stand up for bastards!

Enter GLOUCESTER.

Gloucester. Kent banished thus! And France in choler
parted!
And the king gone to-night! subscrib'd his power!
Confin'd to exhibition! All this done   25
Upon the gad! Edmund, how now! what news?
Edmund. So please your lordship, none.

[*Putting up the letter.*

Gloucester. Why so earnestly seek you to put up that
letter?
Edmund. I know no news, my lord.   30
Gloucester. What paper were you reading?

9 **honest madam's:** the true wife.   11 **stealth:** secret act.
nature: (sexual) desire [*N*].   14 **fops:** fools.   15 **Got:** be-
gotten.   18 **as:** as much as.   21 **top:** get the better of [*N*].
23 **choler:** anger.   **parted:** departed.   24 **to-night:** last night.
subscrib'd: surrendered.   25 **exhibition:** an allowance (cf. university use).   26 **upon the gad:** suddenly (as if pricked by a
gad, = goad).   28 **put up:** put away.

Edmund. Nothing, my lord.

Gloucester. No? What needed then that terrible dispatch of it into your pocket? the quality of nothing hath not such need to hide itself. Let's see; come; if it be nothing, I shall not need spectacles.　36

Edmund. I beseech you, sir, pardon me; it is a letter from my brother that I have not all o'er-read, and for so much as I have perused, I find it not fit for your o'er-looking.

Gloucester. Give me the letter, sir.　40

Edmund. I shall offend, either to detain or give it. The contents, as in part I understand them, are to blame.

Gloucester. Let's see, let's see.

Edmund. I hope, for my brother's justification, he wrote this but as an essay or taste of my virtue.　45

Gloucester. 'This policy and reverence of age makes the world bitter to the best of our times; keeps our fortunes from us till our oldness cannot relish them. I begin to find an idle and fond bondage in the oppression of aged tyranny, who sways, not as it hath power,　50 but as it is suffered. Come to me, that of this I may speak more. If our father would sleep till I waked him, you should enjoy half his revenue for ever, and live the beloved of your brother, EDGAR.'—Hum! Conspiracy! 'Sleep till I waked him, you should enjoy half his　55 revenue.'—My son Edgar! Had he a hand to write this? a heart and brain to breed it in? When came this to you? Who brought it?

Edmund. It was not brought me, my lord; there's the

---

33 **terrible**: frightened (*not* our slang use).　**dispatch**: haste in putting away.　37 **pardon me**: excuse me from showing it you. 38 **for**: as for.　39 **o'er-looking**: examination.　45 **essay**: trial.　46 **policy and reverence of age**: policy of reverence for old age [*N*].　47 **the best . . . times**: our best days, i.e. men in their prime.　49 **fond**: foolish.　50 **aged tyranny**: my aged father (abstract for concrete, as often).　**sways**: rules.

cunning of it; I found it thrown in at the casement of my
closet.   61

Gloucester. You know the character to be your brother's?

Edmund. If the matter were good, my lord, I durst swear
it were his; but, in respect of that, I would fain think it
were not.   65

Gloucester. It is his.

Edmund. It is his hand, my lord; but I hope his heart is
not in the contents.

Gloucester. Hath he never heretofore sounded you in this
business?   70

Edmund. Never, my lord: but I have often heard him
maintain it to be fit that, sons at perfect age, and fathers
declined, the father should be as ward to the son, and the
son manage his revenue.   74

Gloucester. O villain, villain! His very opinion in the
letter! Abhorred villain! Unnatural, detested, brutish
villain! worse than brutish! Go, sirrah, seek him; I'll
apprehend him. Abominable villain! Where is he?

Edmund. I do not well know, my lord. If it shall
please you to suspend your indignation against my   80
brother till you can derive from him better testimony
of his intent, you shall run a certain course; where, if
you violently proceed against him, mistaking his purpose, it would make a great gap in your own honour,
and shake in pieces the heart of his obedience. I dare   85
pawn down my life for him, that he hath writ this to
feel my affection to your honour, and to no other pretence of danger.

60 **casement:** (open) window.   62 **character:** hand-writing.
64 **that:** its goodness or lack of it, i.e. (in this case) its badness.
72 **perfect age:** the prime of life.   73 **declined:** in years.
82 **run a certain course:** act safely.   **where:** whereas.   84 **gap:**
breach.   86 **pawn:** see I. i. 154.   87 **feel:** try.
87–88 **to no . . . danger:** not with a view to any (other) dangerous
design.

Gloucester. Think you so? 89

Edmund. If your honour judge it meet, I will place you where you shall hear us confer of this, and by an auricular assurance have your satisfaction; and that without any further delay than this very evening.

Gloucester. He cannot be such a monster—

Edmund. Nor is not, sure. 95

Gloucester.—to his father, that so tenderly and entirely loves him. Heaven and earth! Edmund, seek him out; wind me into him, I pray you; frame the business after your own wisdom. I would unstate myself to be in a due resolution. 100

Edmund. I will seek him, sir, presently; convey the business as I shall find means, and acquaint you withal.

Gloucester. These late eclipses in the sun and moon portend no good to us: though the wisdom of nature can reason it thus and thus, yet nature finds itself 105 scourged by the sequent effects. Love cools, friendship falls off, brothers divide: in cities, mutinies; in countries, discord; in palaces, treason; and the bond cracked between son and father. This villain of mine comes under the prediction; there's son against father: 110 the king falls from bias of nature; there's father against child. We have seen the best of our time: machinations, hollowness, treachery, and all ruinous

91 **auricular:** through the ear.   98 **wind me into him:** insinuate yourself, get into familiar talk with him, please (**me** is not the object of 'wind' but the so-called ethic dative).   99 **unstate myself:** give up my position.   99–100 **to be ... resolution:** to have my doubts resolved.   101 **presently:** immediately.   **convey:** carry out.   102 **acquaint you withal:** inform you of it.   104–5 **the wisdom ... thus and thus:** natural philosophy can give good explanations.   106 **sequent effects:** effects that follow (eclipses) [*N*].   107 **mutinies:** disturbances.   111 **from bias of nature:** away from natural inclination [*N*] (i.e. of affection towards Cordelia).   113 **machinations:** plots.   **hollowness:** insincerity.

disorders, follow us disquietly to our graves. Find out
this villain, Edmund; it shall lose thee nothing: do it   115
carefully. And the noble and true-hearted Kent banished! his offence, honesty! 'Tis strange!   [*Exit.*

Edmund. This is the excellent foppery of the world,
that, when we are sick in fortune,—often the surfeit
of our own behaviour,—we make guilty of our disas-   120
ters the sun, the moon, and the stars; as if we were
villains by necessity, fools by heavenly compulsion,
knaves, thieves, and treachers by spherical predominance, drunkards, liars, and adulterers by an enforced
obedience of planetary influence; and all that we are   125
evil in, by a divine thrusting on: an admirable evasion
of whoremaster man, to lay his goatish disposition to
the charge of a star! My father compounded with my
mother under the dragon's tail, and my nativity was
under Ursa Major; so that it follows I am rough and   130
lecherous. 'Sfoot! I should have been that I am had
the maidenliest star in the firmament twinkled on my
bastardizing. Edgar—

Enter EDGAR.

and pat he comes, like the catastrophe of the old
comedy: my cue is villanous melancholy, with a sigh   135
like Tom o' Bedlam. O, these eclipses do portend these
divisions! Fa, sol, la, mi.

---

118 **foppery**: folly [*N*].   119 **surfeit**: evil result.   123
treachers: traitors.   **spherical predominance**: dominance of
some special star.   126 **evasion**: of responsibility.   127 **whoremaster**: lecherous.   127 **goatish**: lascivious.   129 **dragon's
tail**: in astronomy, 'The descending node of the moon's orbit with
the ecliptic' (*Shorter O.E.D.*).   130 **Ursa Major**: the Great
Bear.   133 **bastardizing**: unlawful begetting.   134 **pat**:
just at the right moment.   **the old**: any old [*N*].   135 **cue**:
part.   136 **Tom o' Bedlam**: beggar feigning madness [*N*].
137 **Fa . . . mi**: Edmund sings or hums a series of musical notes.

Edgar. How now, brother Edmund! What serious contemplation are you in?

Edmund. I am thinking, brother, of a prediction I read this other day, what should follow these eclipses.   141

Edgar. Do you busy yourself with that?

Edmund. I promise you the effects he writes of succeed unhappily; as of unnaturalness between the child and the parent; death, dearth, dissolutions of ancient 145 amities; divisions in state; menaces and maledictions against king and nobles; needless diffidences, banishment of friends, dissipation of cohorts, nuptial breaches, and I know not what.   149

Edgar. How long have you been a sectary astronomical?

Edmund. Come, come; when saw you my father last?

Edgar. The night gone by.

Edmund. Spake you with him?

Edgar. Ay, two hours together.

Edmund. Parted you in good terms? Found you no displeasure in him by word or countenance?   156

Edgar. None at all.

Edmund. Bethink yourself wherein you may have offended him; and at my entreaty forbear his presence till some little time hath qualified the heat of his dis- 160 pleasure, which at this instant so rageth in him that with the mischief of your person it would scarcely allay.

Edgar. Some villain hath done me wrong.

Edmund. That's my fear. I pray you have a conti- 165 nent forbearance till the speed of his rage goes slower, and, as I say, retire with me to my lodging, from

141 (as to) **what.**   143–4 **succeed:** turn out.   147 **diffidences:** distrust (of others).   148 **dissipation of cohorts:** just possibly 'troops deserting' [*N*].   150 **sectary astronomical:** follower of, believer in astrology.   159 **forbear:** avoid.   160 **qualified:** reduced.   163 **allay:** subside. **165–6 a continent forbearance:** the restraint to keep away.

whence I will fitly bring you to hear my lord speak.
Pray you, go; there's my key. If you do stir abroad
go armed. 170

Edgar. Armed, brother!

Edmund. Brother, I advise you to the best; go armed; I
am no honest man if there be any good meaning toward
you; I have told you what I have seen and heard; but
faintly, nothing like the image and horror of it; pray you,
away. 176

Edgar. Shall I hear from you anon?

Edmund. I do serve you in this business. [*Exit* EDGAR.
A credulous father, and a brother noble,
Whose nature is so far from doing harms 180
That he suspects none; on whose foolish honesty
My practices ride easy! I see the business.
Let me, if not by birth, have lands by wit:
All with me's meet that I can fashion fit. [*Exit.*

Scene III. A Room in the Duke of Albany's Palace

Enter GONERIL *and* OSWALD *her* Steward.

Goneril. Did my father strike my gentleman for chiding
of his fool?

Oswald. Ay, madam.

Goneril. By day and night he wrongs me; every hour
He flashes into one gross crime or other, 5
That sets us all at odds: I'll not endure it:
His knights grow riotous, and himself upbraids us
On every trifle. When he returns from hunting

---

168 **fitly**: at a suitable time.   173 **meaning**: intentions.
175 **image and horror**: horrible reality.   182 **practices**: plots.
184 **fit**: to my purpose.   4 **By day and night**: *probably* 'continually', rather than an oath.   5 **flashes into**: breaks out into.
crime: offence.   6 **sets . . . at odds**: upsets.

I will not speak with him; say I am sick:
If you come slack of former services, 10
You shall do well; the fault of it I'll answer.

Oswald. He's coming, madam; I hear him.

[*Horns within.*

Goneril. Put on what weary negligence you please,
You and your fellows; I'd have it come to question:
If he distaste it, let him to my sister, 15
Whose mind and mine, I know, in that are one,
Not to be over-rul'd. Idle old man,
That still would manage those authorities
That he hath given away! Now, by my life,
Old fools are babes again, and must be us'd 20
With checks as flatteries, when they are seen abus'd.
Remember what I have said.

Oswald. Well, madam.

Goneril. And let his knights have colder looks among you;
What grows of it, no matter; advise your fellows so:
I would breed from hence occasions, and I shall, 25
That I may speak: I'll write straight to my sister
To hold my very course. Prepare for dinner. [*Exeunt.*

Scene IV. A Hall in the Same

Enter KENT, *disguised.*

Kent. If but as well I other accents borrow,
That can my speech defuse, my good intent

---

11 **answer:** (for), be responsible for.   14 **I'd . . . question:**
I want it discussed.   15 **distaste:** dislike (as Q reads).   17
Idle: foolish.   18 **manage those authorities:** exercise the
powers.   20–21 **us'd . . . abus'd** rebuked as well as flattered
when they are seen to be misled (by their followers) *or* deluded.
24 **grows of it:** results from it.   25 **occasions:** opportunities
27 **my very course:** exactly my course.   2 **defuse:** confuse,
disguise.   **my good intent . . . issue:** I may be able to bring off
the purpose.

May carry through itself to that full issue
For which I raz'd my likeness. Now, banish'd Kent,
If thou canst serve where thou dost stand condemn'd,   5
So may it come, thy master, whom thou lovest,
Shall find thee full of labours.

Horns within. Enter LEAR, Knights, *and* Attendants.

Lear. Let me not stay a jot for dinner: go, get it ready.
[*Exit an* Attendant.] How now! what art thou?

Kent. A man, sir.   10

Lear. What dost thou profess? What wouldst thou with
us?

Kent. I do profess to be no less than I seem; to serve him
truly that will put me in trust; to love him that is honest;
to converse with him that is wise, and says little; to fear
judgment; to fight when I cannot choose; and to eat no
fish.   17

Lear. What art thou?

Kent. A very honest-hearted fellow, and as poor as the
king.   20

Lear. If thou be as poor for a subject as he is for a king,
thou art poor enough. What wouldst thou?

Kent. Service.

Lear. Whom wouldst thou serve?

Kent. You.   25

Lear. Dost thou know me, fellow?

Kent. No, sir; but you have that in your countenance
which I would fain call master.

Lear. What's that?

---

4 **raz'd**: erased.   8 **stay a jot**: wait a moment.   11
What... profess?: what is your business, job? (But Kent takes
the word in the sense of 'claim'.)   15 **converse**: have to do
with (Lat. *conversari*).   16 **judgment**: here *or* hereafter.   16–
17 **eat no fish**: be a loyal subject (not fast like a Papist).   27
countenance: bearing.

Kent. Authority.   30

Lear. What services canst thou do?

Kent. I can keep honest counsel, ride, run, mar a curious tale in telling it, and deliver a plain message bluntly: that which ordinary men are fit for, I am qualified in, and the best of me is diligence.   35

Lear. How old art thou?

Kent. Not so young, sir, to love a woman for singing, nor so old to dote on her for any thing; I have years on my back forty-eight.   39

Lear. Follow me; thou shalt serve me: if I like thee no worse after dinner I will not part from thee yet. Dinner, ho! dinner! Where's my knave? my fool? Go you and call my fool hither.   [*Exit an* Attendant.

Enter OSWALD.

You, you, sirrah, where's my daughter?   44

Oswald. So please you,—   [*Exit.*

Lear. What says the fellow there? Call the clotpoll back. [*Exit* a Knight.] Where's my fool, ho? I think the world's asleep. How now! where's that mongrel?

Re-enter Knight.

Knight. He says, my lord, your daughter is not well.

Lear. Why came not the slave back to me when I called him?   51

Knight. Sir, he answered me in the roundest manner, he would not.

Lear. He would not!

Knight. My lord, I know not what the matter is; but,   55

---

32 **honest counsel:** an honourable secret.   **curious:** elaborate, difficult (Kent is only a plain man).   37 (as) **to love.**   42
knave: boy (as in a pack of cards).   45 **So please you:** excuse me (as he goes out).   46 **clotpoll:** clodpate, blockhead.   48
mongrel: i.e. Oswald.   52 **roundest:** plainest.

to my judgment, your highness is not entertained with
that ceremonious affection as you were wont; there's a
great abatement of kindness appears as well in the
general dependants as in the duke himself also and
your daughter.   60

Lear. Ha! sayest thou so?

Knight. I beseech you, pardon me, my lord, if I be mistaken; for my duty cannot be silent when I think your
highness wronged.

Lear. Thou but rememberest me of mine own con-   65
ception: I have perceived a most faint neglect of late;
which I have rather blamed as mine own jealous
curiosity than as a very pretence and purpose of unkindness: I will look further into 't. But where's my
fool? I have not seen him this two days.   70

Knight. Since my young lady's going into France, sir,
the fool hath much pined him away.

Lear. No more of that; I have noted it well. Go you and
tell my daughter I would speak with her.   74

          [Exit an Attendant.

Go you, call hither my fool.   *[Exit an Attendant.*

Re-enter OSWALD.

O! you sir, you, come you hither, sir. Whom am I, sir?

Oswald. My lady's father.

Lear. 'My lady's father!' my lord's knave: you whoreson
dog! you slave! you cur!

Oswald. I am none of these, my lord; I beseech your
pardon.   81

Lear. Do you bandy looks with me, you rascal?

            [Striking him.

---

63 my duty cannot be: my sense of duty forbids me to be. **66
faint:** slight *or* (possibly) cold. **68 curiosity:** watchfulness,
suspicion. **very pretence:** real intention. **82 bandy:** exchange
(originally in tennis).

Oswald. I'll not be struck, my lord.

Kent. Nor tripped neither, you base football player.

[*Tripping up his heels.*

Lear. I thank thee, fellow; thou servest me, and I'll love
thee.   86

Kent. Come, sir, arise, away! I'll teach you differences:
away, away! If you will measure your lubber's length
again, tarry; but away! Go to; have you wisdom? so. 89

[*Pushes* OSWALD *out.*

Lear. Now, my friendly knave, I thank thee: there's
earnest of thy service.   [*Gives* KENT *money.*

Enter Fool.

Fool. Let me hire him too: here's my coxcomb.

[*Offers* KENT *his cap.*

Lear. How now, my pretty knave! how dost thou?

Fool. Sirrah, you were best take my coxcomb.

Kent. Why, fool?   95

Fool. Why? for taking one's part that's out of
favour. Nay, an thou canst not smile as the wind sits,
thou'lt catch cold shortly: there, take my coxcomb.
Why, this fellow has banished two on's daughters, and
did the third a blessing against his will: if thou follow 100
him thou must needs wear my coxcomb. How now,
nuncle! Would I had two coxcombs and two daughters!

Lear. Why, my boy?

---

87 **differences:** i.e. of rank (between you and a king).   89
Go to: Pshaw! (expression of impatience).   **have you wisdom?**
are you **in** your senses?   **so:** good (as Oswald goes out).   91
earnest a pledge (of further reward).   92 **coxcomb:** fool's cap.
94 **you were best:** you had better (*literally* it were, i.e. would be,
best for you).   97 **an:** if.   **smile as the wind sits:** see which
way things are going, trim your sail to the breeze.   99 **on's:**
of his [*N*].   102 **nuncle:** contracted for 'mine uncle', a regular
address of fools to their master.

Fool. If I gave them all my living, I'd keep my coxcombs myself. There's mine; beg another of thy daughters.   106

Lear. Take heed, sirrah; the whip.

Fool. Truth's a dog must to kennel; he must be whipped out when Lady the brach may stand by the fire and stink.

Lear. A pestilent gall to me!   110

Fool. [*To* KENT.] Sirrah, I'll teach thee a speech.

Lear. Do.

Fool. Mark it, nuncle:—

> Have more than thou showest,
> Speak less than thou knowest,   115
> Lend less than thou owest,
> Ride more than thou goest,
> Learn more than thou trowest,
> Set less than thou throwest;
> Leave thy drink and thy whore,   120
> And keep in-a-door,
> And thou shalt have more
> Than two tens to a score.

Kent. This is nothing, fool.   124

Fool. Then 'tis like the breath of an unfee'd lawyer, you gave me nothing for't. Can you make no use of nothing, nuncle?

Lear. Why, no, boy; nothing can be made out of nothing.

Fool. [*To* KENT.] Prithee, tell him, so much the rent of his land comes to: he will not believe a fool.   130

Lear. A bitter fool!

Fool. Dost thou know the difference, my boy, between a bitter fool and a sweet fool?

Lear. No, lad; teach me.

---

109 brach: bitch.   **110 gall:** irritant *or* bitterness [*N*].   **116 owest:** owenest.   **117 goest:** walkest   **118** i.e. (probably) don't believe all you hear.   **119** i.e. stake less than you win (at a throw).   **121 in-a-door:** indoors.   **122–3** i.e. you'll do well.

Fool. That lord that counsell'd thee   135
  To give away thy land,
  Come place him here by me,
  Do thou for him stand:
  The sweet and bitter fool
  Will presently appear;   140
  The one in motley here,
  The other found out there.

Lear. Dost thou call me fool, boy?

Fool. All thy other titles thou hast given away; that thou
was born with.   145

Kent. This is not altogether fool, my lord.

Fool. No, faith, lords and great men will not let me; if I
had a monopoly out, they would have part on 't, and ladies
too: they will not let me have all fool to myself; they'll be
snatching. Nuncle, give me an egg, and I'll give thee two
crowns.   151

Lear. What two crowns shall they be?

Fool. Why, after I have cut the egg i' the middle and
eat up the meat, the two crowns of the egg. When
thou clovest thy crown i' the middle, and gavest away   155
both parts, thou borest thine ass on thy back o'er the
dirt: thou hadst little wit in thy bald crown when
thou gavest thy golden one away. If I speak like myself in this, let him be whipped that first finds it so.

  Fools had ne'er less grace in a year;   160
   For wise men are grown foppish,
  And know not how their wits to wear,
   Their manners are so apish.

141 **motley**: fool's dress (as I am). 147 **let me**: (be the complete fool). 148 **out**: taken out, granted (as often by Stuart
kings). 154 **crowns**: i.e. half shells. 156–7 **borest ... dirt**:
reversed the proper order of things (from a fable of Aesop). 158–9
like myself: foolishly [*N*]. 160 **had ... grace**: were never
less in favour. 161 **foppish**: foolish. 162 **their wits to
wear**: show their wisdom.

Lear. When were you wont to be so full of songs, sirrah?

Fool. I have used it, nuncle, ever since thou madest thy daughters thy mothers; for when thou gavest them the rod and puttest down thine own breeches,   167

> Then they for sudden joy did weep,
>   And I for sorrow sung,
> That such a king should play bo-peep,   170
>   And go the fools among.

Prithee, nuncle, keep a schoolmaster that can teach thy fool to lie: I would fain learn to lie.

Lear. An you lie, sirrah, we'll have you whipped.

Fool. I marvel what kin thou and thy daughters are: 175 they'll have me whipped for speaking true, thou'lt have me whipped for lying; and sometimes I am whipped for holding my peace. I had rather be any kind o' thing than a fool; and yet I would not be thee, nuncle; thou hast pared thy wit o' both sides, and left 180 nothing i' the middle: here comes one o' the parings.

Enter GONERIL.

Lear. How now, daughter! what makes that frontlet on? Methinks you are too much of late i' the frown.

Fool. Thou wast a pretty fellow when thou hadst no need to care for her frowning; now thou art an O 185 without a figure. I am better than thou art now; I am a fool, thou art nothing. [*To* GONERIL.] Yes, forsooth, I will hold my tongue; so your face bids me, though you say nothing.

---

165 **used it**: made it my habit. 170 **play bo-peep**: behave like a child.   180-1 **pared . . . middle**: i.e. by giving away both halves of thy kingdom.   182 **makes**: means.   **frontlet**: i.e. frown (*lit.* cloth worn on forehead).   185-6 **an O . . . figure**: a mere cipher, thing of nought.

Mum, mum;   190
He that keeps nor crust nor crumb,
Weary of all, shall want some.

That's a shealed peascod.   [*Pointing to* LEAR.
  Goneril. Not only, sir, this your all-licens'd fool,
But other of your insolent retinue   195
Do hourly carp and quarrel, breaking forth
In rank and not-to-be-endured riots. Sir,
I had thought, by making this well known unto you,
To have found a safe redress; but now grow fearful,
By what yourself too late have spoke and done,   200
That you protect this course, and put it on
By your allowance; which if you should, the fault
Would not 'scape censure, nor the redresses sleep,
Which, in the tender of a wholesome weal,
Might in their working do you that offence,   205
Which else were shame, that then necessity
Will call discreet proceeding.
  Fool. For you trow, nuncle,
      The hedge-sparrow fed the cuckoo so long,
      That it had it head bit off by it young.   210
So out went the candle, and we were left darkling.
  Lear. Are you our daughter?
  Goneril. I would you would make use of your good wis-
      dom,

193 **shealed peascod:** pod without peas (provincial form of
'shelled').   197 **rank:** gross.   199 **safe redress:** sure
remedy.   201 **put it on:** encourage it.   204 **in the
tender . . . weal:** in their regard for a healthy state of affairs.
206 **Which . . . shame:** which would be disgraceful if the motive
(behind my remedial action) were not good.   **that then . . .
proceeding:** i.e. although, considering the need, people would
approve my conduct ('that'='which' again—an awkward construction).   210 **it young:** its (as often) apparent young, i.e.
the young cuckoo (corresponding to Goneril).   211 **darkling:**
in the dark [*N*].

Whereof I know you are fraught; and put away
These dispositions which of late transform you   215
From what you rightly are.

Fool. May not an ass know when the cart draws the
horse? Whoop, Jug! I love thee.

Lear. Does any here know me? This is not Lear:
Does Lear walk thus? speak thus? Where are his eyes?
Either his notion weakens, his discernings   221
Are lethargied. Ha! waking? 'tis not so.
Who is it that can tell me who I am?

Fool. Lear's shadow.   224

Lear. I would learn that; for, by the marks of sove-
reignty, knowledge and reason, I should be false persuaded
I had daughters.

Fool. Which they will make an obedient father.

Lear. Your name, fair gentlewoman?

Goneril. This admiration, sir, is much o' the favour   230
Of other your new pranks. I do beseech you
To understand my purposes aright:
As you are old and reverend, should be wise.
Here do you keep a hundred knights and squires;
Men so disorder'd, so debosh'd, and bold,   235
That this our court, infected with their manners,
Shows like a riotous inn: epicurism and lust
Make it more like a tavern or a brothel
Than a grac'd palace. The shame itself doth speak

214 **fraught**: stored.   215 **dispositions**: moods.   217 cf.
l. 156.   221 **notion**: understanding.   **discernings**:
powers of discernment.   222 **lethargied**: dulled.   **waking?**: am
I awake?   225 **I would**: I must.   226 **false**: falsely.
228 **Which**: whom (Lear's shadow).   230 **admiration**: (feigned)
surprise.   **favour**: nature.   231 **other** (of) **your**.   233 (you)
should.   235 **disorder'd**: disorderly.   **debosh'd**: debauched.
237 **epicurism**: epicureanism, luxury.   239 **grac'd**: honourable.   239–40 **speak for**: demand.

For instant remedy; be then desir'd   **240**
By her that else will take the thing she begs,
A little to disquantity your train;
And the remainder, that shall still depend,
To be such men as may besort your age,
Which know themselves and you.

Lear.   Darkness and devils!
Saddle my horses; call my train together.   **246**
Degenerate bastard! I'll not trouble thee:
Yet have I left a daughter.

Goneril. You strike my people, and your disorder'd
rabble
Make servants of their betters.   **250**

Enter ALBANY.

Lear. Woe, that too late repents;
                [*To* ALBANY.] O! sir, are you come?
Is it your will? Speak, sir. Prepare my horses.
Ingratitude, thou marble-hearted fiend,
More hideous, when thou show'st thee in a child,
Than the sea-monster.

Albany.   Pray, sir, be patient. **255**

Lear. [*To* GONERIL.] Detested kite! thou liest:
My train are men of choice and rarest parts,
That all particulars of duty know,
And in the most exact regard support
The worships of their name. O most small fault,   **260**

---

240 **be then desir'd:** let yourself be requested.   242 **disquantity:** reduce the number of.   243 **the remainder . . . to
be:** allow the remainder to be. **depend:** serve you. 244 **besort:**
suit.   251 **Woe, that:**Woe to him who.   255 **the:** a (generic
use, cf. I. ii. 134) [*N*].   259 **in the most exact regard:** with
scrupulous care.   260 **worships:** honour (plural sometimes used
when a plurality of persons is concerned).   **O . . . fault:** i.e. Cordelia's obstinacy.

How ugly didst thou in Cordelia show!
Which, like an engine, wrench'd my frame of nature
From the fix'd place, drew from my heart all love,
And added to the gall. O Lear, Lear, Lear!
Beat at this gate, that let thy folly in,

[Striking his head.

And thy dear judgment out! Go, go, my people.   266
  Albany. My lord, I am guiltless, as I am ignorant
Of what hath mov'd you.
  Lear.   It may be so, my lord.
Hear, Nature, hear! dear goddess, hear!
Suspend thy purpose, if thou didst intend   270
To make this creature fruitful!
Into her womb convey sterility!
Dry up in her the organs of increase,
And from her derogate body never spring
A babe to honour her! If she must teem,   275
Create her child of spleen, that it may live
And be a thwart disnatur'd torment to her!
Let it stamp wrinkles in her brow of youth,
With cadent tears fret channels in her cheeks,
Turn all her mother's pains and benefits   280
To laughter and contempt, that she may feel
How sharper than a serpent's tooth it is
To have a thankless child! Away, away!   [*Exit.*
  Albany. Now, gods that we adore, whereof comes this?
  Goneril. Never afflict yourself to know the cause;   285
But let his disposition have that scope
That dotage gives it.

---

   262 **engine:** the rack (a torture, wrenching the body apart).
frame of nature: system of natural affection.   266 **dear:** precious.   274 **derogate:** debased.   275 **teem:** bear children.
277 **thwart:** cross, perverse.   **disnatur'd:** unnatural.   279
cadent: falling.   **fret:** wear away.   280 **benefits:** kindness
done to the child.   286 **disposition:** cf. l. 215.

Re-enter LEAR.

LEAR. What! fifty of my followers at a clap,
Within a fortnight?
   Albany.   What's the matter, sir?
   Lear. I'll tell thee. [*To* GONERIL.] Life and death! I am
      asham'd   290
That thou hast power to shake my manhood thus,
That these hot tears, which break from me perforce,
Should make thee worth them. Blasts and fogs upon
    thee!
Th' untented woundings of a father's curse
Pierce every sense about thee! Old fond eyes,   295
Beweep this cause again, I'll pluck ye out,
And cast you, with the waters that you lose,
To temper clay. Yea, is it come to this?
Let it be so: I have another daughter,
Who, I am sure, is kind and comfortable: 300
When she shall hear this of thee, with her nails
She'll flay thy wolvish visage. Thou shalt find
That I'll resume the shape which thou dost think
I have cast off for ever; thou shalt, I warrant thee.
              [*Exeunt* LEAR, KENT, *and* Attendants.
   Goneril. Do you mark that?   305
   Albany. I cannot be so partial, Goneril,
To the great love I bear you.—
   Goneril. Pray you, content. What, Oswald, ho!
[*To* the Fool.] You, sir, more knave than fool, after your
    master.

---

288 **at a clap**: at a stroke, all at once [*N*].   294 **untented**:
unexplored, deep, and so incurable (a surgeon probed a wound
with a 'tent' or roll of lint).   295 **fond**: foolish.   296
Beweep: if you weep for.   297 **lose**: waste.   298 **temper**:
moisten.   300 **comfortable**: comforting.   306–7 i.e. so pre-
judiced by my love for you (as to approve your conduct now).
308 (be) **content**: calm, almost 'shut up!'.

Fool. Nuncle Lear, nuncle Lear! tarry, and take the fool
with thee. 311

> A fox, when one has caught her,
> And such a daughter,
> Should sure to the slaughter,
> If my cap would buy a halter; 315
> So the fool follows after. [*Exit.*

Goneril. This man hath had good counsel. A hundred
  knights!
'Tis politic and safe to let him keep
At point a hundred knights; yes, that on every dream,
Each buzz, each fancy, each complaint, dislike, 320
He may enguard his dotage with their powers,
And hold our lives in mercy. Oswald, I say!

Albany. Well, you may fear too far.

Goneril. Safer than trust too far.
Let me still take away the harms I fear,
Not fear still to be taken: I know his heart. 325
What he hath utter'd I have writ my sister;
If she sustain him and his hundred knights,
When I have show'd the unfitness,—

Re-enter OSWALD.

How now, Oswald!
What! have you writ that letter to my sister?

Oswald. Ay, madam. 330

Goneril. Take you some company, and away to horse:
Inform her full of my particular fear;
And thereto add such reasons of your own

314 **Should sure:** should surely go. 317 **This man:** Lear (the
whole speech is ironical). 319 **At point:** armed and ready.
320 **buzz:** rumour. 321 **enguard:** guard. 322 **in mercy:**
at his mercy. 324 **still:** always. 325 **taken:** overtaken
by harm. **his heart:** i.e. (perhaps) that he is plotting to recover
his throne. 329 **What!:** Well! 332 **full:** fully. **particular:** personal.

As may compact it more. Get you gone,
And hasten your return. [*Exit* OSWALD.] No, no, my lord,
This milky gentleness and course of yours   336
Though I condemn not, yet, under pardon,
You are much more attask'd for want of wisdom
Than prais'd for harmful mildness.

   Albany. How far your eyes may pierce I cannot tell:
Striving to better, oft we mar what's well.   341

   Goneril. Nay, then—

   Albany. Well, well; the event.   [*Exeunt.*

Scene V. COURT BEFORE THE SAME

Enter LEAR, KENT, *and* Fool.

   Lear. Go you before to Gloucester with these letters.
Acquaint my daughter no further with any thing you
know than comes from her demand out of the letter. If
your diligence be not speedy I shall be there before you.

   Kent. I will not sleep, my lord, till I have delivered your
letter.   [*Exit.*

   Fool. If a man's brains were in 's heels, were 't not in
danger of kibes?   8

   Lear. Ay, boy.

   Fool. Then, I prithee, be merry; thy wit shall not go
slip-shod.   11

   Lear. Ha, ha, ha!

   Fool. Shalt see thy other daughter will use thee kindly;

334 compact: strengthen.   **336 gentleness and course:**
gentleness of your course (hendiadys) [*N*].   **338 attask'd:** blamed,
held to account [*N*].   **339 harmful mildness:** a mildness which
can only prove harmful to us.   **343 the event:** (let us see) what
turns out.   **1 Gloucester:** the town, not the Earl [*N*].   **these
letters:** this letter (Latin *litterae*).   **3 demand out of:** questions arising out of.   **7 't:** it, his brain(s).   **8 kibes:** chaps
or chilblains.   **11 slip-shod:** in slippers (to ease chilblains on the
heel) [*N*].   **13 kindly:** (1) affectionately, (2) after her kind,
or nature (the Fool foresees the second).

for though she's as like this as a crab is like an apple, yet I
can tell what I can tell.   15

  Lear. What canst tell, boy?

  Fool. She will taste as like this as a crab does to a crab.
Thou canst tell why one's nose stands i' the middle on's face?

  Lear. No.

  Fool. Why, to keep one's eyes of either side's nose, that
what a man cannot smell out, he may spy into.   21

  Lear. I did her wrong,—

  Fool. Canst tell how an oyster makes his shell?

  Lear. No.

  Fool. Nor I either; but I can tell why a snail has a house.

  Lear. Why?   26

  Fool. Why, to put his head in; not to give it away to his
daughters, and leave his horns without a case.

  Lear. I will forget my nature. So kind a father! Be my
horses ready?   30

  Fool. Thy asses are gone about 'em. The reason why the
seven stars are no more than seven is a pretty reason.

  Lear. Because they are not eight?

  Fool. Yes, indeed: thou wouldst make a good fool.

  Lear. To take it again perforce! Monster ingratitude! 35

  Fool. If thou wert my fool, nuncle, I'd have thee beaten
for being old before thy time.

  Lear. How's that?

  Fool. Thou shouldst not have been old before thou hadst
been wise.   40

  Lear. O! let me not be mad, not mad, sweet heaven;
Keep me in temper; I would not be mad!

---

14 **this:** Goneril   **crab:** (apple).   20 **'s nose:** of one's nose.
29 **my nature:** my natural affection (for my daughters).   **31 Thy
asses:** those who are fools enough to serve you still.   **31–32 the
seven stars:** the Pleiades.   35 *Either* Lear contemplates trying
to resume his royal power by force, *or* he is thinking of Goneril's
withdrawing the privileges he had been allowed.

Enter Gentleman.

How now! Are the horses ready?

Gentleman. Ready, my lord.

Lear. Come, boy.   **45**

Fool. She that's a maid now, and laughs at my departure,
Shall not be a maid long, unless things be cut shorter.

[*Exeunt.*

46–47 i.e. 'The maid who sees only the funny side of the Fool's
gibes and does not realize that Lear is going on a tragic journey is
such a simpleton that she won't know how to preserve her virginity'
(K. Muir) [*N*].

ACT II

Scene I. A COURT WITHIN THE CASTLE OF THE EARL OF GLOUCESTER

Enter EDMUND *and* CURAN, *meeting.*

Edmund. Save thee, Curan.

Curan. And you, sir. I have been with your father, and given him notice that the Duke of Cornwall and Regan his duchess will be here with him to-night.

Edmund. How comes that?　　　　　　　　　　　　　　5

Curan. Nay, I know not. You have heard of the news abroad? I mean the whispered ones, for they are yet but ear-kissing arguments?

Edmund. Not I: pray you, what are they?

Curan. Have you heard of no likely wars toward, 'twixt the Dukes of Cornwall and Albany?　　　　　　　　11

Edmund. Not a word.

Curan. You may do then, in time. Fare you well, sir.

　　　　　　　　　　　　　　　　　　　　　　[*Exit.*

Edmund. The duke be here to-night! The better! best! This weaves itself perforce into my business.　　　15

Enter EDGAR

My father hath set guard to take my brother;
And I have one thing, of a queasy question,
Which I must act. Briefness and fortune, work!
Brother, a word; descend: brother, I say!

1 (God) **save thee** [*N*].　　　7 **ones**: news.　　　8 **ear-kissing arguments**: subjects of secret conversation (as with the mouth close to the hearer's ear).　　10 **toward**: in view.　　14 (all) **the better.**　　17 **of a queasy question**: awkward, ticklish to handle.　　18 **Briefness**: swift action.　　19 **descend**: Edgar would have entered on the upper stage.

My father watches: O sir! fly this place;   20
Intelligence is given where you are hid;
You have now the good advantage of the night.
Have you not spoken 'gainst the Duke of Cornwall?
He's coming hither, now, i' the night, i' the haste,
And Regan with him; have you nothing said   25
Upon his party 'gainst the Duke of Albany?
Advise yourself.

Edgar.   I am sure on't, not a word.

Edmund. I hear my father coming; pardon me;
In cunning I must draw my sword upon you;
Draw; seem to defend yourself; now 'quit you well.   30
Yield;—come before my father. Light, ho! here!
Fly, brother. Torches! torches! So, farewell.

                                                   [*Exit* EDGAR.

Some blood drawn on me would beget opinion

                                                   [*Wounds his arm.*

Of my more fierce endeavour: I have seen drunkards
Do more than this in sport. Father! father!   35
Stop, stop! No help?

          Enter GLOUCESTER, *and* Servants *with torches.*

Gloucester. Now, Edmund, where's the villain?

Edmund. Here stood he in the dark, his sharp sword out,
Mumbling of wicked charms, conjuring the moon
To stand auspicious mistress.

Gloucester.   But where is he?   40

Edmund. Look, sir, I bleed.

Gloucester.   Where is the villain, Edmund?

24 **i' the haste:** in haste [*N*].   26 **Upon his party 'gainst:**
about the party formed by him against [*N*].   29 **In cunning:**
in pretence (as if we were enemies).   31 **Yield:** said louder, for
Gloucester to hear.   33–34 **beget . . . endeavour:** make men
think that I have really been fighting seriously.   40 **stand
auspicious mistress:** favour him as if she were his mistress (as
she was of Endymion in classical mythology).

III. Act II, Sc. iv. 'Who stocked my servant?'
(Laurence Olivier as Lear and Alec Guinness as the Fool, in an Old Vic production at the New Theatre, 1946)

IV. Act V, Sc. iii. 'Look on her, look, her lips'
(Yvonne Mitchell as Cordelia and Michael Redgrave as Lear, at
Stratford-on-Avon, 1953)

Edmund. Fled this way, sir. When by no means he
    could—

Gloucester. Pursue him, ho! Go after. [*Exeunt some*
    Servants.] 'By no means' what?

    Edmund. Persuade me to the murder of your lordship;

But that I told him, the revenging gods   45
'Gainst parricides did all their thunders bend;
Spoke with how manifold and strong a bond
The child was bound to the father; sir, in fine,
Seeing how loathly opposite I stood
To his unnatural purpose, in fell motion,   50
With his prepared sword he charges home
My unprovided body, lanc'd mine arm:
But when he saw my best alarum'd spirits
Bold in the quarrel's right, rous'd to the encounter,
Or whether gasted by the noise I made,   55
Full suddenly he fled.

    Gloucester.   Let him fly far:
Not in this land shall he remain uncaught;
And found—dispatch. The noble duke my master,
My worthy arch and patron, comes to-night:
By his authority I will proclaim it,   60
That he which finds him shall deserve our thanks,
Bringing the murderous coward to the stake;
He that conceals him, death.

    Edmund. When I dissuaded him from his intent,
And found him pight to do it, with curst speech   65
I threaten'd to discover him: he replied,

45 **But that . . . him:** without my telling him (in reply) that.
49 **loathly opposite:** opposed, with loathing, to.   50 **fell
motion:** fierce thrust.   51 **charges home:** makes a home
(effective) thrust at.   52 **unprovided:** unprotected.   53 **best
alarum'd spirits:** my best spirits stirred up.   55 **gasted:**
frightened [*N*].   58 **found—dispatch:** when he is found, the
order will be 'dispatch him!'   59 **arch:** chief.   65 **pight:**
determined.

'Thou unpossessing bastard! dost thou think,
If I would stand against thee, would the reposal
Of any trust, virtue, or worth, in thee
Make thy words faith'd? No: what I should deny,—
As this I would; ay, though thou didst produce   71
My very character,—I'd turn it all
To thy suggestion, plot, and damned practice:
And thou must make a dullard of the world,
If they not thought the profits of my death   75
Were very pregnant and potential spurs
To make thee seek it.'
   Gloucester.   Strong and fasten'd villain!
Would he deny his letter? I never got him.
                       [*Tucket within.*
Hark! the duke's trumpets. I know not why he comes.
All ports I'll bar; the villain shall not 'scape;   80
The duke must grant me that: besides, his picture
I will send far and near, that all the kingdom
May have due note of him; and of my land,
Loyal and natural boy, I'll work the means
To make thee capable.   85

    Enter CORNWALL, REGAN, *and* Attendants.

   Cornwall. How now, my noble friend! since I came
    hither,—
Which I can call but now,—I have heard strange news.
   Regan. If it be true, all vengeance comes too short

---

67 **unpossessing**: as unable to inherit.   68 **would**: should.
72 **character**: handwriting.   73 **suggestion**: temptation.
practice: treachery.   74 **make ... world**: suppose people
very stupid.   75 **not thought**: should not think.   76 **pregnant**: clear, obvious (of different derivation from the word meaning
'with child').   **potential spurs**: powerful inducements.   77
fasten'd: confirmed.   78 **got**: begot.   84 **natural**: true,
affectionate (with a glance at the meaning of 'born out of wedlock').
85 **capable**: legally able to inherit (cf. l. 67).

Which can pursue the offender. How dost, my lord?

  Gloucester. O! madam, my old heart is crack'd, it's
crack'd.   90

  Regan. What! did my father's godson seek your life?
He whom my father nam'd? your Edgar?

  Gloucester. O! lady, lady, shame would have it hid.

  Regan. Was he not companion with the riotous knights
That tend upon my father?   95

  Gloucester. I know not, madam; 'tis too bad, too bad.

  Edmund. Yes, madam, he was of that consort.

  Regan. No marvel then though he were ill affected;
'Tis they have put him on the old man's death,
To have the expense and waste of his revenues.   100
I have this present evening from my sister
Been well-inform'd of them, and with such cautions
That if they come to sojourn at my house,
I'll not be there.

  Cornwall.   Nor I, assure thee, Regan.
Edmund, I hear that you have shown your father   105
A child-like office.

  Edmund.   'Twas my duty, sir.

  Gloucester. He did bewray his practice; and receiv'd
This hurt you see, striving to apprehend him.

  Cornwall. Is he pursu'd?

  Gloucester.   Ay, my good lord.

  Cornwall. If he be taken he shall never more   110
Be fear'd of doing harm; make your own purpose,
How in my strength you please. For you, Edmund,

---

    92 nam'd: in baptism.   **97 consort:** (accent consórt) com-
pany.   **99 put him on:** egged him on to (attempt).   **100 to
have . . . waste of:** that he might be able to spend wastefully.
106 child-like: truly filial [*N*].   **107 bewray:** reveal.   **practice:** plot.   **111 of doing:** lest he should do.   **make . . .
please:** use my authority and resources as you like in carrying out
your purpose.

Whose virtue and obedience doth this instant
So much commend itself, you shall be ours:
Natures of such deep trust we shall much need;   115
You we first seize on.

   Edmund.   I shall serve you, sir,
Truly, however else.

   Gloucester.   For him I thank your Grace.

   Cornwall. You know not why we came to visit you,—

   Regan. Thus out of season, threading dark-ey'd night:
Occasions, noble Gloucester, of some prize,   120
Wherein we must have use of your advice,
Our father he hath writ, so hath our sister,
Of differences, which I best thought it fit
To answer from our home; the several messengers
From hence attend dispatch. Our good old friend,   125
Lay comforts to your bosom, and bestow
Your needful counsel to our businesses,
Which craves the instant use.

   Gloucester.   I serve you, madam.
Your Graces are right welcome.   [*Exeunt.*

Scene II. BEFORE GLOUCESTER'S CASTLE

Enter KENT *and* OSWALD, *severally.*

Oswald. Good dawning to thee, friend: art of this house?

Kent. Ay.

Oswald. Where may we set our horses?

Kent. I' the mire.

Oswald. Prithee, if thou lovest me, tell me.   5

113 **virtue and obedience**: virtuous obedience (hence verb in
singular).   117 **else**: successfully or not.   119 **threading
dark-ey'd**: (with a pun on the eye of a needle) [*N*].   120
Occasions . . . prize: incidents of some importance have occurred.
124 **from**: away from.   125 **attend dispatch**: wait to be sent
out.   128 **craves . . . use**: demands immediate execution.
1 **of this house**: a dependant, servant.

Kent. I love thee not.

Oswald. Why, then I care not for thee.

Kent. If I had thee in Lipsbury pinfold, I would make thee care for me.

Oswald. Why dost thou use me thus? I know thee not.

Kent. Fellow, I know thee.   11

Oswald. What dost thou know me for?

Kent. A knave, a rascal, an eater of broken meats; a base, proud, shallow, beggarly, three-suited, hundred-pound, filthy, worsted-stocking knave; a lily-liver'd,   15
action-taking knave; a whoreson, glass-gazing, super-serviceable, finical rogue; one-trunk-inheriting slave; one that wouldst be a bawd, in way of good service, and art nothing but the composition of a knave, beg-gar, coward, pandar, and the son and heir of a mongrel   20
bitch: one whom I will beat into clamorous whining if thou deniest the least syllable of thy addition.

Oswald. Why, what a monstrous fellow art thou, thus to rail on one that is neither known of thee nor knows thee!

Kent. What a brazen-faced varlet art thou, to deny   25
thou knowest me! Is it two days since I tripped up thy heels and beat thee before the king? Draw, you rogue; for, though it be night, yet the moon shines: I'll make a sop o' the moonshine of you. [*Drawing his sword.*]
Draw, you whoreson, cullionly, barber-monger, draw.   30

8 **in Lipsbury pinfold:** possibly 'in my jaws' [*N*].   13 **eater
. . . broken meats:** finisher up of scraps [*N*].   14 **three-
suited:** the allowance of some servants.   **hundred-pound:** owning
only a hundred pounds (the qualification for a jury then)   15
worsted: woollen (as opposed to silk).   **lily-liver'd:** see IV. ii. 50.
16 **action-taking:** resorting to legal protection (instead of defend-
ing himself).   **glass-gazing:** vain.   **super-serviceable:** *either*
above his work, *or* over officious.   17 **finical:** affected.   **one-
trunk-inheriting:** whose possessions would all go in one chest.
18 **in way of:** in order to perform.   19 **composition:** mixture.
22 **thy addition:** these titles.   30 **cullionly:** rascally.   **barber-
monger:** frequenter of barbers, fop.

Oswald. Away! I have nothing to do with thee.

Kent. Draw, you rascal; you come with letters against
the king, and take Vanity the puppet's part against the
royalty of her father. Draw, you rogue, or I'll so carbonado
your shanks: draw, you rascal; come your ways.   35

Oswald. Help, ho! murder! help!

Kent. Strike, you slave; stand, rogue, stand; you neat
slave, strike.   [*Beating him.*

Oswald. Help, oh! murder! murder!

Enter EDMUND, *with his rapier drawn.*

Edmund. How now! What's the matter?   40
                                        [*Parting them.*

Kent. With you, goodman boy, if you please: come, I'll
flesh ye; come on, young master.

Enter CORNWALL, REGAN, GLOUCESTER, *and* Servants.

Gloucester. Weapons! arms! What's the matter here?

Cornwall. Keep peace, upon your lives:
He dies that strikes again. What is the matter?   45

Regan. The messengers from our sister and the king.

Cornwall. What is your difference? speak.

Oswald. I am scarce in breath, my lord.

Kent. No marvel, you have so bestirred your valour.
You cowardly rascal, nature disclaims in thee: a tailor
made thee.   51

Cornwall. Thou art a strange fellow; a tailor make a
man?

Kent. Ay, a tailor, sir: a stone-cutter or a painter could

33 **Vanity the puppet's:** i.e. Goneril's [*N*].   34 **carbonado:**
slice, slash.   35 **come your ways:** come on   37 **neat:**
dandified *or* utter.   41 **With you:** my matter, quarrel is with
you *or* I'm your man (for a fight).   42 **flesh:** initiate (into blood-
shed).   47 **difference:** (ground of) quarrel.   50 **disclaims:**
disown (any share).   54 **stone-cutter:** sculptor.

not have made him so ill, though they had been but two
hours o' the trade. 56

Cornwall. Speak yet, how grew your quarrel?

Oswald. This ancient ruffian, sir, whose life I have spar'd
at suit of his grey beard,— 59

Kent. Thou whoreson zed! thou unnecessary letter! My
lord, if you will give me leave, I will tread this unbolted
villain into mortar, and daub the wall of a jakes with him.
Spare my grey beard, you wagtail?

Cornwall. Peace, sirrah!
You beastly knave, know you no reverence? 65

Kent. Yes, sir; but anger hath a privilege.

Cornwall. Why art thou angry?

Kent. That such a slave as this should wear a sword,
Who wears no honesty. Such smiling rogues as these,
Like rats, oft bite the holy cords a-twain 70
Which are too intrinse t' unloose; smooth every passion
That in the natures of their lords rebel;
Bring oil to fire, snow to their colder moods,
Renege, affirm, and turn their halcyon beaks
With every gale and vary of their masters, 75
Knowing nought, like dogs, but following.
A plague upon your epileptic visage!
Smile you my speeches, as I were a fool?
Goose, if I had you upon Sarum plain,
I'd drive ye cackling home to Camelot. 80

Cornwall. What! art thou mad, old fellow?

---

61 **unbolted:** perhaps 'unmitigated' (bolt = sift flour). 62
jakes: privy. 63 **wagtail:** probably 'obsequious', from its
bouncing or bobbing. 70 **the holy cords:** of intimate relationship. 71 **intrinse:** intricate, tight. **smooth:** flatter, fall
in with. 74 **Renege:** deny [N]. 75 **gale and vary:**
varying breeze. 77 **epileptic:** distorted and pale, as in an
epileptic fit. 78 **Smile you:** do you smile at? 79 **Sarum:**
Salisbury. 80 **Camelot:** supposed to be near Winchester
[N].

Gloucester. How fell you out? say that.

Kent. No contraries hold more antipathy
Than I and such a knave.

Cornwall. Why dost thou call him knave? What is his
    fault?   85

Kent. His countenance likes me not.

Cornwall. No more, perchance, does mine, nor his, nor
    hers.

Kent. Sir, 'tis my occupation to be plain:
I have seen better faces in my time
Than stands on any shoulder that I see   90
Before me at this instant.

Cornwall.   This is some fellow,
Who, having been prais'd for bluntness, doth affect
A saucy roughness, and constrains the garb
Quite from his nature: he cannot flatter, he,
An honest mind and plain, he must speak truth: 95
An they will take it, so; if not, he's plain.
These kind of knaves I know, which in this plainness
Harbour more craft and more corrupter ends
Than twenty silly-ducking observants,
That stretch their duties nicely.   100

Kent. Sir, in good sooth, in sincere verity,
Under the allowance of your grand aspect,
Whose influence, like the wreath of radiant fire   103
On flickering Phœbus' front,—

Cornwall.   What mean'st by this?

---

86 **likes**: pleases.   88 **occupation**: business, habit.   93–94
constrains the garb . . . nature: is behaving in a manner quite
unnatural to him (garb = fashion, manner, but not of *dress* in
Shakespeare).   96 **so**: well and good.   98 **more corrupter**:
double comparative, not uncommon in Shakespeare.   99 **silly-
ducking observants**: obsequious attendants foolishly bowing and
scraping (observe = pay court to).   100 **stretch . . . nicely**:
are over-particular in the performance of.   102 **aspect**: power,
influence (astrological).

Kent. To go out of my dialect, which you discommend so
much. I know, sir, I am no flatterer: he that beguiled you
in a plain accent was a plain knave; which for my part I
will not be, though I should win your displeasure to entreat
me to 't.

Cornwall. What was the offence you gave him?   110
Oswald. I never gave him any:
It pleas'd the king his master very late
To strike at me, upon his misconstruction;
When he, conjunct, and flattering his displeasure,
Tripp'd me behind; being down, insulted, rail'd,   115
And put upon him such a deal of man,
That worthied him, got praises of the king
For him attempting who was self-subdu'd;
And, in the fleshment of this dread exploit,   119
Drew on me here again.

Kent.   None of these rogues and cowards
But Ajax is their fool.

Cornwall.   Fetch forth the stocks!
You stubborn ancient knave, you reverend braggart,
We'll teach you.

Kent.   Sir, I am too old to learn,
Call not your stocks for me; I serve the king,
On whose employment I was sent to you;   125
You shall do small respect, show too bold malice
Against the grace and person of my master,

106 **he that:** i.e. the 'kind of knaves' referred to in l. 97.   107
a plain knave: a real knave (which I am not) [*N*].   108 **your
displeasure:** you, in your displeasure.   109 **to 't:** to flatter
you [*N*].   113 **upon his misconstruction:** misunderstanding
me; see I. iv. 82.   114 **conjunct:** joining in with (Lear).   116–
17 **put upon . . . worthied him:** made such a show of valour as to
win the reputation of honour.   118 **him attempting:** attacking
a man.   119 **fleshment:** excitement resulting from first success,
see l. 42.   121 **their fool:** a fool compared to them [*N*].   122
reverend: grey-headed, old enough to know better.

Stocking his messenger.

Cornwall. Fetch forth the stocks! As I have life and honour,
There shall he sit till noon.   130

Regan. Till noon! Till night, my lord; and all night too.

Kent. Why, madam, if I were your father's dog,
You should not use me so.

Regan.   Sir, being his knave, I will.

Cornwall. This is a fellow of the self-same colour
Our sister speaks of. Come, bring away the stocks.   135

                                        [*Stocks brought out.*

Gloucester. Let me beseech your Grace not to do so.
His fault is much, and the good king his master
Will check him for't: your purpos'd low correction
Is such as basest and contemned'st wretches
For pilferings and most common trespasses   140
Are punish'd with: the king must take it ill,
That he, so slightly valu'd in his messenger,
Should have him thus restrain'd.

Cornwall.   I'll answer that.

Regan. My sister may receive it much more worse
To have her gentleman abus'd, assaulted,   145
For following her affairs. Put in his legs.

                                [KENT *is put in the stocks.*

Come, my good lord, away.

                          [*Exeunt all but* GLOUCESTER *and* KENT.

Gloucester. I am sorry for thee, friend; 'tis the duke's
    pleasure,
Whose disposition, all the world well knows,
Will not be rubb'd nor stopp'd: I'll entreat for thee.   150

Kent. Pray, do not, sir. I have watch'd and travell'd hard;

---

128 **stocking**: putting in stocks.   134 **colour**: complexion,
kind.   135 **bring away**: bring in.   139 **contemned'st**:
most despicable.   143 **answer**: take responsibility for.   150
rubb'd: hindered (a 'rub' is an obstacle in bowls).   151 **watch'd**:
lain awake at night.

Some time I shall sleep out, the rest I'll whistle.
A good man's fortune may grow out at heels:
Give you good morrow!   154
   Gloucester. The duke's to blame in this; 'twill be ill taken.
                                         [Exit.

   Kent. Good king, that must approve the common saw,
Thou out of heaven's benediction comest
To the warm sun.
Approach, thou beacon to this under globe,
That by thy comfortable beams I may   160
Peruse this letter. Nothing almost sees miracles
But misery: I know 'tis from Cordelia,
Who hath most fortunately been inform'd
Of my obscured course; and shall find time
From this enormous state, seeking to give   165
Losses their remedies. All weary and o'er-watch'd,
Take vantage, heavy eyes, not to behold
This shameful lodging.   168
Fortune, good night, smile once more; turn thy wheel!
                                       [He sleeps.

Scene III. A Part of the Heath

Enter EDGAR.

   Edgar. I heard myself proclaim'd;
And by the happy hollow of a tree

   153 **out at heels:** a metaphor for 'in a bad way', like 'out at
elbow' or 'down at heel'.   156 **approve:** prove (the truth of).
saw: proverb.   157–8 i.e. from better to worse (a surprising sense,
but proved by other examples).   159 **thou beacon:** the sun.   **this
under globe:** our world, as opposed to heaven (157).   162 **misery:**
the wretched [*N*].   164 **my obscured course:** what has
happened to me who appear to have disappeared.   164–6 **and
who will find the opportunity to deliver us from this unnatural
state of affairs, putting right what is wrong [*N*].   167 **vantage:**
advantage (of the opportunity).   1 **proclaim'd:** see II. i. 61.
2 **happy:** luckily found.

Escap'd the hunt. No port is free; no place,
That guard, and most unusual vigilance,
Does not attend my taking. While I may 'scape   5
I will preserve myself; and am bethought
To take the basest and most poorest shape
That ever penury, in contempt of man,
Brought near to beast; my face I'll grime with filth,
Blanket my loins, elf all my hair in knots,   10
And with presented nakedness outface
The winds and persecutions of the sky.
The country gives me proof and precedent
Of Bedlam beggars, who with roaring voices,
Strike in their numb'd and mortified bare arms   15
Pins, wooden pricks, nails, sprigs of rosemary;
And with this horrible object, from low farms,
Poor pelting villages, sheep-cotes, and mills,
Sometime with lunatic bans, sometime with prayers,
Enforce their charity. Poor Turlygood! poor Tom!   20
That's something yet: Edgar I nothing am.   [*Exit.*

Scene IV. BEFORE GLOUCESTER'S CASTLE. KENT IN
THE STOCKS

Enter LEAR, Fool, *and* Gentleman.

Lear. 'Tis strange that they should so depart from home,
And not send back my messenger.
Gentleman.   As I learn'd,
The night before there was no purpose in them

---

4 **That:** i.e. where.   5 **attend my taking:** wait to arrest me.
6–7 **am bethought to take:** have bethought myself of taking.
10 **elf:** tangle (as an elf might).   11 **presented:** *either* assumed
or exposed to view [*N*].   14 **Bedlam:** cf. I. ii. 136.   15 **Strike:**
drive.   16 **pricks:** skewers.   17 **object:** appearance.
18 **pelting:** petty.   19 **bans:** curses.   20 **Turlygood:** no
certain explanation.   21 **Edgar . . . am:** *either* I am Edgar no
more, *or* As Edgar I no longer exist.   1 **they:** Cornwall and Regan.

Of this remove.

Kent.   Hail to thee, noble master!

Lear. Ha!   5

Mak'st thou this shame thy pastime?

Kent.   No, my lord.

Fool. Ha, ha! he wears cruel garters. Horses are tied by
the head, dogs and bears by the neck, monkeys by the
loins, and men by the legs: when a man is over-lusty at
legs, then he wears wooden nether-stocks.   10

Lear. What's he that hath so much thy place mistook
To set thee here?

Kent.   It is both he and she,
Your son and daughter.

Lear. No.

Kent. Yes.   15

Lear. No, I say.

Kent. I say, yea.

Lear. No, no; they would not.

Kent. Yes, they have.

Lear. By Jupiter, I swear, no.   20

Kent. By Juno, I swear, ay.

Lear.   They durst not do 't;
They could not, would not do 't; 'tis worse than murder,
To do upon respect such violent outrage.
Resolve me, with all modest haste, which way
Thou mightst deserve, or they impose, this usage,   25
Coming from us.

Kent.   My lord, when at their home
I did commend your highness' letters to them,

---

4 **remove:** change of residence.   7 **cruel:** with a pun on
'crewel' = worsted yarn.   10 **nether-stocks:** stockings (as
opposed to 'upper stocks' = breeches).   11 **place:** rank, status
as my envoy.   23 **upon respect:** deliberately.   24 **Resolve me:**
explain to me.   **modest:** becoming.   26 **Coming from us:**
seeing that you came from me.

Ere I was risen from the place that show'd
My duty kneeling, there came a reeking post,
Stew'd in his haste, half breathless, panting forth   30
From Goneril his mistress salutations;
Deliver'd letters, spite of intermission,
Which presently they read: on whose contents
They summon'd up their meiny, straight took horse;
Commanded me to follow, and attend   35
The leisure of their answer; gave me cold looks:
And meeting here the other messenger,
Whose welcome, I perceiv'd, had poison'd mine,—
Being the very fellow which of late
Display'd so saucily against your highness,—   40
Having more man than wit about me, drew:
He rais'd the house with loud and coward cries.
Your son and daughter found this trespass worth
The shame which here it suffers.

Fool. Winter's not gone yet, if the wild geese fly that
way.   46

> Fathers that wear rags
>   Do make their children blind,
> But fathers that bear bags
>   Shall see their children kind.   50
> Fortune, that arrant whore,
> Ne'er turns the key to the poor.

But for all this thou shalt have as many dolours for thy
daughters as thou canst tell in a year.

29 **post**: messenger.   30 **Stew'd** sweating.   32 **spite of
intermission**: in spite of the fact he was interrupting me.   33
presently: immediately.   34 **meiny**: household, company.
37 **And meeting**: And I, meeting.   40 **Display'd**: showed off.
41 **man**: courage (cf. ii. ii. 116).   45 i.e. We are not out of trouble.
48 **blind**: to filial duty.   49 **bags**: of money .   52 **turns
the key**: to admit.   53 **dolours**: griefs (with pun on 'dollars'=
money).   **for**: from, because of.   54 **tell**: (1) recount griefs,
(2) count money.

Lear. O! how this mother swells up toward my heart;
Hysterica passio! down, thou climbing sorrow! 56
Thy element's below. Where is this daughter?

Kent. With the earl, sir: here within.

Lear. Follow me not; stay here. [*Exit.*

Gentleman. Made you no more offence than what you
speak of? 61

Kent. None.
How chance the king comes with so small a number?

Fool. An thou hadst been set i' the stocks for that question, thou hadst well deserved it. 65

Kent. Why, fool?

Fool. We'll set thee to school to an ant, to teach
thee there's no labouring i' the winter. All that follow
their noses are led by their eyes but blind men; and
there's not a nose among twenty but can smell him 70
that's stinking. Let go thy hold when a great wheel
runs down a hill, lest it break thy neck with following
it; but the great one that goes up the hill, let him draw
thee after. When a wise man gives thee better counsel, give me mine again: I would have none but 75
knaves follow it, since a fool gives it.

> That sir which serves and seeks for gain,
> And follows but for form,
> Will pack when it begins to rain,
> And leave thee in the storm. 80
> But I will tarry; the fool will stay,
> And let the wise man fly:

---

55 **mother:** hysteria [*N*]. 56 **Hysterica passio!:** suffering in
the 'mother' (archaic for womb, Gk. hystera), so-called as commoner
in women. 64–65 i.e. you should know that people desert a
losing cause. 70–71 i.e. it does not take the keen smell of a
blind man to smell out the poor state of Lear's fortunes [*N*].
77 **sir:** gentleman. 79 **pack:** clear off. 82 **wise:** i.e.
worldly wise.

    The knave turns fool that runs away;
      The fool no knave, perdy.

Kent. Where learn'd you this, fool?   85
Fool. Not i' the stocks, fool.

Re-enter LEAR, *with* GLOUCESTER.

  Lear. Deny to speak with me! They are sick! they are
    weary!
They have travell'd hard to-night! Mere fetches,
The images of revolt and flying off.
Fetch me a better answer.

  Gloucester.   My dear lord,   90
You know the fiery quality of the duke;
How unremovable and fix'd he is
In his own course.

  Lear. Vengeance! plague! death! confusion!
Fiery! what quality? Why, Gloucester, Gloucester,   95
I'd speak with the Duke of Cornwall and his wife.

  Gloucester. Well, my good lord, I have inform'd them so.

  Lear. Inform'd them! Dost thou understand me, man?

  Gloucester. Ay, my good lord.

  Lear. The king would speak with Cornwall; the dear
    father   100
Would with his daughter speak, commands her service:
Are they inform'd of this? My breath and blood!
Fiery! the fiery duke! Tell the hot duke that—
No, but not yet; may be he is not well:
Infirmity doth still neglect all office   105
Whereto our health is bound; we are not ourselves

---

    83 turns fool: i.e. judged from a higher, less self-interested point
of view.   **84 The fool:** the Fool, I.   **perdy:** par Dieu.
87 Deny: refuse.   **88 fetches:** tricks, excuses (with pun in l. 90).
89 images: tokens *or* embodiment (cf. IV. vi. 158).   **flying off:**
desertion.   **91 quality:** nature.   **103 hot:** hot-tempered.
105 Infirmity: a sick man.   **office:** duty.   **106 Whereto . . .
bound:** which, if well, we should feel bound to perform.

When nature, being oppress'd, commands the mind
To suffer with the body. I'll forbear;
And am fall'n out with my more headier will,
To take the indispos'd and sickly fit   110
For the sound man. Death on my state! [*Looking on*
    KENT.] Wherefore
Should he sit here? This act persuades me
That this remotion of the duke and her
Is practice only. Give me my servant forth.
Go, tell the duke and 's wife I'd speak with them,   115
Now, presently: bid them come forth and hear me,
Or at their chamber-door I'll beat the drum
Till it cry sleep to death.

   Gloucester. I would have all well betwixt you.   [*Exit.*
   Lear. O, me! my heart, my rising heart? but, down!   120
   Fool. Cry to it, nuncle, as the cockney did to the eels
when she put 'em i' the paste alive; she knapped 'em o' the
coxcombs with a stick, and cried, 'Down, wantons, down!'
'Twas her brother that, in pure kindness to his horse,
buttered his hay.   125

   Enter CORNWALL, REGAN, GLOUCESTER, *and* Servants.

   Lear. Good morrow to you both.
   Cornwall.   Hail to your Grace.
                              [KENT *is set at liberty.*
   Regan. I am glad to see your highness.
   Lear. Regan, I think you are; I know what reason
I have to think so: if thou shouldst not be glad,

---

   109 i.e. I turn back from my overhasty determination.   113
remotion: removal (from their home).   114 **practice:** a trick.
118 **cry sleep to death:** drown sleep with its noise (as Macbeth heard
a voice 'murder' sleep, Macbeth II. ii. 36–37).   121 **cockney:**
(probably) an affected woman.   122 **knapped:** rapped, struck.
123 **coxcombs:** heads.   **wantons:** pert, cheeky creatures [*N*].
125 **buttered his hay:** i.e. did something equally silly [*N*].

I would divorce me from thy mother's tomb,   130
Sepulchring an adultress.—[*To* KENT.] O! are you free?
Some other time for that. Beloved Regan,
Thy sister's naught: O Regan! she hath tied
Sharp-tooth'd unkindness, like a vulture, here:

                                   [*Points to his heart.*
I can scarce speak to thee; thou'lt not believe   135
With how deprav'd a quality—O Regan!
  Regan. I pray you, sir, take patience. I have hope
You less know how to value her desert
Than she to scant her duty.
  Lear.   Say, how is that?
  Regan. I cannot think my sister in the least   140
Would fail her obligation: if, sir, perchance
She have restrain'd the riots of your followers,
'Tis on such ground, and to such wholesome end,
As clears her from all blame.
  Lear. My curses on her.
  Regan.   O, sir! you are old;   145
Nature in you stands on the very verge
Of her confine: you should be rul'd and led
By some discretion that discerns your state
Better than you yourself. Therefore I pray you
That to our sister you do make return;   150
Say, you have wrong'd her, sir.
  Lear.   Ask her forgiveness?
Do you but mark how this becomes the house:
'Dear daughter, I confess that I am old;
Age is unnecessary: on my knees I beg   [*Kneeling.*

131 **Sepulchring**: (as it would then be) the tomb of.   136
quality: manner (she treated me).   138 **desert**: merits [*N*].
139 **Than she** (knows how) **to scant**: is capable of falling short of.
147 **confine**: boundary, utmost limit.   148 **discretion**:
discreet people.   150 **make return**: return.   152 **the
house**: our family relationship *or* the royal house.   154 **unnecessary**: useless, has no right to exist [*N*].

That you'll vouchsafe me raiment, bed, and food.'   155
   Regan. Good sir, no more; these are unsightly tricks:
Return you to my sister.
   Lear.   [*Rising.*] Never, Regan.
She hath abated me of half my train;
Look'd black upon me; struck me with her tongue,
Most serpent-like, upon the very heart.   160
All the stor'd vengeances of heaven fall
On her ingrateful top! Strike her young bones,
You taking airs, with lameness!
   Cornwall.   Fie, sir, fie!
   Lear. You nimble lightnings, dart your blinding flames
Into her scornful eyes! Infect her beauty,   165
You fen-suck'd fogs, drawn by the powerful sun,
To fall and blast her pride!
   Regan. O the blest gods! So will you wish on me,
When the rash mood is on.
   Lear. No, Regan, thou shalt never have my curse: 170
Thy tender-hefted nature shall not give
Thee o'er to harshness: her eyes are fierce, but thine
Do comfort and not burn. 'Tis not in thee
To grudge my pleasures, to cut off my train,
To bandy hasty words, to scant my sizes,   175
And, in conclusion, to oppose the bolt
Against my coming in: thou better know'st
The offices of nature, bond of childhood,
Effects of courtesy, dues of gratitude;
Thy half o' the kingdom hast thou not forgot,   180
Wherein I thee endow'd.

---

  158 **abated**: curtailed.   162 **top**: head.   163 **taking**:
infecting, infectious [*N*].   169 **the rash mood**: cf. i. i. 288.
171 **tender-hefted**: (probably) set in a delicate bodily frame (heft
= haft = handle), womanly.   175 **sizes**: allowances (cf. sizar
= exhibitioner, sometimes at Cambridge).   176 **oppose the
bolt**: bar the door.   179 **Effects**: manifestations.

Regan.   Good sir, to the purpose.
Lear. Who put my man i' the stocks?   [*Tucket within.*
Cornwall.   What trumpet's that?
Regan. I know't, my sister's; this approves her letter,
That she would soon be here. Is your lady come?

Enter OSWALD.

Lear. This is a slave, whose easy-borrow'd pride   185
Dwells in the fickle grace of her he follows.
Out, varlet, from my sight!
Cornwall.   What means your Grace?

Enter GONERIL.

Lear. Who stock'd my servant? Regan, I have good
    hope
Thou didst not know on't. Who comes here? O heavens,
If you do love old men, if your sweet sway   190
Allow obedience, if yourselves are old,
Make it your cause; send down and take my part!
[*To* GONERIL.] Art not asham'd to look upon this beard?
O Regan, wilt thou take her by the hand?
Goneril. Why not by the hand, sir? How have I offended?
All's not offence that indiscretion finds   196
And dotage terms so.
Lear.   O sides! you are too tough;
Will you yet hold? How came my man i' the stocks?
Cornwall. I set him there, sir: but his own disorders
Deserv'd much less advancement.
Lear.   You! did you?   200

181 **to the purpose**: come to the point.   183 **approves**:
confirms.   185 **easy-borrow'd**: assumed without justification.
186 **fickle**: unreliable (as not given for merit).   191 **Allow**:
approve.   192 **Make it your cause**: identify yourselves with my
side.   196 **indiscretion**: cf. 148.   **finds**: holds.   200 **much
less advancement**: greater disgrace.

Regan. I pray you, father, being weak, seem so.
If, till the expiration of your month,
You will return and sojourn with my sister,
Dismissing half your train, come then to me:
I am now from home, and out of that provision   205
Which shall be needful for your entertainment.
    Lear. Return to her? and fifty men dismiss'd!
No, rather I abjure all roofs, and choose
To wage against the enmity o' the air;
To be a comrade with the wolf and owl,   210
Necessity's sharp pinch! Return with her!
Why, the hot-blooded France, that dowerless took
Our youngest born, I could as well be brought
To knee his throne, and, squire-like, pension beg
To keep base life afoot. Return with her!   215
Persuade me rather to be slave and sumpter
To this detested groom.   [*Pointing at* OSWALD.
    Goneril.   At your choice, sir.
    Lear. I prithee, daughter, do not make me mad:
I will not trouble thee, my child; farewell.
We'll no more meet, no more see one another;   220
But yet thou art my flesh, my blood, my daughter;
Or rather a disease that's in my flesh,
Which I must needs call mine: thou art a boil,
A plague-sore, an embossed carbuncle,
In my corrupted blood. But I'll not chide thee   225
Let shame come when it will, I do not call it:
I do not bid the thunder-bearer shoot,

---

201 **seem so:** admit it, behave accordingly.   205 **from:**
away from.   209 **wage** (war) **against:** contend with.   211
Necessity's sharp pinch: straits to which need will reduce me (cf.
'Necessitie must first pinch you by the throat' in Florio's *Montaigne*).
214 **knee:** kneel before.   216 **sumpter:** beast of burden.
224 **embossed:** swollen.   227 **the thunder-bearer:** *Juppiter
tonans.*   **shoot:** strike with lightning [*N*].

Nor tell tales of thee to high-judging Jove.
Mend when thou canst; be better at thy leisure:
I can be patient; I can stay with Regan,   230
I and my hundred knights.

    Regan.   Not altogether so:
I look'd not for you yet, nor am provided
For your fit welcome. Give ear, sir, to my sister;
For those that mingle reason with your passion
Must be content to think you old, and so—   235
But she knows what she does.

    Lear.   Is this well spoken?

    Regan. I dare avouch it, sir: what! fifty followers?
Is it not well? What should you need of more?
Yea, or so many, sith that both charge and danger
Speak 'gainst so great a number? How, in one house,
Should many people, under two commands,   241
Hold amity? 'Tis hard; almost impossible.

    Goneril. Why might not you, my lord, receive attendance
From those that she calls servants, or from mine?

    Regan. Why not, my lord? If then they chanc'd to slack
    you   245
We could control them. If you will come to me,
For now I spy a danger, I entreat you
To bring but five-and-twenty; to no more
Will I give place or notice.

    Lear. I gave you all—

    Regan.   And in good time you gave it.

    Lear. Made you my guardians, my depositaries,   251

228 **high-judging**: supreme judge *or* judge in heaven. 234
mingle . . . passion: examine your passionate utterances in the
light of reason (but the figure is probably from mixing drinks).
235 **and so—**: *sc.* not take you seriously (or something similar) [*N*].
239 **sith**: since. **charge**: the expense. **danger**: i.e. of disturbance. 242 **amity**: friendship. 245 **slack you**: be
negligent in serving you. 249 **notice**: recognition. 251
depositaries: trustees.

But kept a reservation to be follow'd
With such a number. What! must I come to you
With five-and-twenty? Regan, said you so?   254
  Regan. And speak 't again, my lord; no more with me.
  Lear. Those wicked creatures yet do look well-favour'd,
When others are more wicked; not being the worst
Stands in some rank of praise. [*To* GONERIL.] I'll go with
    thee:
Thy fifty yet doth double five-and-twenty,
And thou art twice her love.
  Goneril.   Hear me, my lord.   260
What need you five-and-twenty, ten, or five,
To follow in a house, where twice so many
Have a command to tend you?
  Regan.   What need one?
  Lear. O! reason not the need; our basest beggars
Are in the poorest thing superfluous: 265
Allow not nature more than nature needs,
Man's life is cheap as beast's. Thou art a lady;
If only to go warm were gorgeous,
Why, nature needs not what thou gorgeous wear'st,   269
Which scarcely keeps thee warm. But, for true need,—
You heavens, give me that patience, patience I need!
You see me here, you gods, a poor old man,
As full of grief as age; wretched in both!

252 **kept a reservation**: made a saving clause or exception (see
I. i. 132).   256 **Those . . . creatures**: i.e. Goneril.   260
art twice her love: show me twice as much love.   264 **reason
not**: don't argue about [*N*]. 265 **superfluous**: possessing more than
they actually need.   266 **Allow not nature**: if you don't allow
men to possess.   267 **cheap as**: of as little value as.   268–70
i.e. If the need for warmth were the only purpose of wearing (fine)
clothes, well, your body does not need the fine clothes you wear—
which incidentally hardly do keep you warm. (The first 'gorgeous'
is not the logical word but is effective).   270 **for true need**: as
for what I really need most.   271 **that**: the omission of this word
would improve sense and metre.

If it be you that stir these daughters' hearts
Against their father, fool me not so much   275
To bear it tamely; touch me with noble anger,
And let not women's weapons, water-drops,
Stain my man's cheeks! No, you unnatural hags,
I will have such revenges on you both
That all the world shall—I will do such things,—   280
What they are yet I know not,—but they shall be
The terrors of the earth. You think I'll weep;
No, I'll not weep:
I have full cause of weeping, but this heart
Shall break into a hundred thousand flaws   285
Or ere I'll weep. O fool! I shall go mad.

       [*Exeunt* LEAR, GLOUCESTER, KENT, *and* Fool.
  Cornwall. Let us withdraw; 'twill be a storm.

       [*Storm heard at a distance.*
  Regan. This house is little; the old man and his people
Cannot be well bestow'd.
  Goneril. 'Tis his own blame; hath put himself from rest,
And must needs taste his folly.   291
  Regan. For his particular, I'll receive him gladly,
But not one follower.
  Goneril.   So am I purpos'd.
Where is my Lord of Gloucester?   294
  Cornwall. Follow'd the old man forth. He is return'd.

Re-enter GLOUCESTER.

  Gloucester. The king is in high rage.
  Cornwall.   Whither is he going?
  Gloucester. He calls to horse; but will I know not whither.

275 **fool me . . . To:** do not make me such a fool as to (perhaps
with reference to a Fool who has to endure what his master does to
him).   285 **flaws:** cracks *and/or* fragments.   286 **Or ere:**
before (which each word means).   289 **bestow'd:** accommodated.   290 **hath:** he hath.   **from:** out of.   292 **his
particular:** himself alone.

Cornwall. 'Tis best to give him way; he leads himself.

Goneril. My lord, entreat him by no means to stay.

Gloucester. Alack! the night comes on, and the bleak
    winds   300
Do sorely ruffle; for many miles about
There's scarce a bush.

Regan.   O! sir, to wilful men,
The injuries that they themselves procure
Must be their schoolmasters. Shut up your doors;
He is attended with a desperate train,   305
And what they may incense him to, being apt
To have his ear abus'd, wisdom bids fear.

Cornwall. Shut up your doors, my lord; 'tis a wild night:
My Regan counsels well: come out o' the storm.   [*Exeunt.*

298 **give him way**: let him be.   **leads himself**: insists on his
own way.   301 **ruffle**: bluster.   305 **with**: by [*N*].   307
abus'd: misled [*N*].

ACT III

Scene I. A Heath

A storm, with thunder and lightning. Enter KENT *and a*
Gentleman, *meeting.*

Kent. Who's here, beside foul weather?

Gentleman. One minded like the weather, most unquietly.

Kent. I know you. Where's the king?

Gentleman. Contending with the fretful elements;
Bids the wind blow the earth into the sea,　　　　　5
Or swell the curled waters 'bove the main,
That things might change or cease; tears his white hair,
Which the impetuous blasts, with eyeless rage,
Catch in their fury, and make nothing of;
Strives in his little world of man to out-scorn　　10
The to-and-fro-conflicting wind and rain.
This night, wherein the cub-drawn bear would couch,
The lion and the belly-pinched wolf
Keep their fur dry, unbonneted he runs,
And bids what will take all.

Kent.　　　　　　　　But who is with him?　　15

Gentleman. None but the fool, who labours to out-jest
His heart-struck injuries.

Kent.　　　　　　　　Sir, I do know you;
And dare, upon the warrant of my note,

---

6 main: mainland (as in 'Spanish main'). **7 things:** the
order of the world, *natura rerum.* **8 eyeless:** blind. **9
make nothing of:** show no respect for. **12 cub-drawn:**
drained by her cubs (and so ravenous). **couch:** lie down. **14 unbonneted:** bare-headed (reminding us also of the *crown* he has
given up). **15 what will take all:** everything go hang (a
gesture of despair). **16 out-jest:** jest him out of. **17
heart-struck:** which have struck him to the heart (cf. II. iv. 160).
18 upon ... note: on the strength of my knowledge.

Commend a dear thing to you. There is division,
Although as yet the face of it be cover'd   20
With mutual cunning, 'twixt Albany and Cornwall;
Who have—as who have not, that their great stars
Thron'd and set high?—servants, who seem no less,
Which are to France the spies and speculations
Intelligent of our state; what hath been seen,   25
Either in snuffs and packings of the dukes,
Or the hard rein which both of them have borne
Against the old kind king; or something deeper,
Whereof perchance these are but furnishings;
But, true it is, from France there comes a power   30
Into this scatter'd kingdom; who already,
Wise in our negligence, have secret feet
In some of our best ports, and are at point
To show their open banner. Now to you:
If on my credit you dare build so far   35
To make your speed to Dover, you shall find
Some that will thank you, making just report
Of how unnatural and bemadding sorrow
The king hath cause to plain.
I am a gentleman of blood and breeding,   40
And from some knowledge and assurance offer
This office to you.
    Gentleman. I will talk further with you.

  19 **dear:** important.   23 **seem no less:** at any rate appear
to be servants.   24 **speculations:** observers, spies (abstract for
concrete, as often).   25 **Intelligent of:** giving information
about.   26 **snuffs:** resentments, quarrels.   **packings:** plots.
27 **hard rein:** metaphor from curbing a horse severely.   29
furnishings: the trimmings.   30 **power:** army.   31 **scatter'd:** divided.   32 **secret feet:** landed secretly.   33 **at
point:** ready.   34 **Now to you:** to come to your part   35 **on
my credit ... build:** trust me.   37 **making:** when you make.
39 **plain:** complain of.   41 **knowledge and assurance:** sure
knowledge.

Kent.   No, do not.
For confirmation that I am much more
Than my out-wall, open this purse, and take   45
What it contains. If you shall see Cordelia,—
As doubt not but you shall,—show her this ring,
And she will tell you who your fellow is
That yet you do not know. Fie on this storm!
I will go seek the king.   50
    Gentleman. Give me your hand. Have you no more to
        say?
    Kent. Few words, but, to effect, more than all yet;
That, when we have found the king,—in which your pain
That way, I'll this,—he that first lights on him
Holla the other.   55
                            [*Exeunt severally.*

Scene II. ANOTHER PART OF THE HEATH. STORM STILL

                Enter LEAR *and* Fool.

    Lear. Blow, winds, and crack your cheeks! rage! blow!
You cataracts and hurricanoes, spout
Till you have drench'd our steeples, drown'd the cocks!
You sulphurous and thought-executing fires,
Vaunt-couriers to oak-cleaving thunderbolts,   5
Singe my white head! And thou, all-shaking thunder,
Strike flat the thick rotundity o' the world!
Crack nature's moulds, all germens spill at once

---

   45 **out—wall:** exterior (suggests).   48 **fellow:** (present) companion.   52 **to effect:** in importance.   53–54 **your pain . . .
I'll this:** let it be your task to go that way while I go this way.
2 **cataracts:** waterspouts (from heaven). **hurricanoes:** emphatic
form of 'hurricanes'.   3 **cocks:** weathercocks.   4 **thought-
executing:** *either* swift as thought *or* executing Jove's wishes [*N*].
5 **Vaunt-couriers:** precursors.   8 **nature's moulds:** the moulds
in which things are made. **germens:** seeds. **spill:** destroy [*N*].

That make ingrateful man!   9

Fool. O nuncle, court holy-water in a dry house is better
than this rain-water out o' door. Good nuncle, in, and ask
thy daughters' blessing; here's a night pities neither wise
man nor fool.

Lear. Rumble thy bellyful! Spit, fire! spout, rain!
Nor rain, wind, thunder, fire, are my daughters: 15
I tax not you, you elements, with unkindness;
I never gave you kingdom, call'd you children,
You owe me no subscription: then, let fall
Your horrible pleasure; here I stand, your slave,
A poor, infirm, weak, and despis'd old man.   20
But yet I call you servile ministers,
That have with two pernicious daughters join'd
Your high-engender'd battles 'gainst a head
So old and white as this. O! O! 'tis foul.

Fool. He that has a house to put his head in has a good
head-piece.   26

The cod-piece that will house
   Before the head has any,
The head and he shall louse;
   So beggars marry many.   30
The man that makes his toe
   What he his heart should make,
Shall of a corn cry woe,
   And turn his sleep to wake.

10 **court holy-water**: flattery (a common phrase at the time).
11–12 **ask . . . blessing**: apologize to and make peace with.   16
tax: charge (cf. I. iv. 338 and notes).   18 **subscription**:
submission.   21 **ministers**: agents.   23 **high-engender'd
battles**: battalions bred in the sky.   26 **head-piece**: *both* head-
covering *and* brain.   27–34 i.e. the man who prefers a meaner
part of his body to the more honourable will get himself into trouble.
27 **cod-piece**: covering worn by men between legs under close-fitting
hose.   28 **any**: house.   29 **louse**: be lousy, infected with lice.
30 **So . . . many**: (perhaps) in that condition many beggars marry.

For there was never yet fair woman but she made mouths
in a glass.   36

Enter KENT.

Lear. No, I will be the pattern of all patience;
I will say nothing.

Kent. Who's there?

Fool. Marry, here's grace and a cod-piece; that's a wise
man and a fool.   41

Kent. Alas! sir, are you here? things that love night
Love not such nights as these; the wrathful skies
Gallow the very wanderers of the dark,
And make them keep their caves. Since I was man 45
Such sheets of fire, such bursts of horrid thunder,
Such groans of roaring wind and rain, I never
Remember to have heard; man's nature cannot carry
The affliction nor the fear.

Lear.   Let the great gods,
That keep this dreadful pother o'er our heads,   50
Find out their enemies now. Tremble, thou wretch,
That hast within thee undivulged crimes,
Unwhipp'd of justice; hide thee, thou bloody hand;
Thou perjur'd, and thou simular of virtue
That art incestuous; caitiff, to pieces shake,   55
That under covert and convenient seeming
Hast practis'd on man's life; close pent-up guilts,
Rive your concealing continents, and cry

35 **made mouths**: made faces, preened herself [*N*].   40 **grace**:
the king's grace.   **a cod-piece**: something comparatively worthless.
44 **gallow**: frighten (now only in dialect).   45 **keep ... caves**:
cf. III. i. 12–14.   48 **carry**: bear.   50 **pother**: disturbance,
commotion.   53 **of**: by.   54 **perjur'd** (man)   **simular
of**: pretender to.   55 **caitiff**: wretch.   **to pieces shake**: i.e. with
fear and trembling.   56 **covert**: secret.   **seeming**: pretence,
hypocrisy.   57 **practis'd on**: plotted against.   **close**: (adjective.)
guilts: crimes (for criminals).   58 **Rive ... continents**: burst
open the receptacles that hide you.   **cry ... grace**: beg mercy from.

These dreadful summoners grace. I am a man
More sinn'd against than sinning.

    Kent.   Alack! bare-headed!
Gracious my lord, hard by here is a hovel;   61
Some friendship will it lend you 'gainst the tempest;
Repose you there while I to this hard house,—
More harder than the stone whereof 'tis rais'd,—
Which even but now, demanding after you,   65
Denied me to come in, return and force
Their scanted courtesy.

    Lear.   My wits begin to turn.
Come on, my boy. How dost, my boy? Art cold?
I am cold myself. Where is this straw, my fellow?
The art of our necessities is strange,   70
That can make vile things precious. Come, your hovel.
Poor fool and knave, I have one part in my heart
That's sorry yet for thee.

Fool.

        He that has a little tiny wit,
           With hey, ho, the wind and the rain,   75
        Must make content with his fortunes fit,
           Though the rain it raineth every day.

    Lear. True, my good boy. Come, bring us to this hovel.

                         [*Exeunt* LEAR *and* KENT.

    Fool. This is a brave night to cool a courtezan.
I'll speak a prophecy ere I go: 80
        When priests are more in word than matter;

---

    59 summoners: officers who summon to justice [N].   62
lend: afford.   **63 hard:** cruel.   **64 rais'd:** built.   66
Denied . . . in: refused me admittance.   **70 The art . . .
necessities:** necessity is an art, like alchemy, which can change the
nature of things.   **71 vile:** worthless.   **76 make . . . fit:**
make content fit his fortunes, make the best of what he has [N].
79 brave: fine [N].   **81 more . . . matter:** preach more than
they practise [N].

When brewers mar their malt with water;
When nobles are their tailors' tutors;
No heretics burn'd, but wenches' suitors;
When every case in law is right;   85
No squire in debt, nor no poor knight;
When slanders do not live in tongues;
Nor cutpurses come not to throngs;
When usurers tell their gold i' the field;
And bawds and whores do churches build;   90
Then shall the realm of Albion
Come to great confusion:
Then comes the time, who lives to see 't,
That going shall be us'd with feet.   94
This prophecy Merlin shall make; for I live before his time.
                                           [*Exit.*

Scene III. A Room in Gloucester's Castle

Enter GLOUCESTER *and* EDMUND.

Gloucester. Alack, alack! Edmund, I like not this
unnatural dealing. When I desired their leave that I
might pity him, they took from me the use of mine
own house; charged me, on pain of their perpetual
displeasure, neither to speak of him, entreat for him,   5
nor any way sustain him.

Edmund. Most savage, and unnatural!

Gloucester. Go to; say you nothing. There is division
between the dukes, and a worse matter than that. I
have received a letter this night; 'tis dangerous to be   10

---

83 **are . . . tutors:** teach their tailors the latest fashions.
84 **wenches' suitors:** i.e. lovers burn with lust and its results.
86 **no poor knight:** no knight poor.   89 **tell:** count out.
91 **Albion:** England.   93 **who lives:** for whoever lives.   94
going . . . feet: feet shall be used to walk on (the lame conclusion is
intentional).   3 **pity:** show pity, i.e. relieve (cf. l. 6 'sustain').
8 **Go to:** come!   9 **a worse matter:** the French landing.

spoken; I have locked the letter in my closet. These
injuries the king now bears will be revenged home;
there's part of a power already footed; we must incline to the king. I will seek him and privily relieve
him; go you and maintain talk with the duke, that my   15
charity be not of him perceived. If he ask for me, I am
ill and gone to bed. If I die for it, as no less is threa-
tened me, the king, my old master, must be relieved.
There is some strange thing toward, Edmund; pray
you, be careful.   [*Exit.*

Edmund. This courtesy, forbid thee, shall the duke   21
Instantly know; and of that letter too:
This seems a fair deserving, and must draw me
That which my father loses; no less than all: 24
The younger rises when the old doth fall.   [*Exit.*

Scene IV. The Heath. Before a Hovel

Enter LEAR, KENT, *and* Fool.

Kent. Here is the place, my lord; good my lord, enter:
The tyranny of the open night's too rough
For nature to endure.   [*Storm still.*

Lear.   Let me alone.

Kent. Good my lord, enter here.

Lear.   Wilt break my heart?

Kent. I'd rather break mine own. Good my lord, enter.

Lear. Thou think'st 'tis much that this contentious storm
Invades us to the skin: so 'tis to thee;   7

12 **home:** fully (cf. II. i. 51).   13 **power:** force.   **footed:**
see III. i. 32.   13-14 **incline to:** side with.   19 **toward:**
imminent.   21 **courtesy, forbid thee:** (bit of) kindness which
was forbidden you.   23 **deserving:** that for which one deserves
well, service.   1 **Here:** see III. ii. 61.   2 **the open night:**
night in the open.   3 **nature:** human nature, man.   4 **Wilt
. . . heart:** explained by 23-25.   6 **contentious:** quarrelsome,
contending with us.

But where the greater malady is fix'd,
The lesser is scarce felt. Thou'dst shun a bear;
But if thy flight lay toward the roaring sea,   10
Thou'dst meet the bear i' the mouth. When the mind's
    free
The body's delicate; the tempest in my mind
Doth from my senses take all feeling else
Save what beats there. Filial ingratitude!
Is it not as this mouth should tear this hand   15
For lifting food to 't? But I will punish home:
No, I will weep no more. In such a night
To shut me out! Pour on; I will endure.
In such a night as this! O Regan, Goneril!
Your old kind father, whose frank heart gave all,·   20
O! that way madness lies; let me shun that;
No more of that.
   Kent.   Good, my lord, enter here.
   Lear. Prithee, go in thyself; seek thine own ease:
This tempest will not give me leave to ponder
On things would hurt me more. But I'll go in.   25
[*To the* Fool.] In, boy; go first. You houseless poverty,—
Nay, get thee in. I'll pray, and then I'll sleep.

                                [Fool *goes in.*

Poor naked wretches, wheresoe'er you are,
That bide the pelting of this pitiless storm,
How shall your houseless heads and unfed sides,   30
Your loop'd and window'd raggedness, defend you
From seasons such as these? O! I have ta'en
Too little care of this. Take physic, pomp;
Expose thyself to feel what wretches feel,

---

11 **free**: at ease.   12 **delicate**: fastidious (about its comfort).
14 **there**: i.e. in the mind (when the thought that throbs is 'Filial
ingratitude').   15 **as**: as if.   24 **will ... leave**: does not leave
me free.   26 **poverty**: (abstract for concrete.)   29 **bide**: endure.
31 **loop'd ... raggedness**: clothes full of holes (loop = hole).

That thou mayst shake the superflux to them,   35
And show the heavens more just.

   Edgar. [*Within.*] Fathom and half, fathom and half!
     Poor Tom!   [*The* Fool *runs out from the hovel.*
   Fool. Come not in here, nuncle; here's a spirit.
Help me! help me!

   Kent. Give me thy hand. Who's there?   40

   Fool. A spirit, a spirit: he says his name's poor Tom.

   Kent. What art thou that dost grumble there i' the straw?
Come forth.

     Enter EDGAR *disguised as a madman.*

   Edgar. Away! the foul fiend follows me!
     Through the sharp hawthorn blow the winds.   45
     Hum! go to thy cold bed and warm thee.

   Lear. Didst thou give all to thy two daughters?
And art thou come to this?

   Edgar. Who gives anything to poor Tom? whom
the foul fiend hath led through fire and through flame,   50
through ford and whirlpool, o'er bog and quagmire;
that hath laid knives under his pillow, and halters in
his pew; set ratsbane by his porridge; made him
proud of heart, to ride on a bay trotting-horse over
four-inched bridges, to course his own shadow for a   55
traitor. Bless thy five wits! Tom's a-cold. O! do de,
do de, do de. Bless thee from whirlwinds, star-blasting, and taking! Do poor Tom some charity, whom
the foul fiend vexes. There could I have him now,
and there, and there again, and there.   [*Storm still.*

35 **the superflux**: your superfluity (metaphor from an overladen
tree).   37 **Fathom and half**: suggested by the heavy rain.
Poor Tom: cf. ii. iii. 20.   55 **four-inched**: four inches wide.
course: pursue.   56–57 **do . . . de**: represents chattering
teeth and shivering.   57–58 **star-blasting**: being struck by
the evil influence of stars.   **taking**: infection (cf. ii. iv. 163).
59 **There**: as he pretends to feel the devil biting some part of his
body, perhaps in the form of vermin (see 153).

Lear. What! have his daughters brought him to this pass?   61

Couldst thou save nothing? Didst thou give them all?

Fool. Nay, he reserved a blanket, else we had been all shamed.

Lear. Now all the plagues that in the pendulous air   65
Hang fated o'er men's faults light on thy daughters!

Kent. He hath no daughters, sir.

Lear. Death, traitor! nothing could have subdu'd nature
To such a lowness, but his unkind daughters.
Is it the fashion that discarded fathers   70
Should have thus little mercy on their flesh?
Judicious punishment! 'twas this flesh begot
Those pelican daughters.

Edgar. Pillicock sat on Pillicock-hill:
Halloo, halloo, loo, loo!   75

Fool. This cold night will turn us all to fools and madmen.

Edgar. Take heed o' the foul fiend. Obey thy parents;
keep thy word justly; swear not; commit not with man's
sworn spouse; set not thy sweet heart on proud array.
Tom's a-cold.   80

Lear. What hast thou been?

Edgar. A servingman, proud in heart and mind; that
curled my hair, wore gloves in my cap, served the lust
of my mistress's heart, and did the act of darkness
with her; swore as many oaths as I spake words, and   85
broke them in the sweet face of heaven; one that slept
in the contriving of lust, and waked to do it. Wine
loved I deeply, dice dearly, and in woman out-para-

65 **pendulous**: hanging over us.   66 **fated**: full of fate.
69 **unkind**: unnatural (also suggesting 'cruel').   73 pelicans
were supposed to feed their young on their life-blood.   74 **Pillicock**: darling, pretty knave (the line, adapted from an old one, was
suggested by the word 'pelican').   75 **loo**: properly a cry to encourage hounds.   78 **commit**: sin.   82 **servingman**: *either*
lover *or* servant [*N*].   83 **gloves**: as a favour.

moured the Turk: false of heart, light of ear, bloody of
hand; hog in sloth, fox in stealth, wolf in greediness,   90
dog in madness, lion in prey. Let not the creaking of
shoes nor the rustling of silks betray thy poor heart to
woman: keep thy foot out of brothels, thy hand out of
plackets, thy pen from lenders' books, and defy the
foul fiend. Still through the hawthorn blows the cold   95
wind; says suum, mun ha no nonny. Dolphin my boy,
my boy; sessa! let him trot by.   [*Storm still.*

Lear. Why, thou wert better in thy grave than to
answer with thy uncovered body this extremity of the
skies. Is man no more than this? Consider him well.   100
Thou owest the worm no silk, the beast no hide, the
sheep no wool, the cat no perfume. Ha! here's three
on 's are sophisticated; thou art the thing itself; unaccommodated man is no more but such a poor, bare,
forked animal as thou art. Off, off, you lendings!   105
Come; unbutton here.   [*Tearing off his clothes.*

Enter GLOUCESTER, *with a torch.*

Fool. Prithee, nuncle, be contented; 'tis a naughty night
to swim in. Now a little fire in a wide field were like an old
lecher's heart; a small spark, all the rest on 's body cold.
Look! here comes a walking fire.   110

Edgar. This is the foul fiend Flibbertigibbet: he begins at

---

89 **the Turk:** the Sultan with his many wives.   **light of ear:**
quick to believe evil.   94 **plackets:** openings in petticoats or
skirts.   **lenders:** money lenders.   96 **suum . . . nonny:**
the refrain of a song.   **Dolphin:** perhaps addressing an imaginary
horse (but Dolphin = Dauphin of France).   97 **sessa:** an
interjection of uncertain meaning (perhaps = cessez, stop!, perhaps
'off with you').   99 **answer:** expose yourself to.   101 **Thou:**
man (in Edgar's state).   103 **sophisticated:** adulterated,
unnatural.   103-4 **unaccommodated:** without the advantages
(*Lat.* commoda) of civilization.   105 **lendings:** borrowed
articles, things not man's own.   107 **naughty:** bad [*N*].

curfew, and walks till the first cock; he gives the web and
the pin, squinies the eye, and makes the harelip; mildews
the white wheat, and hurts the poor creature of earth.

Swithold footed thrice the old;   115
He met the night-mare, and her nine-fold;
    Bid her alight,
    And her troth plight,
And aroint thee, witch, aroint thee!

Kent. How fares your Grace?   120
Lear. What's he?
Kent. Who's there? What is't you seek?
Gloucester. What are you there? Your names?
Edgar. Poor Tom; that eats the swimming frog; the
toad, the tadpole, the wall-newt, and the water; that 125
in the fury of his heart, when the foul fiend rages, eats
cow-dung for sallets; swallows the old rat and the
ditch-dog; drinks the green mantle of the standing
pool; who is whipped from tithing to tithing, and
stock-punished, and imprisoned; who hath had three 130
suits to his back, six shirts to his body, horse to ride,
and weapon to wear;

But mice and rats and such small deer
Have been Tom's food for seven long year.   134

---

112 **first cock**: cockrow, see *Hamlet* I. i. 147–57.   112–13 **the
web and the pin**: cataract, an eye disease.   113 **squinies**: makes
it squint [*N*].   114 **white**: ripening.   **the poor creature of
earth**: mankind.   115 **Swithold**: St. Withold [*N*].   **old**:
wold.   116 **night-mare**: incubus, demon (*not* female horse).
nine-fold: brood.   118 **her troth plight**: give her pledge
(not to vex men).   119 **aroint**: begone.   121 **he**: i.e.
Gloucester.   125 **wall–newt**: lizard.   **water**: newt.
127 **sallets**: salads.   128 **mantle**: covering, screen.   129
tithing: hamlet (originally holding *ten* families).   130 **stock-
punish'd**: punished by being put in the stocks.   133 **deer**:
beasts [*N*].

Beware my follower. Peace, Smulkin! peace, thou fiend.

Gloucester. What! hath your Grace no better company?

Edgar. The prince of darkness is a gentleman; Modo he's call'd, and Mahu.

Gloucester. Our flesh and blood, my lord, is grown so vile,
That it doth hate what gets it. 140

Edgar. Poor Tom's a-cold.

Gloucester. Go in with me. My duty cannot suffer
To obey in all your daughters' hard commands:
Though their injunction be to bar my doors,
And let this tyrannous night take hold upon you, 145
Yet have I ventur'd to come seek you out
And bring you where both fire and food is ready.

Lear. First let me talk with this philosopher.
What is the cause of thunder? 149

Kent. Good my lord, take his offer; go into the house.

Lear. I'll talk a word with this same learned Theban.
What is your study?

Edgar. How to prevent the fiend, and to kill vermin.

Lear. Let me ask you one word in private,

Kent. Importune him once more to go, my lord; 155
His wits begin to unsettle.

Gloucester. Canst thou blame him?

[*Storm still.*

His daughters seek his death. Ah! that good Kent;
He said it would be thus, poor banish'd man!
Thou sayst the king grows mad. I'll tell thee, friend,
I am almost mad myself. I had a son, 160
Now outlaw'd from my blood; he sought my life,
But lately, very late; I lov'd him, friend,

---

135 **follower**: familiar spirit. 139 **Our . . . blood**: our children [*N*]. 140 **gets**: begets. 142 **suffer**: submit, agree. 143 **in all**: in everything. 152 **study**: pursuit, brand of learning. 153 **prevent**: anticipate, so defeat. 161 **outlaw'd . . . blood**: disinherited.

No father his son dearer; true to tell thee,

                               [*Storm continues.*

The grief hath craz'd my wits. What a night's this!
I do beseech your Grace,—

   Lear.   O! cry you mercy, sir.   165
Noble philosopher, your company.

   Edgar. Tom's a-cold.

   Gloucester. In, fellow, there into the hovel: keep thee
warm.

   Lear. Come, let's in all.

   Kent.   This way, my lord.

   Lear.   With him;
I will keep still with my philosopher.   170

   Kent. Good my lord, soothe him; let him take the fellow.

   Gloucester. Take him you on.

   Kent. Sirrah, come on; go along with us.

   Lear. Come, good Athenian.

   Gloucester.   No words, no words: hush.

   Edgar. Child Rowland to the dark tower came,   175
          His word was still, Fie, foh, and fum,
          I smell the blood of a British man.   [*Exeunt.*

Scene V. A Room in Gloucester's Castle

Enter CORNWALL *and* EDMUND.

   Cornwall. I will have my revenge ere I depart his house.

   Edmund. How, my lord, I may be censured, that nature
thus gives way to loyalty, something fears me to think of.

   Cornwall. I now perceive it was not altogether your
brother's evil disposition made him seek his death; but a

165 **cry you mercy:** (I) beg your pardon.   171 **soothe:**
humour.   175 **Child:** Sir (title of a young knight).   **Row-**
land: Roland (Charlemagne's hero) [*N*].   176 **His:** the giant's.
2–3 i.e. I am rather afraid what people will think of me for allowing my natural affection to give way to my sense of duty.   5 **his:**
Gloucester's.   5–7 **a provoking ... in himself:** i.e. (probably)

provoking merit, set a-work by a reproveable badness in
himself.   7

Edmund. How malicious is my fortune, that I must
repent to be just! This is the letter he spoke of, which
approves him an intelligent party to the advantages of
France. O heavens! that this treason were not, or not I
the detector!   12

Cornwall. Go with me to the duchess.

Edmund. If the matter of this paper be certain, you have
mighty business in hand.   15

Cornwall. True, or false, it hath made thee Earl of
Gloucester. Seek out where thy father is, that he may be
ready for our apprehension.

Edmund. [*Aside.*] If I find him comforting the king it
will stuff his suspicion more fully. I will persever in my
course of loyalty, though the conflict be sore between that
and my blood.   22

Cornwall. I will lay trust upon thee; and thou shalt find
a dearer father in my love.   [*Exeunt.*

Scene VI. A Chamber in a Farmhouse adjoining the Castle

Enter GLOUCESTER, LEAR, KENT, Fool, *and* EDGAR.

Gloucester. Here is better than the open air; take it
thankfully. I will piece out the comfort with what addition
I can: I will not be long from you.

Gloucester's deserts inviting punishment, which, however, was
only brought into action by Edgar's own wickedness.   **9 to be
just:** of being loyal.   **the letter:** see III. iii. 10.   **10 approves:** proves. **intelligent party:** person giving intelligence,
informer.   **18 apprehension:** arrest.   **19 comforting:**
supporting, strengthening [*N*].   **20 stuff . . . fully:** make our
suspicion of him more justified.   **persever:** persevere.   **22
blood:** natural temperament.   **2 piece out:** increase.

Kent. All the power of his wits has given way to his impatience. The gods reward your kindness! 5

[*Exit* GLOUCESTER.

Edgar. Frateretto calls me, and tells me Nero is an angler in the lake of darkness. Pray, innocent, and beware the foul fiend.

Fool. Prithee, nuncle, tell me whether a madman be a gentleman or a yeoman! 10

Lear. A king, a king!

Fool. No; he's a yeoman that has a gentleman to his son; for he's a mad yeoman that sees his son a gentleman before him.

Lear. To have a thousand with red burning spits 15
Come hizzing in upon 'em,—

Edgar. The foul fiend bites my back.

Fool. He's mad that trusts in the tameness of a wolf, a horse's health, a boy's love, or a whore's oath.

Lear. It shall be done; I will arraign them straight. 20
[*To* EDGAR.] Come, sit thou here, most learned justicer;
[*To the* Fool.] Thou, sapient sir, sit here. Now, you she foxes!

Edgar. Look, where he stands and glares! wantest thou eyes at trial, madam?

Come o'er the bourn, Bessy, to me,— 25

6 **Frateretto**: an imaginary familiar spirit; so Hopdance (30) (both from Harsnett) [*N*]. 7 **innocent**: simple man [*N*]. 12 **has . . . his son**: has his son a gentleman (i.e. a reversal of nature, like your daughters' conduct). 15 Lear is brooding over the very course he would like to see the Furies take on his daughters. 16 **hizzing**: a variant of 'hissing', perhaps in order to sound like 'whizzing'. 18–19 **a horse's health**: perhaps as described by the vendor; or simply as horses are delicate animals. 21 **justicer**: judge [*N*]. 23 **he**: a fiend *or* (possibly) Lear. 23–24 **wantest thou eyes**: do you want people to look at you? *or* can't you see him? 24 **madam**: Goneril or Regan (present on trial in fancy). 25 **bourn**: stream (the line is a fragment of an old song).

Fool. Her boat hath a leak,
          And she must not speak
     Why she dares not come over to thee.

Edgar. The foul fiend haunts poor Tom in the voice of a
nightingale. Hopdance cries in Tom's belly for two white
herring. Croak not, black angel; I have no food for thee.

Kent. How do you, sir? Stand you not so amaz'd: Will
you lie down and rest upon the cushions?   33

Lear. I'll see their trial first. Bring in their evidence.
[*To* EDGAR.] Thou robed man of justice, take thy place;
[*To the* Fool.] And thou, his yoke-fellow of equity,   36
Bench by his side. [*To* KENT.] You are o' the commission,
Sit you too.

Edgar. Let us deal justly.
          Sleepest or wakest thou, jolly shepherd?   40
          Thy sheep be in the corn;
          And for one blast of thy minikin mouth,
          Thy sheep shall take no harm.
Purr! the cat is grey.   44

Lear. Arraign her first; 'tis Goneril. I here take my oath
before this honourable assembly, she kicked the poor king
her father.

Fool. Come hither, mistress. Is your name Goneril?

Lear. She cannot deny it.

Fool. Cry you mercy, I took you for a joint-stool.   50

Lear. And here's another, whose warp'd looks proclaim

30 **white:** (probably) fresh.   31 **Croak:** in the stomach, from
hunger.   32 **amaz'd:** dumbfounded.   34 **their evidence:**
the witnesses against them.   37 **o' the commission:** com-
missioned, appointed a justice of the peace.   42 i.e. while you
turn aside to play us a tune.   **minikin:** dainty.   43 perhaps
ironical, as the sheep would harm the corn more than the corn them.
44 **the cat:** a 'familiar' again, called 'Purr' (in Harsnett), or Purr
may be only the sound.   50 **joint-stool:** stool made carefully
by a joiner (in fact Lear took the stool for Goneril).   51 **another:** i.e. Regan.   **warp'd:** crooked, perverse.

What store her heart is made on. Stop her there!
Arms, arms, sword, fire! Corruption in the place!
False justicer, why hast thou let her 'scape?

   Edgar. Bless thy five wits!   55

   Kent. O pity! Sir, where is the patience now
That you so oft have boasted to retain?

   Edgar. [*Aside.*] My tears begin to take his part so much,
They'll mar my counterfeiting.

   Lear. The little dogs and all,   60
Tray, Blanch, and Sweet-heart, see, they bark at me.

   Edgar. Tom will throw his head at them. Avaunt, you
curs!

> Be thy mouth or black or white,
> Tooth that poisons if it bite;   65
> Mastiff, greyhound, mongrel grim,
> Hound or spaniel, brach or lym;
> Or bobtail tike or trundle-tail;
> Tom will make them weep and wail:
> For, with throwing thus my head,   70
> Dogs leap the hatch, and all are fled.

Do de, de, de. Sessa! Come, march to wakes and fairs and
market-towns. Poor Tom, thy horn is dry.

   Lear. Then let them anatomize Regan, see what
breeds about her heart. Is there any cause in nature   75
that makes these hard hearts? [*To* EDGAR.] You, sir,
I entertain you for one of my hundred; only I do not
like the fashion of your garments: you will say, they
are Persian attire; but let them be changed.

---

   52 store: material (but probably a corruption, perhaps for
'stone', since 'store' can hardly mean stuff).   **64 or . . . or:**
either . . . or.   **67 lym:** a kind of bloodhound [*N*].   **68
trundle-tail:** long-tailed.   **71 leap the hatch:** make a hurried
exit.   **72 Do de . . . Sessa:** see III. iv. 56 and 97.   **73 horn:**
the Bedlam beggar's drinking flask.   **74 anatomize:** dissect.
77 entertain: take on.   **79 Persian:** proverbial for 'luxurious'
(here ironical) [*N*].

Kent. Now, good my lord, lie here and rest awhile.   80
 Lear. Make no noise, make no noise; draw the curtains:
so, so, so. We'll go to supper i' the morning: so, so, so.
Fool. And I'll go to bed at noon.

Re-enter GLOUCESTER.

Gloucester. Come hither, friend: where is the king my
master?   85
 Kent. Here, sir; but trouble him not, his wits are gone.
 Gloucester. Good friend, I prithee, take him in thy arms;
I have o'erheard a plot of death upon him.
There is a litter ready; lay him in 't,
And drive toward Dover, friend, where thou shalt meet
Both welcome and protection. Take up thy master: 91
If thou shouldst dally half an hour, his life,
With thine, and all that offer to defend him,
Stand in assured loss. Take up, take up;
And follow me, that will to some provision   95
Give thee quick conduct.
 Kent.   Oppress'd nature sleeps:
This rest might yet have balm'd thy broken sinews,
Which, if convenience will not allow,
Stand in hard cure.—[*To the* Fool.] Come, help to bear thy
      master;
Thou must not stay behind.
 Gloucester.   Come, come, away.   100
[*Exeunt* KENT, GLOUCESTER, *and the* Fool, *bearing away*
                                                    LEAR.

81 **curtains:** of old-fashioned beds.   88 **upon:** against.   93
offer: presume, dare.   94 **Stand in assured loss:** are certain
to be lost.   95 **some provision:** something provided (l. 89).
96 **conduct:** guidance.   97 **balm'd:** healed like a balm.
broken sinews: racked nerves.   98 **if convenience . . . allow:**
unless circumstances are favourable.   99 **Stand . . . cure:** are
hardly likely to be cured [*N*].

Edgar. When we our betters see bearing our woes,
We scarcely think our miseries our foes.
Who alone suffers suffers most i' the mind,
Leaving free things and happy shows behind;
But then the mind much sufferance doth o'er-skip,   105
When grief hath mates, and bearing fellowship.
How light and portable my pain seems now,
When that which makes me bend makes the king bow;
He childed as I father'd! Tom, away!
Mark the high noises, and thyself bewray   110
When false opinion, whose wrong thought defiles thee,
In thy just proof repeals and reconciles thee.
What will hap more to-night, safe 'scape the king!
Lurk, lurk.   [*Exit.*

Scene *VII*. A Room in Gloucester's Castle

Enter CORNWALL, REGAN, GONERIL, EDMUND, *and* Servants.

Cornwall. Post speedily to my lord your husband; show
him this letter: the army of France is landed. Seek out the
traitor Gloucester.   [*Exeunt some of the* Servants.
Regan. Hang him instantly.
Goneril. Pluck out his eyes.   5

101 **our woes:** the same trouble as we have.   103 emphasize
alone.   104 **free:** carefree, free from distress.   **shows:** sights.
106 **bearing:** when suffering (has).   107 **portable:** easy to bear.
109 **childed as I father'd:** treated by his children as I by my
father.   110 **high noises:** disturbances in the state, in high
quarters.   **thyself bewray:** only reveal who you really are.
111 **false opinion:** wrong suspicions (felt about you).   112 **In
thy just proof:** when your character is vindicated.   **repeals:**
recalls you (from banishment).   **reconciles:** restores you to your
position and reconciles you to your father.   113 **What . . . hap:**
whatever happens.   114 **Lurk:** hide yourself, lie low.   1
addressed to Goneril.

Cornwall. Leave him to my displeasure. Edmund,
keep you our sister company: the revenges we are
bound to take upon your traitorous father are not fit
for your beholding. Advise the duke, where you are
going, to a most festinate preparation: we are bound   10
to the like. Our posts shall be swift and intelligent
betwixt us. Farewell, dear sister: farewell, my Lord
of Gloucester.

Enter OSWALD.

How now? Where's the king?

  Oswald. My Lord of Gloucester hath convey'd him
    hence: 15
Some five or six and thirty of his knights,
Hot questrists after him, met him at gate;
Who, with some other of the lord's dependants,
Are gone with him toward Dover, where they boast
To have well-armed friends.

  Cornwall.   Get horses for your mistress.

  Goneril. Farewell, sweet lord, and sister.   21

  Cornwall. Edmund, farewell.

             [*Exeunt* GONERIL, EDMUND, *and* OSWALD.

                 Go seek the traitor Gloucester,
Pinion him like a thief, bring him before us.

                    [*Exeunt other* Servants.

Though well we may not pass upon his life
Without the form of justice, yet our power   25
Shall do a courtesy to our wrath, which men
May blame but not control. Who's there? The traitor?

---

10 **festinate:** speedy.   10–11 **bound to:** purposed to, pro-
posing (so also, probably in 8).   11 **posts:** messengers.
intelligent: bringing good information.   13 **Gloucester:**
see III. v. 16–17.   17 **questrists:** seekers (*Lat.* quaero).   24
pass (sentence) **upon.**   26 **do a courtesy to:** bow before, give
way to [*N*].

Re-enter Servants, *with* GLOUCESTER.

Regan. Ingrateful fox! 'tis he.

Cornwall. Bind fast his corky arms.

Gloucester. What mean your Graces? Good my friends,
    consider   30
You are my guests: do me no foul play, friends.

Cornwall. Bind him, I say.   [*Servants* bind him.

Regan.   Hard, hard. O filthy traitor!

Gloucester. Unmerciful lady as you are, I'm none.

Cornwall. To this chair bind him. Villain, thou shalt
    find—   [REGAN *plucks his beard.*

Gloucester. By the kind gods, 'tis most ignobly done   35
To pluck me by the beard.

Regan. So white, and such a traitor!

Gloucester.   Naughty lady,
These hairs, which thou dost ravish from my chin,
Will quicken, and accuse thee: I am your host:
With robbers' hands my hospitable favours   40
You should not ruffle thus. What will you do?

Cornwall. Come, sir, what letters had you late from
    France?

Regan. Be simple-answer'd, for we know the truth.

Cornwall. And what confederacy have you with the
    traitors
Late footed in the kingdom?   45

Regan. To whose hands have you sent the lunatic king?
Speak.

Gloucester. I have a letter guessingly set down,

29 **corky:** dry (as he is old).   32 **filthy:** beastly, disgraceful.
37 **Naughty:** wicked (not then a childish word).   39 **quicken:**
come to life.   40 **my hospitable favours:** the features of me,
your host.   41 **ruffle:** disturb, violate (cf. II. iv. 301 where,
however, it was intransitive).   42 **late:** lately.   43 **Be
simple-answer'd:** answer straightforwardly.   45 **footed:**
see III. i. 32.   48 **guessingly set down:** written from conjecture, not knowledge.

Which came from one that's of a neutral heart,
And not from one oppos'd.

    Cornwall.   Cunning.

    Regan.   And false   50

    Cornwall. Where hast thou sent the king?

    Gloucester.   To Dover.

    Regan. Wherefore to Dover? Wast thou not charg'd at
    peril—

    Cornwall. Wherefore to Dover? Let him answer that.

    Gloucester. I am tied to the stake, and I must stand the
    course.

    Regan. Wherefore to Dover?   55

    Gloucester. Because I would not see thy cruel nails
Pluck out his poor old eyes; nor thy fierce sister
In his anointed flesh stick boarish fangs.
The sea, with such a storm as his bare head
In hell-black night endur'd, would have buoy'd up,   60
And quench'd the stelled fires;
Yet, poor old heart, he holp the heavens to rain.
If wolves had at thy gate howl'd that dern time,
Thou shouldst have said, 'Good porter, turn the key,'
All cruels else subscrib'd: but I shall see   65
The winged vengeance overtake such children.

    Cornwall. See 't shalt thou never. Fellows, hold the chair.
Upon these eyes of thine I'll set my foot.

    Gloucester. He that will think to live till he be old,
Give me some help! O cruel! O ye gods!   70

                          [GLOUCESTER's *eye put out.*

---

    54 course: attack of the dogs in bear-baiting [*N*].   58
anointed: royal   **60 buoy'd up:** risen up, like a buoy.   61
stelled: *either* starry *or* (more probably) fixed (Middle Eng. stellen =
fix), or part of both.   **62 holp:** encouraged (lit. helped).   63
dern: dreary, dread.   **64 turn the key:** i.e. admit them.   **65 All
cruels else: all other** cruel things (except the storm).   **subscrib'd:**
being admitted [*N*].   **66 winged vengeance:** vengeance of heaven
(as in Jove's arrows).

Regan. One side will mock another; the other too.

Cornwall. If you see vengeance.—

First Servant.   Hold your hand, my lord:
I have serv'd you ever since I was a child,
But better service have I never done you
Than now to bid you hold.

Regan.   How now, you dog!   75

First Servant. If you did wear a beard upon your chin,
I'd shake it on this quarrel.

Regan.   What do you mean?   77

Cornwall. My villain!   [*Draws.*

First Servant. Nay then, come on, and take the chance
    of anger.   [*Draws. They fight.*
                [CORNWALL *is wounded.*

Regan. Give me thy sword. A peasant stand up thus!
        [*Takes a sword, and runs at him behind.*

First Servant. O! I am slain. My lord, you have one eye
    left   81
To see some mischief on him. O!   [*Dies.*

Cornwall. Lest it see more, prevent it. Out, vile jelly!
Where is thy lustre now?

Gloucester. All dark and comfortless. Where 's my son
    Edmund?   85
Edmund, enkindle all the sparks of nature
To quit this horrid act.

Regan.   Out, treacherous villain!
Thou call'st on him that hates thee; it was he
That made the overture of thy treasons to us,
Who is too good to pity thee.   90

---

71 **the other** (eye) **too.**   77 **shake it:** i.e. challenge you to
fight [*N*].   78 **villain:** serf (perhaps also in modern sense as in
l. 96).   79 **take . . . anger:** take the chance result where anger,
not skill, directs the weapons.   82 **him:** Cornwall.   83 **Lest
. . . prevent it:** prevent it from seeing more.   87 **quit:** requite,
avenge [*N*].   89 **overture:** disclosure.

Gloucester. O my follies! Then Edgar was abus'd.
Kind gods, forgive me that, and prosper him!
  Regan. Go thrust him out at gates, and let him smell
His way to Dover. [*Exit one with* GLOUCESTER.] How is 't,
    my lord? How look you?
  Cornwall. I have receiv'd a hurt. Follow me, lady.   95
Turn out that eyeless villain; throw this slave
Upon the dunghill. Regan, I bleed apace:
Untimely comes this hurt. Give me your arm.
                            [*Exit* CORNWALL, *led by* REGAN.
  Second Servant. I'll never care what wickedness I do
If this man come to good.
  Third Servant.   If she live long,   100
And, in the end, meet the old course of death,
Women will all turn monsters.
  Second Servant. Let's follow the old earl, and get the
    Bedlam
To lead him where he would: his roguish madness
Allows itself to any thing.   105
  Third Servant. Go thou; I'll fetch some flax, and whites
    of eggs,
To apply to his bleeding face. Now, heaven help him!
                            [*Exeunt severally.*

  91 **abus'd:** deceived.   94 **How look you?:** What do you
appear like (almost) How do you feel?   101 **old:** usual, ordinary.
104 **would:** like to be led.   104–5 **his roguish . . . any thing:**
as he (the Bedlamite, Edgar) is a mad vagrant he will lend himself
to anything, go anywhere he is asked, *or* his madness affords him
licence to do what he likes.

ACT IV

Scene I. The Heath

Enter EDGAR.

Edgar. Yet better thus, and known to be contemn'd,
Than still contemn'd and flatter'd. To be worst,
The lowest and most dejected thing of fortune,
Stands still in esperance, lives not in fear:
The lamentable change is from the best;   5
The worst returns to laughter. Welcome, then,
Thou unsubstantial air that I embrace:
The wretch that thou hast blown unto the worst
Owes nothing to thy blasts. But who comes here?

Enter GLOUCESTER, *led by an* Old Man.

My father, poorly led? World, world, O world!   10
But that thy strange mutations make us hate thee,
Life would not yield to age.
   Old Man.   O my good lord!
I have been your tenant, and your father's tenant,
These fourscore years.
   Gloucester. Away, get thee away; good friend, be gone;
Thy comforts can do me no good at all;   16
Thee they may hurt.
   Old Man.   You cannot see your way.

1 **Yet** (it is better to be) **thus.**   **known ... contemn'd:** known
to yourself to be, conscious of being despised.   2 **still:** all the
same.   3 **most ... fortune:** the thing (i.e. creature) cast
down lowest by fortune.   4 **Stands ... esperance:** puts you
in a situation of permanent hopefulness.   6 **returns to**
laughter: may yet see you happy again.   9 **Owes nothing to:**
has paid his full debt to, and has therefore nothing more to fear
from.   10 **poorly led:** led by a poor man [*N*].   11 **But**
that: if it were not that.   12 **Life ... age:** we should not be
reconciled to old age and death.

Gloucester. I have no way, and therefore want no eyes;
I stumbled when I saw. Full oft 'tis seen,
Our means secure us, and our mere defects   20
Prove our commodities. Ah! dear son Edgar,
The food of thy abused father's wrath;
Might I but live to see thee in my touch,
I'd say I had eyes again.
    Old Man.   How now! Who's there?
    Edgar. [*Aside.*] O gods! Who is 't can say, 'I am at the
        worst'?   25
I am worse than e'er I was.
    Old Man.   'Tis poor mad Tom.
    Edgar. [*Aside.*] And worse I may be yet; the worst is not,
So long as we can say, 'This is the worst.'
    Old Man. Fellow, where goest?
    Gloucester.   Is it a beggar-man?
    Old Man. Madman and beggar too.   30
    Gloucester. He has some reason, else he could not beg.
I' the last night's storm I such a fellow saw,
Which made me think a man a worm: my son
Came then into my mind; and yet my mind
Was then scarce friends with him: I have heard more since.
As flies to wanton boys, are we to the gods;   36
They kill us for their sport.
    Edgar.   [*Aside.*] How should this be?
Bad is the trade that must play fool to sorrow,

20 **Our means . . . us:** our resources make us careless (Lat.
securus).   20-21 **our mere . . . commodities:** it is precisely our
weaknesses that turn out to our advantage [*N*].   22 **food:** object.
abused: misled.   24 **I'd say . . . again:** i.e. it would be as good
as recovering his sight.   31 **He has some reason:** he's not quite
mad.   33 **my son:** see III. iv. 160.   35 **more:** viz. III.
vii. 88–90.   36 **wanton:** playful [*N*].   37 **How should this
be?:** probably refers to second half of 35.   38 i.e. it's a bad
job when we have to pretend to folly in the presence of sorrow (as
I am now doing).

Angering itself and others.—[*To* GLOUCESTER.] Bless thee,
    master!

Gloucester. Is that the naked fellow?

Old Man.   Ay, my lord.   40

Gloucester. Then, prithee, get thee gone. If, for my sake,
Thou wilt o'ertake us, hence a mile or twain,
I' the way toward Dover, do it for ancient love;
And bring some covering for this naked soul
Who I'll entreat to lead me.

Old Man.   Alack, sir! he is mad.   45

Gloucester. 'Tis the times' plague, when madmen lead the
    blind.
Do as I bid thee, or rather do thy pleasure;
Above the rest, be gone.

Old Man. I'll bring him the best 'parel that I have,
Come on 't what will.   [*Exit.*

Gloucester. Sirrah, naked fellow,—   51

Edgar. Poor Tom's a-cold. [*Aside.*] I cannot daub it further.

Gloucester. Come hither, fellow.

Edgar. [*Aside.*] And yet I must. Bless thy sweet eyes,
    they bleed.

Gloucester. Know'st thou the way to Dover?   55

Edgar. Both stile and gate, horse-way and footpath.
Poor Tom hath been scared out of his good wits: bless
thee, good man's son, from the foul fiend! Five fiends
have been in poor Tom at once; of lust, as Obidicut;
Hobbididance, prince of dumbness; Mahu, of stealing;   60
Modo, of murder; and Flibbertigibbet, of mopping
and mowing; who since possesses chambermaids and
waiting-women. So, bless thee, master!

46 **'Tis the times' plague:** the world's in a bad way.   48
Above the rest: above all things.   49 **'parel:** apparel.   50
on 't: of it.   52 **daub it:** dissemble, pretend (lit. cover up with
plaster).   57–58 **bless thee ... from:** God preserve thee from.
61–62 **mopping and mowing:** grimacing, making faces (Fr. *moue*).

Gloucester. Here, take this purse, thou whom the heavens'
  plagues
Have humbled to all strokes: that I am wretched 65
Makes thee the happier: heavens, deal so still!
Let the superfluous and lust-dieted man,
That slaves your ordinance, that will not see
Because he doth not feel, feel your power quickly;
So distribution should undo excess, 70
And each man have enough. Dost thou know Dover?
  Edgar. Ay, master.
  Gloucester. There is a cliff, whose high and bending head
Looks fearfully in the confined deep;
Bring me but to the very brim of it, 75
And I'll repair the misery thou dost bear
With something rich about me; from that place
I shall no leading need.
  Edgar. Give me thy arm:
Poor Tom shall lead thee. [*Exeunt.*

Scene II. Before the Duke of Albany's Palace

Enter GONERIL *and* EDMUND.

Goneril. Welcome, my lord; I marvel our mild husband
Not met us on the way. [*Enter* OSWALD.] Now, where's
  your master?
  Oswald. Madam, within; but never man so chang'd.

65 **humbled to:** humbled into bearing. 67 **superfluous:**
having more than he needs (cf. II. iv. 265), spoilt. **lust-dieted:**
gluttonous or (perhaps) indulgent to his sexual appetite (cf. III.
iv. 85 and 88) [*N*]. 68 **slaves your ordinance:** makes your
commands his slaves, enslaves them (esp. the command to charity).
69 **feel** (sympathy for others). 73 **bending:** overhanging.
74 **fearfully:** frighteningly. **in:** into. **confined:** bounded by it
[*N*]. 1 **Welcome:** to our house (see III. vii. 1–7 for their
journey together). **mild:** sarcastic, cf. 12. 2 **Not met:** did
not meet (so in 53).

I told him of the army that was landed;
He smil'd at it: I told him you were coming;   5
His answer was, 'The worse:' of Gloucester's treachery,
And of the loyal service of his son,
When I inform'd him, then he call'd me sot,
And told me I had turn'd the wrong side out:
What most he should dislike seems pleasant to him;   10
What like, offensive.

   Goneril. [*To* EDMUND.] Then, shall you go no further.
It is the cowish terror of his spirit
That dares not undertake; he'll not feel wrongs
Which tie him to an answer. Our wishes on the way
May prove effects. Back, Edmund, to my brother;   15
Hasten his musters and conduct his powers:
I must change arms at home, and give the distaff
Into my husband's hands. This trusty servant
Shall pass between us; ere long you are like to hear,
If you dare venture in your own behalf,   20
A mistress's command. Wear this; spare speech;
                                [*Giving a favour.*
Decline your head: this kiss, if it durst speak,
Would stretch thy spirits up into the air.
Conceive, and fare thee well.   24

   Edmund. Yours in the ranks of death.

   Goneril.   My most dear Gloucester!
                              [*Exit* EDMUND.

   8 sot: fool (*not* drunkard).   **9 turn'd . . . out:** got things
inside out, inverted right and wrong.   **11 What** (he should
like, seems) **offensive.**   **12 cowish:** cowardly (cf. 50 below and
I. iv. 336 'milky gentleness') [*N*].   **13 undertake:** venture
take up enterprises.   **14 tie him to:** demand, require.
14–15 Our wishes . . . may prove effects: What we wished for
may be realized (i.e. that you should replace him).   **15 brother:**
(-in-law) Cornwall.   **16 conduct his powers:** lead his forces.
17 change arms: i.e. take in exchange (for the distaff) his warlike
weapons.   **22 Decline:** put down (for a kiss).   **24 Conceive:**
take my meaning.

O! the difference of man and man!
To thee a woman's services are due:
My fool usurps my bed.

 Oswald.   Madam, here comes my lord. [*Exit.*

     Enter ALBANY.

 Goneril. I have been worth the whistle.
 Albany.   O Goneril!
You are not worth the dust which the rude wind 30
Blows in your face. I fear your disposition
That nature, which contemns its origin,
Cannot be border'd certain in itself;
She that herself will sliver and disbranch
From her material sap, perforce must wither 35
And come to deadly use.
 Goneril. No more; the text is foolish.
 Albany. Wisdom and goodness to the vile seem vile;
Filths savour but themselves. What have you done?
Tigers, not daughters, what have you perform'd? 40
A father, and a gracious aged man,
Whose reverence the head-lugg'd bear would lick,
Most barbarous, most degenerate! have you madded.
Could my good brother suffer you to do it?
A man, a prince, by him so benefited! 45

---

 28 My fool: My husband who is a fool [*N*]. **29 worth the whistle:** worth something to you (cf. proverb 'It's a poor dog that is not worth the whistling'). **31 fear:** fear for (what it may lead to). **33 border'd certain:** contained within fixed bounds, trusted not to break the limits (of right). **34 sliver:** tear off (as a twig from a branch). **35 material:** forming the substance of a thing, essential. **36 deadly use:** come to a bad end, the only use for dead wood is burning. **37 text:** subject of your moral (cf. 58) discourse, sermons. **39 Filths . . . but themselves:** filthy creatures enjoy only things that are filthy. **42** i.e. whose grey hairs even a beast would respect. **head-lugg'd:** tugged about by the head ('by the nose' in Harsnett!). **43 madded:** maddened. **45 him:** Lear.

If that the heavens do not their visible spirits
Send quickly down to tame these vile offences,
It will come,
Humanity must perforce prey on itself,
Like monsters of the deep.

Goneril.   Milk-liver'd man!   50
That bear'st a cheek for blows, a head for wrongs;
Who hast not in thy brows an eye discerning
Thine honour from thy suffering; that not know'st
Fools do those villains pity who are punish'd
Ere they have done their mischief. Where 's thy drum?
France spreads his banners in our noiseless land,   56
With plumed helm thy state begins to threat,
Whilst thou, a moral fool, sitt'st still, and criest
'Alack! why does he so?'

Albany.   See thyself, devil!
Proper deformity seems not in the fiend   60
So horrid as in woman.

Goneril.   O vain fool!

Albany. Thou changed and self-cover'd thing, for shame,
Be-monster not thy feature. Were 't my fitness
To let these hands obey my blood,
They are apt enough to dislocate and tear   65

46 **visible**: in visible form.   47 **offences**: offenders.   48
It: punishment [*N*].   50 **Milk-liver'd**: cowardly (cf. 'the liver
white and pale, which is the badge of pusillanimity and cowardice',
2 Henry IV, IV. iii. 103) [*N*].   51 i.e. you are the sort of man
to 'turn the other cheek' (Matthew v. 39).   52–53 **discerning . . .
suffering**: able to distinguish between what your honour can let you
endure and what it cannot.   54 **those villains**: in the case
(probably) Lear.   56 **noiseless**: with no sound of drums or
other preparations for war.   57 **state . . . threat**: begins to
threaten thy power, position.   58 **moral**: moralizing.   60
Proper: which belongs to him (rightly).   62 **self-cover'd**:
veiling thy true (devilish) self [*N*].   63 **feature**: appearance.
my fitness: befitting me.   64 **my blood**: my instinct.   65
apt: ready.

Thy flesh and bones; howe'er thou art a fiend,
A woman's shape doth shield thee.
  Goneril. Marry, your manhood.—Mew!

Enter a Messenger.

  Albany. What news?
  Messenger. O! my good lord, the Duke of Cornwall's dead;
Slain by his servant, going to put out   71
The other eye of Gloucester.
  Albany.   Gloucester's eyes!
  Messenger. A servant that he bred, thrill'd with remorse,
Oppos'd against the act, bending his sword
To his great master; who, thereat enrag'd,   75
Flew on him, and amongst them fell'd him dead;
But not without that harmful stroke, which since
Hath pluck'd him after.
  Albany.   This shows you are above,
You justicers, that these our nether crimes
So speedily can venge! But, O poor Gloucester!   80
Lost he his other eye?
  Messenger.   Both, both, my lord.
This letter, madam, craves a speedy answer;
'Tis from your sister.
  Goneril. [*Aside.*] One way I like this well;
But being widow, and my Gloucester with her,
May all the building in my fancy pluck   85

  66 **howe'er:** although.   68 **Mew!:** pooh! A fig for it [*N*].   73
thrill'd: excited.   **remorse:** pity (as often).   74 **bending:**
directing.   75 **To:** against.   76 **amongst them:** between
them they (he and Regan).   78 **pluck'd him after:** snatched
away him too (to death).   79 **justicers:** judges (as in III. vi. 21,
where it was a conjecture).   **nether:** committed on earth (the
lower world as opposed to heaven).   84 i.e. the fact that Regan
is a widow and Gloucester, whom I desire, is with her.   85–86
i.e. may pull down all my fine schemes and so make my life hateful
to me.

Upon my hateful life; another way,
This news is not so tart. [*To* Messenger.] I'll read and
    answer.   [*Exit.*

Albany. Where was his son when they did take his eyes?
Messenger. Come with my lady hither.
Albany.   He is not here.
Messenger. No, my good lord; I met him back again.
Albany. Knows he the wickedness?   91
Messenger. Ay, my good lord; 'twas he inform'd against
    him,
And quit the house on purpose that their punishment
Might have the freer course.
Albany.   Gloucester, I live
To thank thee for the love thou show'dst the king,   95
And to revenge thine eyes. Come hither, friend:
Tell me what more thou knowest.   [*Exeunt.*

Scene III. THE FRENCH CAMP, NEAR DOVER

Enter KENT *and a* Gentleman.

Kent. Why the King of France is so suddenly gone back
know you the reason?

Gentleman. Something he left imperfect in the state,
which since his coming forth is thought of; which imports
to the kingdom so much fear and danger, that his personal
return was most required and necessary.   6

Kent. Who hath he left behind him general?

Gentleman. The Marshal of France, Monsieur la Far.

Kent. Did your letters pierce the queen to any demonstra-
tion of grief?   10

---

  86 **another way:** the 'one way' cf. 83. Goneril sees a chance of
the whole kingdom.   87 **tart:** bitter.   90 **back:** going
back (Edmund had only escorted Goneril home).   4 **imports:**
involves, carries with it.   9 **pierce:** wound, excite.

Gentleman. Ay, sir; she took them, read them in my
    presence;
And now and then an ample tear trill'd down
Her delicate cheek; it seem'd she was a queen
Over her passion; who, most rebel-like,
Sought to be king o'er her.

Kent.   O! then it mov'd her.   15

Gentleman. Not to a rage; patience and sorrow strove
Who should express her goodliest. You have seen
Sunshine and rain at once; her smiles and tears
Were like a better way; those happy smilets
That play'd on her ripe lip seem'd not to know   20
What guests were in her eyes; which parted thence,
As pearls from diamonds dropp'd. In brief,
Sorrow would be a rarity most belov'd,
If all could so become it.

Kent.   Made she no verbal question?

Gentleman. Faith, once or twice she heav'd the name of
    'father'   25
Pantingly forth, as if it press'd her heart;
Cried, 'Sisters! sisters! Shame of ladies! sisters!
Kent! father! sisters! What, i' the storm? i' the night?
Let pity not be believed!' There she shook
The holy water from her heavenly eyes,   30
And clamour-moisten'd, then away she started
To deal with grief alone.

Kent.   It is the stars,

---

14 **passion:** emotion (*not* anger). **who:** which. 17 **Who
... goodliest:** as to which should become her best. 19 **like a
better way:** like that (sunshine and rain together), only better (a
comma could be inserted after 'like'). 21 **which:** the guest,
i.e. tears. 22 **diamonds:** her eyes. 24 **become:** suit.
Made ... question?: Didn't she *say* anything? 29 **believed:**
to exist, if people can do such things (but 'not believe it' is a likely
reading). 31 **clamour-moisten'd:** having her outburst,
emotion, calmed by a flood of tears [*N*].

The stars above us, govern our conditions;
Else one self mate and make could not beget
Such different issues. You spoke not with her since?   35
  Gentleman. No.
  Kent. Was this before the king return'd?
  Gentleman.   No, since.
  Kent. Well, sir, the poor distress'd Lear 's i' the town,
Who sometime, in his better tune, remembers
What we are come about, and by no means   40
Will yield to see his daughter.
  Gentleman.   Why, good sir?
  Kent. A sovereign shame so elbows him: his own unkind-
    ness,
That stripp'd her from his benediction, turn'd her
To foreign casualties, gave her dear rights
To his dog-hearted daughters,—these things sting   45
His mind so venomously that burning shame
Detains him from Cordelia.
  Gentleman.   Alack! poor gentleman.
  Kent. Of Albany's and Cornwall's powers you heard not?
  Gentleman. 'Tis so, they are afoot.
  Kent. Well, sir, I'll bring you to our master Lear,   50
And leave you to attend him. Some dear cause
Will in concealment wrap me up awhile;
When I am known aright, you shall not grieve
Lending me this acquaintance. I pray you, go   54
Along with me.   [*Exeunt.*

33 **conditions**: character.   34 **one self mate and make**: the
same husband and wife ('make' comes from a root meaning 'equal').
37 **the king** (of France).   39 **sometime**(s). **better tune**:
saner moments.   41 **yield**: agree.   42 **sovereign**: (1) all-
powerful, but also (2) worthy of a king. **elbows him**: pushes him
away (from her).   44 **foreign casualties**: the chances of life
abroad.   48 **powers**: forces.   49 **'Tis so**: it is true that.
51 **dear cause**: important reason (cf. III. i. 19) [*N*].   54 **Lending ... acquaintance**: for having got to know me.

Scene IV. The Same. A Tent

Enter with drum and colours, CORDELIA, Doctor, *and*
Soldiers.

Cordelia. Alack! 'tis he: why, he was met even now
As mad as the vex'd sea; singing aloud;
Crown'd with rank fumiter and furrow weeds,
With burdocks, hemlock, nettles, cuckoo-flowers,
Darnel, and all the idle weeds that grow   5
In our sustaining corn. A century send forth;
Search every acre in the high-grown field,
And bring him to our eye.   [*Exit an* Officer.
               What can man's wisdom
In the restoring his bereaved sense?
He that helps him take all my outward worth.   10
   Physician. There is means, madam;
Our foster-nurse of nature is repose,
The which he lacks; that to provoke in him,
Are many simples operative, whose power
Will close the eye of anguish.
   Cordelia.   All bless'd secrets,   15
All you unpublish'd virtues of the earth,
Spring with my tears! be aidant and remediate
In the good man's distress! Seek, seek for him,
Lest his ungovern'd rage dissolve the life
That wants the means to lead it.

2 **vex'd**: stirred up (by winds).   3 **rank**: luxuriant.   **fumiter**:
fumitory.   **furrow weeds**: weeds which grow in ploughed land.
4 **cuckoo-flowers**: (uncertain) [*N*].   6 **sustaining**: life-giving.
century: a hundred men [*N*].   8 **can**: knows, can do.   9
bereaved: lost.   10 **helps**: heals.   **outward worth**: possessions.   12 **Our . . . nature**: the foster-nurse of our nature.
13 **provoke**: induce.   14 **simples operative**: effective (medi-
cinal) plants.   16 **virtues**: properties, (healing) powers.   17
Spring with: spring up watered by.   **remediate**: remedial.
20 i.e. which lacks the power (sanity) to control it(self).

Enter a Messenger.

Messenger.   News, madam;   20
The British powers are marching hitherward.
  Cordelia. 'Tis known before; our preparation stands
In expectation of them. O dear father!
It is thy business that I go about;
Therefore great France   25
My mourning and important tears hath pitied.
No blown ambition doth our arms incite,
But love, dear love, and our ag'd father's right,
Soon may I hear and see him!   [*Exeunt.*

Scene V. A Room in Gloucester's Castle

Enter REGAN *and* OSWALD.

  Regan. But are my brother's powers set forth?
  Oswald.   Ay, madam.
  Regan. Himself in person there?
  Oswald.   Madam, with much ado:
Your sister is the better soldier.
  Regan. Lord Edmund spake not with your lord at home?
  Oswald. No, madam.   5
  Regan. What might import my sister's letter to him?
  Oswald. I know not, lady.
  Regan. Faith, he is posted hence on serious matter.
It was great ignorance, Gloucester's eyes being out,
To let him live; where he arrives he moves   10
All hearts against us. Edmund, I think, is gone,
In pity of his misery, to dispatch
His nighted life; moreover, to descry

25 **France:** the king of France.   26 **important:** importunate,
urgent.   27 **blown:** proud.   1 **brother**(-in-law)**'s.**   2
with much ado: i.e. Goneril had great difficulty in getting Albany
to take up arms in a bad cause.   6 **import:** signify.   9
ignorance: folly.   13 **nighted:** darkened, blinded.

The strength o' the enemy.   **14**

  Oswald. I must needs after him, madam, with my letter.

  Regan. Our troops set forth to-morrow; stay with us,
The ways are dangerous.

  Oswald.   I may not, madam;
My lady charg'd my duty in this business.

  Regan. Why should she write to Edmund? Might not you
Transport her purposes by word? Belike,   **20**
Something—I know not what. I'll love thee much,
Let me unseal the letter.

  Oswald.   Madam, I had rather—

  Regan. I know your lady does not love her husband;
I am sure of that: and at her late being here
She gave strange œilliades and most speaking looks   **25**
To noble Edmund. I know you are of her bosom.

  Oswald. I, madam!

  Regan. I speak in understanding; you are, I know't:
Therefore I do advise you, take this note:
My lord is dead; Edmund and I have talk'd,   **30**
And more convenient is he for my hand
Than for your lady's. You may gather more.
If you do find him, pray you, give him this,
And when your mistress hears thus much from you,
I pray desire her call her wisdom to her: **35**
So, fare you well.
If you do chance to hear of that blind traitor,
Preferment falls on him that cuts him off.

---

    18 charg'd my duty: invoked my sense of duty to her (to deliver
the letter at once).   **20 Belike:** probably.   **22 I had
rather—:** s.d. refusing the letter (Johnson) [*N*].   **25 œilliades:**
glad eyes.   **speaking:** eloquent of her wishes.   **26 of her
bosom:** trusted by her.   **29 take this note:** (probably) take
note of this [*N*].   **30 talk'd:** come to an understanding.
32 gather: infer.   **33 this:** a token *or* letter.   **35 call
her . . . her:** show some sense (remember she has a husband).
38 i.e. you will be promoted if you kill him.

Oswald. Would I could meet him, madam: I would show
What party I do follow.

Regan.   Fare thee well.   [*Exeunt.*

Scene VI. THE COUNTRY NEAR DOVER

Enter GLOUCESTER, *and* EDGAR *dressed like a peasant.*

Gloucester. When shall I come to the top of that same
    hill?

Edgar. You do climb up it now; look how we labour.

Gloucester. Methinks the ground is even.

Edgar.   Horrible steep:
Hark! do you hear the sea?

Gloucester.   No, truly.

Edgar. Why, then your other senses grow imperfect   5
By your eyes' anguish.

Gloucester.   So may it be, indeed.
Methinks thy voice is alter'd, and thou speak'st
In better phrase and matter than thou didst.

Edgar. Y'are much deceived; in nothing am I chang'd
But in my garments.

Gloucester.   Methinks you're better spoken.   10

Edgar. Come on, sir; here's the place: stand still.
How fearful
And dizzy 'tis to cast one's eyes so low!
The crows and choughs that wing the midway air
Show scarce so gross as beetles; half way down   15
Hangs one that gathers samphire, dreadful trade!
Methinks he seems no bigger than his head.
The fishermen that walk upon the beach
Appear like mice, and yond tall anchoring bark
Diminish'd to her cock, her cock a buoy   20

1 **that same hill**: see IV. i. 73.   14 **choughs**: still a cliff bird
in Cornwall.   15 **gross**: large.   16 **samphire**: a herb used
for pickles [*N*].   20 **cock**: cock-boat, ship's boat.

Almost too small for sight. The murmuring surge,
That on the unnumber'd idle pebble chafes,
Cannot be heard so high. I'll look no more,
Lest my brain turn, and the deficient sight
Topple down headlong.
   Gloucester.   Set me where you stand.   25
   Edgar. Give me your hand; you are now within a foot
Of the extreme verge: for all beneath the moon
Would I not leap upright.
   Gloucester.   Let go my hand.
Here, friend, 's another purse; in it a jewel
Well worth a poor man's taking; fairies and gods 30
Prosper it with thee! Go thou further off;
Bid me farewell, and let me hear thee going.
   Edgar. Now fare you well, good sir.
   Gloucester.   With all my heart.
   Edgar. Why I do trifle thus with his despair
Is done to cure it.
   Gloucester.   O you mighty gods!   35
This world I do renounce, and, in your sights,
Shake patiently my great affliction off;
If I could bear it longer, and not fall
To quarrel with your great opposeless wills,
My snuff and loathed part of nature should 40
Burn itself out. If Edgar live, O, bless him!

---

    22 **unnumber'd:** innumerable.   **idle:** moved to no purpose.
pebble: (used as plural.)   24 **the deficient sight:** I, through
failing sight.   28 **leap upright:** he is so near the edge that
even such a movement would be fatal.   29 **another purse:** see
IV. i. 64.   31 **Prosper it with thee:** make the purse lucky for
you (perhaps a reference to a belief that fairies multiplied treasure
trove).   34–35 i.e. The object of my trifling . . . is to cure it (a
mixture of constructions).   39 **quarrel with:** rebel against.
opposeless: irresistible.   40–41 i.e. I would let the miserable
remnant of my life expire naturally, instead of seeking my own death
(snuff = the half-burnt wick).

Now, fellow, fare thee well.

   Edgar.   Gone, sir: farewell.

                         [GLOUCESTER *falls forward.*

[*Aside.* And yet I know not how conceit may rob

The treasury of life when life itself

Yields to the theft; had he been where he thought   45

By this had thought been past. Alive or dead?

[*To* GLOUCESTER.] Ho, you sir! friend! Hear you, sir?
    speak!

Thus might he pass indeed; yet he revives.

What are you, sir?

   Gloucester.   Away and let me die.

   Edgar. Hadst thou been aught but gossamer, feathers, air,

So many fathom down precipitating,   51

Thou'dst shiver'd like an egg; but thou dost breathe,

Hast heavy substance, bleed'st not, speak'st, art sound.

Ten masts at each make not the altitude

Which thou hast perpendicularly fell: 55

Thy life's a miracle. Speak yet again.

   Gloucester. But have I fallen or no?

   Edgar. From the dread summit of this chalky bourn.

Look up a-height; the shrill-gorg'd lark so far

Cannot be seen or heard: do but look up.   60

   Gloucester. Alack! I have no eyes.

Is wretchedness depriv'd that benefit

To end itself by death? 'Twas yet some comfort,

When misery could beguile the tyrant's rage,

---

    42 Gone, sir: answer to 31.   **43 I know not how:** I don't
know how it is that.   **conceit:** imagination.   **44–45 when life
. . . theft:** when there is no longer the will to live.   **47** is spoken
in a different voice as if by a stranger who has found Gloucester at
the foot of the cliff.   **48** (an aside.)   **51 precipitating:** falling
headlong.   **54 at each:** on end.   **58 bourn:** the limit of
the sea (cf. IV. i. 74).   **59 a-height:** on high.   **59 shrill-
gorg'd:** shrill-throated, high-voiced.   **64 beguile:** cheat (by
death).

And frustrate his proud will.

Edgar.   Give me your arm: 65
Up: so. How is't? Feel you your legs? You stand.

Gloucester. Too well, too well.

Edgar.   This above all strangeness.
Upon the crown o' the cliff, what thing was that
Which parted from you?

Gloucester.   A poor unfortunate beggar.

Edgar. As I stood here below methought his eyes 70
Were two full moons; he had a thousand noses,
Horns whelk'd and wav'd like the enridged sea:
It was some fiend; therefore, thou happy father,
Think that the clearest gods, who make them honours
Of men's impossibilities, have preserv'd thee. 75

Gloucester. I do remember now; henceforth I'll bear
Affliction till it do cry out itself
'Enough, enough,' and die. That thing you speak of
I took it for a man; often 'twould say
'The fiend, the fiend:' he led me to that place. 80

Edgar. Bear free and patient thoughts. But who comes
here?

Enter LEAR, *fantastically dressed with flowers.*

The safer sense will ne'er accommodate
His master thus.

Lear. No, they cannot touch me for coining;
I am the king himself. 85

Edgar. O thou side-piercing sight!

72 **whelk'd:** (probably) twisted.   **enridged:** ridged, furrowed.
73 **father:** ambiguous, since it could be addressed to any old man [N].
74 **clearest:** purest, open and righteous.   81 **free:** free from
fear, happy (and so not inclined to suicide) *or* generous towards men
and **patient** towards God.   81–82 s.d. based on IV. iv. 3–6.
82–83 i.e. a man in his right senses would not get himself up like
this ('safer' = saner).   84 **touch:** get at, punish [N].   86
side-piercing: heart-rending.

Lear. Nature's above art in that respect. There's
your press-money. That fellow handles his bow like
a crow-keeper: draw me a clothier's yard. Look, look!
a mouse. Peace, peace! this piece of toasted cheese   90
will do 't. There's my gauntlet; I'll prove it on a
giant. Bring up the brown bills. O! well flown, bird;
i' the clout, i' the clout: hewgh! Give the word.

Edgar. Sweet marjoram.

Lear. Pass.   95

Gloucester. I know that voice.

Lear. Ha! Goneril, with a white beard! They
flatter'd me like a dog, and told me I had white hairs
in my beard ere the black ones were there. To say 'ay'
and 'no' to every thing I said! 'Ay' and 'no' too was   100
no good divinity. When the rain came to wet me once
and the wind to make me chatter, when the thunder
would not peace at my bidding, there I found 'em,
there I smelt 'em out. Go to, they are not men o'
their words: they told me I was every thing; 'tis a lie,   105
I am not ague-proof.

Gloucester. The trick of that voice I do well remember:
Is 't not the king?

Lear.   Ay, every inch a king:
When I do stare, see how the subject quakes.

87 **Nature's above art:** (probably) a king's above a coiner (issuer
of false money).   88 **press-money:** payment given a man forced
into the services (cf. press-gang).   89 **crow-keeper:** scarer of
birds.   **me:** for me to see.   **clothier's yard:** long arrow.   91
gauntlet: mailed glove as a challenge.   92 **brown bills:**
halberds painted brown *or* the bearers of them.   **bird:** here used
for arrow.   93 **clout:** mark, target.   **hewgh:** the whistling
sound of the arrow in the air.   **word:** password.   94 **marjoram:** used as a remedy for madness.   98 **like a dog:** as a
dog fawns on people.   **white hairs:** i.e. the wisdom of age.
101 **no good divinity:** not sound theologically (in view of St. Paul's
words 'For the Son of God, Jesus Christ . . . was not yea and nay,
but in him was yea', 2 Cor. i. 19).   107 **trick:** accent.

I pardon that man's life. What was thy cause?   110
Adultery?
Thou shalt not die: die for adultery! No:
The wren goes to 't, and the small gilded fly
Does lecher in my sight.
Let copulation thrive; for Gloucester's bastard son   115
Was kinder to his father than my daughters
Got 'tween the lawful sheets.
To 't luxury, pell-mell! for I lack soldiers.
Behold yond simpering dame,
Whose face between her forks presageth snow;   120
That minces virtue, and does shake the head
To hear of pleasure's name;
The fitchew nor the soiled horse goes to 't
With a more riotous appetite.
Down from the waist they are Centaurs,   125
Though women all above:
But to the girdle do the gods inherit,
Beneath is all the fiends':
There's hell, there's darkness, there is the sulphurous pit,
Burning, scalding, stench, consumption; fie, fie, fie! pah,
pah! Give me an ounce of civet, good apothecary, to
sweeten my imagination: there's money for thee.   132

   Gloucester. O! let me kiss that hand!

   Lear. Let me wipe it first; it smells of mortality.

   Gloucester. O ruin'd piece of nature! This great world
Shall so wear out to nought. Dost thou know me?   136

---

110 **cause**: crime, subject of accusation.   118 **luxury**: lust.
pell mell: promiscuously.   120 i.e. Whose face would make
you think she had little sexual desire [*N*].   121 **minces**:
affects.   123 **fitchew**: (1) pole-cat, and (2) harlot.   **soil'd**:
overfed.   125 **Centaurs**: half men, half horses, in Greek
mythology.   127 **But to**: only as far as.   **inherit**: own.
131 **civet**: scent.   134 **mortality** (1) humanity, and perhaps
also (2) death.   135 **piece**: (perhaps) masterpiece.   136 **so**:
as you have done.

Lear. I remember thine eyes well enough. Dost thou
squiny at me? No, do thy worst, blind Cupid; I'll not
love. Read thou this challenge; mark but the penning of it.

Gloucester. Were all the letters suns I could not see.   140

Edgar. [*Aside.*] I would not take this from report; it is,
And my heart breaks at it.

Lear. Read.

Gloucester. What! with the case of eyes?   144

Lear. O, ho! are you there with me? No eyes in your
head, nor no money in your purse? Your eyes are in a
heavy case, your purse in a light: yet you see how this
world goes.

Gloucester. I see it feelingly.

Lear. What! art mad? A man may see how this   150
world goes with no eyes. Look with thine ears: see
how yond justice rails upon yon simple thief. Hark,
in thine ear: change places; and, handy-dandy, which
is the justice, which is the thief? Thou hast seen a
farmer's dog bark at a beggar?   155

Gloucester. Ay, sir.

Lear. And the creature run from the cur? There thou
mightst behold the great image of authority; a dog's
obey'd in office.

Thou rascal beadle, hold thy bloody hand!   160
Why dost thou lash that whore? Strip thine own back;
Thou hotly lusts to use her in that kind

---

138 **squiny:** squint.   **blind Cupid:** the sign over brothels (may
recall Gloucester's sin).   144 **case:** sockets.   145 **are you
. . . me?:** Is that what you mean?   146-7 **in a heavy case:**
because in a bad way.   149 **feelingly:** by my sense of feeling
(perhaps also suggests 'I feel it deeply').   152 **simple:** humble.
153 **handy-dandy:** take which you like (from a children's game).
157 **creature:** human being.   158 **image:** type, example.
a dog: even a dog.   159 **in office:** in a position of authority.
160 **beadle:** parish constable [*N*].   162 **in that kind:** i.e.
lustfully [*N*].

For which thou whipp'st her. The usurer hangs the
    cozener.
Through tatter'd clothes small vices do appear;
Robes and furr'd gowns hide all. Plate sin with gold,   165
And the strong lance of justice hurtless breaks;
Arm it in rags, a pigmy's straw doth pierce it.
None does offend, none, I say none; I'll able 'em:
Take that of me, my friend, who have the power
To seal the accuser's lips. Get thee glass eyes;   170
And, like a scurvy politician, seem
To see the things thou dost not. Now, now, now, now;
Pull off my boots; harder, harder; so.
   Edgar. [*Aside.*] O! matter and impertinency mix'd;
Reason in madness!   175
   Lear. If thou wilt weep my fortunes, take my eyes;
I know thee well enough; thy name is Gloucester:
Thou must be patient; we came crying hither:
Thou know'st the first time that we smell the air
We waul and cry. I will preach to thee: mark.   180
   Gloucester. Alack! alack the day!
   Lear. When we are born, we cry that we are come
To this great stage of fools. This' a good block!
It were a delicate stratagem to shoe
A troop of horse with felt; I'll put it in proof,   185
And when I have stol'n upon these sons-in-law,
Then, kill, kill, kill, kill, kill, kill!

---

163 **The usurer ... cozener:** i.e. a magistrate who has a man
hanged for a petty theft may himself lend money for interest (con-
demned by medieval church).   165 **furr'd gowns:** worn by
judges and aldermen. **Plate sin with gold:** give the sinner the
armour of riches [*N*].   166 **hurtless:** inflicting no wound.
168 **able:** vouch for, protect.   171 **scurvy politician:** rascally
schemer. **seem:** pretend.   174 **matter:** good sense. **impertinency:** irrelevance, nonsense.   177 see l. 136.   180
waul: wail (cf. caterwaul).   183 **This':** This is. **block:** (perhaps) a felt hat [*N*].   185 **in proof:** on trial.

Enter Gentleman, *with* Attendants.

Gentleman. O! here he is; lay hand upon him. Sir,
Your most dear daughter—

Lear. No rescue? What! a prisoner? I am even   190
The natural fool of fortune. Use me well;
You shall have ransom. Let me have surgeons;
I am cut to the brains.

Gentleman.   You shall have any thing.

Lear. No seconds? All myself?
Why this would make a man a man of salt,   195
To use his eyes for garden water-pots,
Ay, and laying autumn's dust.

Gentleman.   Good sir,—

Lear. I will die bravely as a bridegroom. What!
I will be jovial: come, come; I am a king,
My masters, know you that?   200

Gentleman. You are a royal one, and we obey you.

Lear. Then there's life in it. Nay, an you get it, you shall
get it by running. Sa, sa, sa, sa.

[*Exit. Attendants* follow.

Gentleman. A sight most pitiful in the meanest wretch,
Past speaking of in a king! Thou hast one daughter, 205
Who redeems nature from the general curse
Which twain have brought her to.

Edgar. Hail, gentle sir!

Gentleman.   Sir, speed you: what's your will?

190 Lear has been found by Cordelia's attendants whom he imagines to be enemies.   191 **The natural fool of:** born to be the
sport, victim of (bad) fortune.   193 **cut to the brains:** cf.
'cut to the heart'.   194 **seconds:** supporters.   195 **a man
of salt:** all tears (but cf. Lot's wife Genesis xix. 26).   198 **as
a bridegroom:** meeting death like a bride.   202 **there's
life in it:** there's still hope for me.   203 **Sa, sa:** a cry
inciting to action, as to hunting dogs.   206 **nature:** human
nature, disgraced by Goneril and Regan [*N*].   208 (God) **speed
you.**

Edgar. Do you hear aught, sir, of a battle toward?

Gentleman. Most sure and vulgar; every one hears that,
Which can distinguish sound.

Edgar. But, by your favour, 211
How near's the other army?

Gentleman. Near, and on speedy foot; the main descry
Stands on the hourly thought.

Edgar. I thank you, sir: that's all.

Gentleman. Though that the queen on special cause is
here, 215
Her army is mov'd on.

Edgar. I thank you, sir.

[*Exit* Gentleman.

Gloucester. You ever-gentle gods, take my breath from
me:
Let not my worser spirit tempt me again
To die before you please!

Edgar. Well pray you, father.

Gloucester. Now, good sir, what are you? 220

Edgar. A most poor man, made tame to fortune's blows;
Who, by the art of known and feeling sorrows,
Am pregnant to good pity. Give me your hand,
I'll lead you to some biding.

Gloucester. Hearty thanks:
The bounty and the benison of heaven 225
To boot, and boot!

209 **toward**: imminent.   210 **vulgar**: commonly known.
213–14 **the main ... thought**: the sight of the main body is expected every hour.   217 i.e. let me die in heaven's good time
[*N*].   218 **my worser spirit**: the worse part of me, my evil
genius (a phrase used in Sonnet 144).   219 **father**: see 73,
and cf. 254 &c.   222 **by the art of**: taught by.   **feeling**: heart-
felt.   223 **pregnant to**: disposed to show.   224 **biding**:
abode, resting place.   225 **benison**: blessing.   226 **To
boot, and boot**: in addition, and may it help you (two meanings of
'boot').

Enter OSWALD.

Oswald.   A proclaim'd prize! Most happy!
That eyeless head of thine was first fram'd flesh
To raise my fortunes. Thou old unhappy traitor,
Briefly thyself remember: the sword is out
That must destroy thee.

Gloucester.   Now let thy friendly hand   230
Put strength enough to 't.   [EDGAR *interposes.*

Oswald.   Wherefore, bold peasant,
Dar'st thou support a publish'd traitor? Hence;
Lest that infection of his fortune take
Like hold on thee. Let go his arm.

Edgar. Chill not let go, zur, without vurther 'casion.   235

Oswald. Let go, slave, or thou diest.

Edgar. Good gentleman, go your gait, and let poor
volk pass. An chud ha' bin zwaggered out of my life,
'twould not ha' bin zo long as 'tis by a vortnight. Nay,
come not near th' old man; keep out, che vor ye, or ise   240
try whether your costard or my ballow be the harder.
Chill be plain with you.

Oswald. Out, dunghill!

Edgar. Chill pick your teeth, zur. Come; no matter vor
your foins.   [*They fight, and* EDGAR *knocks him down.*

Oswald. Slave, thou hast slain me. Villain, take my purse.
If ever thou wilt thrive, bury my body;   247
And give the letters which thou find'st about me

226 **A proclaim'd prize:** a publish'd traitor (232) for whose
arrest a reward had been offered.   227 **fram'd:** made.
229 **thyself remember:** remember your sins, prepare for death.
out: unsheathed.   230 **friendly:** G. desires to die.   233–4 i.e.
lest the same fate overtake you.   235 **Chill:** I will.   '**casion:**
reason [*N*].   237 **gait:** way.   238 **An . . . zwaggered:** If I
could have been bullied.   240 **che vor ye:** I warrant you.
ise: I shall.   241 **costard:** head (lit. a kind of apple).   **ballow:**
cudgel.   244 **pick your teeth:** i.e. fight you.   245 **foins:**
thrusts [*N*].   246 **Villain:** serf.

To Edmund Earl of Gloucester; seek him out
Upon the English party: O! untimely death.   [*Dies.*

  Edgar. I know thee well: a serviceable villain;   251
As duteous to the vices of thy mistress
As badness would desire.

  Gloucester.   What! is he dead?

  Edgar. Sit you down, father; rest you.
Let's see his pockets: these letters that he speaks of   255
May be my friends. He's dead; I am only sorry
He had no other deaths-man. Let us see:
Leave, gentle wax; and, manners, blame us not:
To know our enemies' minds, we'd rip their hearts;
Their papers, is more lawful.   260

   'Let our reciprocal vows be remembered. You have
many opportunities to cut him off; if your will want
not, time and place will be fruitfully offered. There is
nothing done if he return the conqueror; then am I
the prisoner, and his bed my gaol; from the loathed   265
warmth whereof deliver me, and supply the place for
your labour.

   'Your—wife, so I would say—

              'Affectionate servant,
                   'GONERIL.'

O undistinguish'd space of woman's will!   271
A plot upon her virtuous husband's life,
And the exchange my brother! Here, in the sands,
Thee I'll rake up, the post unsanctified
Of murderous lechers; and in the mature time   275

    250 **Upon:** on, among.   **party:** side [*N*].   251 **villain:**
rascal.   258 **Leave:** by your leave.   262 **him:** Albany.
262-3 **want not:** is not deficient.   266 **for:** as a reward for.
271 **undistinguish'd:** indistinguishable, illimitable.   **space:** range.
will: desire, lust (cf. IV. ii. 32-33 with this whole line).   274
rake up: bury.   **post:** messenger, postman.   275 **in the
mature time:** at the right moment.

With this ungracious paper strike the sight
Of the death-practis'd duke. For him 'tis well
That of thy death and business I can tell.

   Gloucester. The king is mad: how stiff is my vile sense,
That I stand up, and have ingenious feeling   280
Of my huge sorrows! Better I were distract:
So should my thoughts be sever'd from my griefs,
And woes by wrong imaginations lose
The knowledge of themselves.   [*Drums afar off.*
   Edgar.   Give me your hand:
Far off, methinks, I hear the beaten drum.   285
Come, father, I'll bestow you with a friend.   [*Exeunt.*

Scene VII. A Tent in the French Camp

   Enter CORDELIA, KENT, *Doctor, and* Gentleman.

   Cordelia. O thou good Kent! how shall I live and work
To match thy goodness? My life will be too short,
And every measure fail me.
   Kent.   To be acknowledg'd, madam, is o'erpaid.
All my reports go with the modest truth,   5
Nor more nor clipp'd, but so.
   Cordelia.   Be better suited:
These weeds are memories of those worser hours:
I prithee, put them off.
   Kent.   Pardon me, dear madam;

---

   276 **ungracious:** disgraceful.   277 **death-practis'd:** whose
death has been plotted.   279 **stiff:** unbending, unfeeling.   280
ingenious: intelligent, conscious.   281 **distract**(ed): mad.
282 i.e. I should not realize my miseries.   283 **wrong imaginations:** illusions.   286 **bestow:** lodge.   2 **match:**
come up to, in recompensing it.   3 **measure:** degree (of
gratitude, compared with Kent's services).   5 **my reports:** the
reports I have given you.   6 **Nor more . . . so:** neither ex-
aggerated nor understated but accurate.   **suited:** dressed [*N*].
7 **weeds:** clothes.

Yet to be known shortens my made intent:
My boon I make it that you know me not   10
Till time and I think meet.

  Cordelia. Then be 't so, my good lord.—[*To the* Doctor.]
    How does the king?

  Doctor. Madam, sleeps still.

  Cordelia. O you kind gods,
Cure this great breach in his abused nature!   15
The untun'd and jarring senses, O! wind up
Of this child-changed father!

  Doctor.   So please your majesty
That we may wake the king? he hath slept long.

  Cordelia. Be govern'd by your knowledge, and proceed
I' the sway of your own will. Is he array'd?   20

    Enter LEAR *in his chair, carried by* Servants.

  Gentleman. Ay, madam; in the heaviness of sleep, We
put fresh garments on him.

  Doctor. Be by, good madam, when we do awake him;
I doubt not of his temperance.

  Cordelia.   Very well.   [*Music.*

  Doctor. Please you, draw near. Louder the music there.

  Cordelia. O my dear father! Restoration, hang   26
Thy medicine on my lips, and let this kiss
Repair those violent harms that my two sisters
Have in thy reverence made!

  Kent.   Kind and dear princess!

---

9 **Yet:** at present.   **my made intent:** the plan I have made.
10 **My boon . . . it:** the favour I ask is.   11 i.e. Till I think the
time ripe.   16 **wind up:** tune.   17 **child-changed:**
(1) changed into a child (in mind), (2) changed by (the cruelty of)
his children—very probably *both.*   **please:** may it please.
20 **I' the sway . . . will:** as you think best.   24 **temperance:**
sanity.   26 **Restoration:** the power of restoring the senses
(personified).

Cordelia. Had you not been their father, these white
    flakes   30
Had challeng'd pity of them. Was this a face
To be expos'd against the warring winds?
To stand against the deep dread-bolted thunder?
In the most terrible and nimble stroke
Of quick cross lightning? to watch—poor perdu!—   35
With this thin helm? Mine enemy's dog,
Though he had bit me, should have stood that night
Against my fire. And wast thou fain, poor father,
To hovel thee with swine and rogues forlorn,
In short and musty straw? Alack, alack!   40
'Tis wonder that thy life and wits at once
Had not concluded all. He wakes; speak to him.

    Doctor. Madam, do you; 'tis fittest.

    Cordelia. How does my royal lord? How fares your
        majesty?

    Lear. You do me wrong to take me out o' the grave;   45
Thou art a soul in bliss; but I am bound
Upon a wheel of fire, that mine own tears
Do scald like molten lead.

    Cordelia.   Sir, do you know me?

    Lear. You are a spirit, I know; when did you die?

    Cordelia. Still, still, far wide.   50

    Doctor. He's scarce awake; let him alone awhile.

    Lear. Where have I been? Where am I? Fair daylight?
I am mightily abus'd. I should even die with pity
To see another thus. I know not what to say.

---

    30 white flakes: his *snowy* hair and beard.   **31 of:** from.
33 deep: deep-voiced.   **dread-bolted:** armed with the dreaded
thunderbolt.   **35 cross:** forked. **watch:** stand exposed [*N*].
36 thin helm: unprotected head.   **38 Against:** in front of.
40 short: cut short (and therefore uncomfortable), and/or scanty.
42 concluded all: entirely ended.   **47 that:** so that.
48 scald: scald me.   **50 wide:** astray (in mind).   **53
abus'd:** deceived, deluded (cf. 77 below.)

I will not swear these are my hands: let's see;   55
I feel this pin prick. Would I were assur'd
Of my condition!

Cordelia.   O! look upon me, sir,
And hold your hands in benediction o'er me,
No, sir, you must not kneel.

   Lear.   Pray, do not mock me:
I am a very foolish fond old man,   60
Fourscore and upward, not an hour more or less;
And, to deal plainly,
I fear I am not in my perfect mind.
Methinks I should know you and know this man;
Yet I am doubtful: for I am mainly ignorant   65
What place this is, and all the skill I have
Remembers not these garments; nor I know not
Where I did lodge last night. Do not laugh at me;
For, as I am a man, I think this lady
To be my child Cordelia.

   Cordelia.   And so I am, I am.   70

   Lear. Be your tears wet? Yes, faith. I pray, weep not:
If you have poison for me, I will drink it.
I know you do not love me; for your sisters
Have, as I do remember, done me wrong:
You have some cause, they have not.

   Cordelia.   No cause, no cause.

   Lear. Am I in France?

   Kent.   In your own kingdom, sir.   76

   Lear. Do not abuse me.

   Doctor. Be comforted, good madam; the great rage,
You see, is kill'd in him; and yet it is danger
To make him even o'er the time he has lost.   80
Desire him to go in; trouble him no more

---

60 **fond:** simple, foolish   65 **mainly:** completely.   78
rage: frenzy, madness.   80 **even o'er:** smooth over, straighten
out, make the recollection continuous.

Till further settling.

   Cordelia. Will't please your highness walk?

   Lear.   You must bear with me.
Pray you now, forget and forgive: I am old and foolish.

        [*Exeunt* LEAR, CORDELIA, Doctor, *and* Attendants.

   Gentleman. Holds it true, sir, that the Duke of Cornwall
was so slain?   86

   Kent. Most certain, sir.

   Gentleman. Who is conductor of his people?

   Kent. As 'tis said, the bastard son of Gloucester.

   Gentleman. They say Edgar, his banished son, is with the
Earl of Kent in Germany.   91

   Kent. Report is changeable. 'Tis time to look about; the
powers of the kingdom approach apace.

   Gentleman. The arbitrement is like to be bloody. Fare
you well, sir.   95

   Kent. My point and period will be thoroughly wrought,
Or well or ill, as this day's battle's fought.   [*Exit.*

---

   82 Till . . . settling: till his mind has had more time to settle
down again.   **83 walk:** withdraw.   **94 arbitrement:**
decision (of the war).   **96 point and period:** object and end.

ACT V

Scene I. THE BRITISH CAMP NEAR DOVER

Enter, with drum and colours, EDMUND, REGAN, Officers, Soldiers, *and others.*

Edmund. Know of the duke if his last purpose hold,
Or whether since he is advis'd by aught
To change the course; he 's full of alteration
And self-reproving; bring his constant pleasure.

                [To an Officer, *who goes out.*

Regan. Our sister's man is certainly miscarried.   5

Edmund. 'Tis to be doubted, madam.

Regan.   Now, sweet lord,
You know the goodness I intend upon you:
Tell me, but truly, but then speak the truth,
Do you not love my sister?

Edmund.   In honour'd love.

Regan. But have you never found my brother's way   10
To the forefended place?

Edmund.   That thought abuses you.

Regan. I am doubtful that you have been conjunct
And bosom'd with her, as far as we call hers.

Edmund. No, by mine honour, madam.

Regan. I never shall endure her: dear my lord,   15

---

1 Know: find out.   **hold:** still holds good.   **2 since:** since then.   **advis'd:** induced.   **4 constant pleasure:** firm decision.   **5 Our sister's man:** Oswald (see IV. vi. 250). **6 doubted:** feared (so 'doubtful' in l. 12 = afraid).   **7 goodness I intend** (to confer) **upon you:** i.e. my hand.   **8 then:** even if it is what I fear.   **9 honour'd:** honourable, not adulterous.   **11 forefended:** forbidden.   **abuses:** deceives.   **13** i.e. intimate with her to the fullest degree.   **15 endure her:** i.e. bear to see her separate us.

Be not familiar with her.

Edmund. Fear me not.
She and the duke her husband!

Enter with drums and colours, ALBANY,
GONERIL, *and* Soldiers.

Goneril [*Aside.*] I had rather lose the battle than that
sister
Should loosen him and me.

Albany. Our very loving sister, well be-met. 20
Sir, this I heard, the king is come to his daughter,
With others; whom the rigour of our state
Forc'd to cry out. Where I could not be honest
I never yet was valiant: for this business,
It toucheth us, as France invades our land, 25
Not bolds the king, with others, whom, I fear,
Most just and heavy causes make oppose.

Edmund. Sir, you speak nobly.

Regan. Why is this reason'd?

Goneril. Combine together 'gainst the enemy
For these domestic and particular broils 30
Are not the question here.

Albany. Let's then determine
With the ancient of war on our proceeding.

Edmund. I shall attend you presently at your tent.

Regan. Sister, you'll go with us?

Goneril. No. 35

Regan. 'Tis most convenient; pray you, go with us.

16 **Fear**: distrust.   20 **be-met**: met.   22 **our state**:
our rule.   23 **cry out**: protest, rebel.   25 **toucheth us, as**:
concerns me in so far as.   26 **Not bolds**: not in so far as the
king of France emboldens (supports).   26–27 **whom ... oppose**:
who, I fear, have good and weighty reasons for taking up arms
against us [*N*].   28 **Why ... reason'd?**: Why all this argument
(about the cause of rebellion)?   30 **particular**: private.   32
the ancient of war: veteran soldiers.   33 **presently**: at once.

Goneril. [*Aside.*] O, ho! I know the riddle. [*Aloud.*] I
   will go.

Enter EDGAR, *disguised.*

Edgar. If e'er your Grace had speech with man so poor,
Hear me one word.
Albany.   I'll overtake you. Speak.

> [*Exeunt* EDMUND, REGAN, GONERIL, Officers,
>   Soldiers, *and* Attendants.

Edgar. Before you fight the battle, ope this letter.   40
If you have victory, let the trumpet sound
For him that brought it: wretched though I seem,
I can produce a champion that will prove
What is avouched there. If you miscarry,
Your business of the world hath so an end,   45
And machination ceases. Fortune love you!
Albany. Stay till I have read the letter.
Edgar.   I was forbid it.
When time shall serve, let but the herald cry,
And I'll appear again.   49
Albany. Why, fare thee well: I will o'erlook thy paper.

> [*Exit* EDGAR.

Re-enter EDMUND.

Edmund. The enemy's in view; draw up your powers.
Here is the guess of their true strength and forces
By diligent discovery; but your haste
Is now urg'd on you.
Albany.   We will greet the time.   [*Exit.*
Edmund. To both these sisters have I sworn my love;
Each jealous of the other, as the stung   56

37 **the riddle:** i.e. what you are after [*N*].   44 **avouched:**
asserted.   45 **Your . . . world:** your worldly concerns, your
life.   46 **machination:** plotting, i.e. Edmund's.   50 **o'erlook:** look over, peruse.   52 **guess:** estimate.   53 **discovery:** inquiry, spying.   54 **greet the time:** go to meet the
occasion, emergency.   56 **jealous:** suspicious [*N*].

Are of the adder. Which of them shall I take?
Both? one? or neither? Neither can be enjoy'd
If both remain alive: to take the widow
Exasperates, makes mad her sister Goneril;　　　　　60
And hardly shall I carry out my side,
Her husband being alive. Now then, we'll use
His countenance for the battle; which being done,
Let her who would be rid of him devise
His speedy taking off. As for the mercy　　　　　65
Which he intends to Lear, and to Cordelia,
The battle done, and they within our power,
Shall never see his pardon; for my state
Stands on me to defend, not to debate.　　　　　[*Exit.*

Scene II. A FIELD BETWEEN THE TWO CAMPS

Alarum within. Enter, with drum and colours, LEAR,
CORDELIA, *and their Forces; and exeunt. Enter* EDGAR
and GLOUCESTER.

Edgar. Here, father, take the shadow of this tree
For your good host; pray that the right may thrive.
If ever I return to you again,
I'll bring you comfort.
　　Gloucester.　　　　　Grace go with you, sir!
　　　　　　　　　　　　　　　　[*Exit* EDGAR.

Alarum; afterwards a retreat. Re-enter EDGAR.

Edgar. Away, old man! give me thy hand: away!　　5
King Lear hath lost, he and his daughter ta'en.
Give me thy hand; come on.

61 **carry out my side:** attain my object, i.e. the throne [*N*].
63 **countenance:** authority, prestige.　　65 **taking off:** murder
(a euphemism like 'liquidation' today).　　68 **Shall:** they shall
(grammatical confusion).　　**state:** position.　　69 **Stands on
me:** (it) concerns me, it is up to me.　　2 **host:** shelterer, protection.

Gloucester. No further, sir; a man may rot even here.

Edgar. What! in ill thoughts again? Men must endure
Their going hence, even as their coming hither: 10
Ripeness is all. Come on.

Gloucester. And that's true too. [*Exeunt.*

Scene III. The British Camp, near Dover

Enter, in conquest, with drum and colours, EDMUND; LEAR
and CORDELIA, *prisoners;* Officers, Soldiers, &c.

Edmund. Some officers take them away: good guard,
Until their greater pleasures first be known
That are to censure them.

Cordelia. We are not the first
Who, with best meaning, have incurr'd the worst.
For thee, oppressed king, am I cast down; 5
Myself could else out-frown false Fortune's frown.
Shall we not see these daughters and these sisters?

Lear. No, no, no, no! Come, let 's away to prison;
We two alone will sing like birds i' the cage:
When thou dost ask me blessing, I'll kneel down, 10
And ask of thee forgiveness: so we'll live,
And pray, and sing, and tell old tales, and laugh
At gilded butterflies, and hear poor rogues
Talk of court news; and we'll talk with them too,
Who loses and who wins; who's in, who's out; 15

9 **endure**: wait for, live patiently until [*N*]. 11 **Ripeness is
all**: the important thing is to be ready for death when it does come.
1 **good guard**: keep good guard over them. 2–3 **their
greater pleasures ... That**: the pleasure (decision as to their fate)
of those higher authorities (Albany, &c.) who. **censure**: judge.
4 **with best meaning**: trying to act for the best. 6 **out-
frown ... frown**: defy misfortune. 9 **cage**: *also* meant a
prison. 13 **gilded butterflies**: court gallants (cf. l. 85) [*N*].

And take upon 's the mystery of things,
As if we were God's spies: and we'll wear out,
In a wall'd prison, packs and sects of great ones
That ebb and flow by the moon.

    Edmund.   Take them away.

    Lear. Upon such sacrifices, my Cordelia,   20
The gods themselves throw incense. Have I caught thee?
He that parts us shall bring a brand from heaven,
And fire us hence like foxes. Wipe thine eyes;
The good years shall devour them, flesh and fell,   24
Ere they shall make us weep: we'll see 'em starve first.
Come.   [*Exeunt* LEAR *and* CORDELIA, *guarded.*

    Edmund. Come hither, captain; hark,
Take thou this note; [*Giving a paper.*] go follow them to
    prison:
One step I have advanc'd thee; if thou dost
As this instructs thee, thou dost make thy way   30
To noble fortunes; know thou this, that men
Are as the time is; to be tender-minded
Does not become a sword; thy great employment
Will not bear question; either say thou'lt do 't,
Or thrive by other means.

    Officer.   I'll do 't, my lord.   35

    Edmund. About it; and write happy when thou hast done.
Mark,—I say, instantly, and carry it so
As I have set it down.

16–17 i.e. imagine we understand the ways of God in the world as
if we were His agents or saw with His eyes [*N*].   **17 wear out:**
outlast.   **18–19 packs . . . moon:** sets and parties at court
who go in and out of favour like the changes of the moon.   **20**
such sacrifices: as our imprisonment [*N*].   **22** i.e. no power on
earth shall separate us.   **23 like foxes:** as foxes are smoked
out of their holes.   **24 The good years:** the Devil.   **fell:**
skin [*N*].   **33 a sword:** i.e. a soldier.   **34 question:**
investigation, discussion.   **36 write happy:** count yourself
happy.   **37 carry it** (out).

Officer. I cannot draw a cart nor eat dried oats;   39
If it be man's work I will do it.   [*Exit.*

Flourish. Enter ALBANY, GONERIL, REGAN, Officers, *and*
Attendants.

Albany. Sir, you have show'd to-day your valiant strain,
And fortune led you well; you have the captives
Who were the opposites of this day's strife;
I do require them of you, so to use them
As we shall find their merits and our safety   45
May equally determine.
Edmund.   Sir, I thought it fit
To send the old and miserable king
To some retention, and appointed guard;
Whose age has charms in it, whose title more,
To pluck the common bosom on his side,   50
And turn our impress'd lances in our eyes
Which do command them. With him I sent the queen;
My reason all the same; and they are ready
To-morrow, or at further space, to appear
Where you shall hold your session. At this time   55
We sweat and bleed; the friend hath lost his friend,
And the best quarrels, in the heat, are curs'd
By those that feel their sharpness;
The question of Cordelia and her father
Requires a fitter place.
Albany.   Sir, by your patience,   60
I hold you but a subject of this war,

41 **strain:** lineage.   43 **the opposites of:** our opponents in.
45 **we:** I and my counsellors.   **merits:** deserts, deeds.   49
Whose: refers back to 'king'.   50 **the common bosom:**
the affections of the common people.   51 **our impress'd**
lances: the soldiers we had conscripted.   **in our eyes:** against ourselves.   57 **the best quarrels:** battles in the best causes.   **in**
the heat (of the moment): before passions have cooled [*N*].   60
by your patience: if you will excuse me saying so.

Not as a brother.

Regan.   That's as we list to grace him:
Methinks our pleasure might have been demanded,
Ere you had spoke so far. He led our powers,
Bore the commission of my place and person;   65
The which immediacy may well stand up,
And call itself your brother.

Goneril.   Not so hot;
In his own grace he doth exalt himself
More than in your addition.

Regan.   In my rights,
By me invested, he compeers the best.   70

Goneril. That were the most, if he should husband you.

Regan. Jesters do oft prove prophets.

Goneril.   Holla, holla!
That eye that told you so look'd but a-squint.

Regan. Lady, I am not well; else I should answer
From a full-flowing stomach. General,   75
Take thou my soldiers, prisoners, patrimony;
Dispose of them, of me; the walls are thine;
Witness the world, that I create thee here
My lord and master.

Goneril.   Mean you to enjoy him?

Albany. The let-alone lies not in your good will.   80

Edmund. Nor in thine, lord.

Albany.   Half-blooded fellow, yes.

Regan. [*To* EDMUND.] Let the drum strike, and prove my
    title thine.

---

62 **list:** choose.   65 **place:** rank.   66 **immediacy:** close-
ness to me.   **well stand up:** i.e. justify him in standing up, &c.
67 **Not so hot:** Don't be in such a hurry.   69 **your addition:**
the position you have claimed for him.   70 **compeers:** equals.
71 **the most** (he could do, even) **if.**   75 **full-flowing stomach:**
the eloquence of passion.   77 **the walls:** of my fortress (metaphorically), i.e. I myself.   80 **let-alone:** power to forbid it.
81 **Half-blooded:** bastard.

Albany. Stay yet; hear reason. Edmund, I arrest thee
On capital treason; and, in thy attaint,
This gilded serpent. [*Pointing to* GONERIL.] For your
　　claim, fair sister,　　　　　　　　　　　　　　85
I bar it in the interest of my wife;
'Tis she is sub-contracted to this lord,
And I, her husband, contradict your bans.
If you will marry, make your love to me,
My lady is bespoke.

Goneril.　　　　　　An interlude!　　　　　90

Albany. Thou art arm'd, Gloucester; let the trumpet
　　sound:
If none appear to prove upon thy person
Thy heinous, manifest, and many treasons,
There is my pledge; [*Throws down a glove.*] I'll prove it on
　　thy heart,
Ere I taste bread, thou art in nothing less　　95
Than I have here proclaim'd thee.

Regan.　　　　　　　　Sick! O sick!

Goneril. [*Aside.*] If not, I'll ne'er trust medicine.

Edmund. There's my exchange: [*Throws down a glove.*]
　　what in the world he is
That names me traitor, villain-like he lies.
Call by thy trumpet: he that dares approach,　　100
On him, on you, who not? I will maintain
My truth and honour firmly.

Albany.　　A herald, ho!

Edmund.　　　　　　A herald, ho! a herald!

Albany. Trust to thy single virtue; for thy soldiers,
All levied in my name, have in my name　　105
Took their discharge.

---

84 **attaint**: impeachment.　　85 **gilded**: gilded-over, fair-
seeming.　　87 **sub-contracted**: betrothed for the second time.
90 **An interlude**: (This is as good as) a play.　　97 **medicine**:
euphemism for 'poison'.　　104 **virtue**: valour (*virtus*).

Regan.   My sickness grows upon me.
Albany. She is not well; convey her to my tent.

                                        [*Exit* REGAN, *led.*
Come hither, herald,—

                    Enter a Herald.

                    Let the trumpet sound,—
And read out this.   109
    Officer. Sound, trumpet!   [*A trumpet sounds.*
    Herald. 'If any man of quality or degree within the lists
of the army will maintain upon Edmund, supposed Earl of
Gloucester, that he is a manifold traitor, let him appear at
the third sound of the trumpet. He is bold in his defence.'
    Edmund. Sound!   [*First Trumpet.*
    Herald. Again!   [*Second Trumpet.*
    Herald. Again!   [*Third Trumpet.*
                            [*Trumpet answers within.*

    Enter EDGAR, *armed, with a Trumpet before him.*

Albany. Ask him his purposes, why he appears   118
Upon this call o' the trumpet.
    Herald.   What are you?
Your name? your quality? and why you answer   120
This present summons?
    Edgar.   Know, my name is lost;
By treason's tooth bare-gnawn and canker-bit:
Yet am I noble as the adversary
I come to cope.
    Albany.   Which is that adversary?
    Edgar. What 's he that speaks for Edmund Earl of
        Gloucester?   125

    111 **lists**: role, muster.   117–18 s.d. **with . . . him**: preceded
by a trumpeter.   120 **quality**: rank.   122 **bare-gnawn**:
gnawed bare.   **canker-bit**: devoured, as by the canker worm [N].
124 **cope**: engage.

Edmund. Himself: what sayst thou to him?

Edgar.   Draw thy sword,
That, if my speech offend a noble heart,
Thy arm may do thee justice; here is mine:
Behold, it is the privilege of mine honours,
My oath, and my profession: I protest,   130
Maugre thy strength, youth, place, and eminence,
Despite thy victor sword and fire-new fortune,
Thy valour and thy heart, thou art a traitor,
False to thy gods, thy brother, and thy father,
Conspirant 'gainst this high illustrious prince,   135
And, from the extremest upward of thy head
To the descent and dust below thy foot,
A most toad-spotted traitor. Say thou 'No',
This sword, this arm, and my best spirits are bent
To prove upon thy heart, whereto I speak,   140
Thou liest.

Edmund. In wisdom I should ask thy name;
But since thy outside looks so fair and warlike,
And that thy tongue some say of breeding breathes,
What safe and nicely I might well delay
By rule of knighthood, I disdain and spurn;   145
Back do I toss these treasons to thy head,
With the hell-hated lie o'erwhelm thy heart,

129 **it**: to fight, to maintain the truth of my assertion.   130
my profession: of knighthood.   131 **Maugre**: in spite of.
132 **victor**: (lately) victorious.   **fire-new**: fresh like coins
from the mint. Edmund is a *novus homo*, a *parvenu*.   133 **heart**:
courage.   135 **Conspirant**: conspiring *or* a conspirer.   136
upward: top.   137 **descent**: lowest part, sole of thy feet.
138 **toad-spotted**: covered with shame as a toad with spots.
143 **say**: suggestion, trace.   144 **What**: i.e. the combat.
safe: safely (from the point of view of honour).   **nicely**: by
insisting on the exact code of honour (which only requires me to
answer an equal; see 153 below).   145 **I disdain and spurn**:
viz. to insist on my rights (change of construction).   146 **to
thy head**: in thy teeth.   147 **hell-hated**: hated like hell.

Which, for they yet glance by and scarcely bruise,
This sword of mine shall give them instant way,
Where they shall rest for ever. Trumpets, speak!   150

                [*Alarums. They fight.* EDMUND *falls.*

  Albany. Save him, save him!

  Goneril.   This is practice, Gloucester:
By the law of arms thou wast not bound to answer
An unknown opposite; thou art not vanquish'd,
But cozen'd and beguil'd.

  Albany.   Shut your mouth, dame,
Or with this paper shall I stop it. Hold, sir;   155
Thou worse than any name, read thine own evil:
No tearing, lady; I perceive you know it.

  Goneril. Say, if I do, the laws are mine, not thine:
Who can arraign me for 't?

  Albany.   Most monstrous!
Know'st thou this paper?

  Goneril.   Ask me not what I know.   160

                        [*Exit.*

  Albany. Go after her: she 's desperate; govern her.

                    [*Exit an* Officer.

  Edmund. What you have charg'd me with, that have I
      done,
And more, much more; the time will bring it out:
'Tis past, and so am I. But what art thou
That hast this fortune on me? If thou'rt noble,   165
I do forgive thee.

  Edgar.   Let 's exchange charity.

---

148 **Which**: treasons.   **for**: because.   149 **give them . . .
way**: press them urgently back (upon you).   151 **practice**:
treachery.   154 **cozen'd**: tricked.   155 **this paper**: the
love-letter of Goneril to Edmund (see IV. vi. 276). **Hold, sir**: wait
a moment (to Edmund) [*N*].   156 **Thou**: Goneril.   161
govern her: control her, e.g. prevent her suicide.   165 **fortune
on me**: advantage given thee by fortune over me.   166 **charity**:
including forgiveness.

I am no less in blood than thou art, Edmund;
If more, the more thou hast wrong'd me.
My name is Edgar, and thy father's son.
The gods are just, and of our pleasant vices   170
Make instruments to plague us:
The dark and vicious place where thee he got
Cost him his eyes.

  Edmund.   Thou hast spoken right, 'tis true;
The wheel is come full circle; I am here.

  Albany. Methought thy very gait did prophesy   175
A royal nobleness: I must embrace thee:
Let sorrow split my heart, if ever I
Did hate thee or thy father.

  Edgar.   Worthy prince, I know 't.

  Albany. Where have you hid yourself?
How have you known the miseries of your father?   180

  Edgar. By nursing them, my lord. List a brief tale;
And, when 'tis told, O that my heart would burst!
The bloody proclamation to escape
That follow'd me so near,—O! our lives' sweetness,
That we the pain of death would hourly die   185
Rather than die at once!—taught me to shift
Into a madman's rags, to assume a semblance
That very dogs disdain'd: and in this habit
Met I my father with his bleeding rings,
Their precious stones new lost; became his guide,   190
Led him, begg'd for him, sav'd him from despair;
Never,—O fault!—reveal'd myself unto him,
Until some half hour past, when I was arm'd;
Not sure, though hoping, of this good success,
I ask'd his blessing, and from first to last   195

---

172 i.e. the act of adultery which led to your birth [*N*].   183
to escape: governs 'the bloody proclamation'.   184 **our lives'
sweetness:** how highly we value our lives!   186 **shift:** change.
189 **rings:** eye-sockets.

Told him my pilgrimage: but his flaw'd heart,—
Alack! too weak the conflict to support;
'Twixt two extremes of passion, joy and grief,
Burst smilingly.

   Edmund.   This speech of yours hath mov'd me,
And shall perchance do good; but speak you on;   200
You look as you had something more to say.

   Albany. If there be more, more woeful, hold it in;
For I am almost ready to dissolve,
Hearing of this.

   Edgar.   This would have seem'd a period
To such as love not sorrow; but another,   205
To amplify too much, would make much more,
And top extremity.
Whilst I was big in clamour came there a man,
Who, having seen me in my worst estate,
Shunn'd my abhorr'd society; but then, finding   210
Who 'twas that so endur'd, with his strong arms
He fasten'd on my neck, and bellow'd out
As he'd burst heaven; threw him on my father;
Told the most piteous tale of Lear and him
That ever ear receiv'd; which in recounting   215
His grief grew puissant, and the strings of life
Began to crack: twice then the trumpet sounded,
And there I left him tranc'd.

   Albany.   But who was this?

   Edgar. Kent, sir, the banish'd Kent; who in disguise
Follow'd his enemy king, and did him service   220
Improper for a slave.

---

   196 **flaw'd**: cracked, worn out.   203 **dissolve**: in tears, melt
away.   204 **period**: limit, ending.   205 **another**: sorrow *or* tale.
206 **To amplify too much**: (probably) by increasing what is already
excessive.   207 **top extremity**: pass the (due) limit.   208 **big**:
loud.   209 **estate**: state.   213 **As**: as if. **him**: himself   216
puissant: (too) powerful.   218 **tranc'd**: insensible.   220
enemy: (turned) hostile.   221 **Improper for**: too humble even for.

Enter a Gentleman, *with a bloody knife.*

Gentleman. Help, help! O help!

Edgar.   What kind of help?

Albany.   Speak, man.

Edgar. What means that bloody knife?

Gentleman.   'Tis hot, it smokes;
It came even from the heart of—O! she 's dead.

Albany. Who dead? speak, man.   225

Gentleman. Your lady, sir, your lady: and her sister
By her is poison'd; she confesses it.

Edmund. I was contracted to them both: all three
Now marry in an instant.

Edgar.   Here comes Kent.

Albany. Produce the bodies, be they alive or dead: 230
This judgment of the heavens, that makes us tremble,
Touches us not with pity.   [*Exit* Gentleman.

Enter KENT.

                        O! is this he?
The time will not allow the compliment
Which very manners urges.

Kent.   I am come
To bid my king and master aye good-night;   235
Is he not here?

Albany.   Great thing of us forgot!
Speak, Edmund, where's the king? and where's Cordelia?
Seest thou this object, Kent?

          [*The bodies of* GONERIL *and* REGAN *are brought in.*

Kent. Alack! why thus?

Edmund.   Yet Edmund was belov'd:
The one the other poison'd for my sake,   240
And after slew herself.

228 **contracted**: engaged, promised.   233 **compliment**:
formal courtesy (as in I. i. 301).   238 **object**: sight, something
thrown in the way (Lat. *obicio*).   241 **after**(wards).

Albany. Even so. Cover their faces.

Edmund. I pant for life: some good I mean to do
Despite of mine own nature. Quickly send,
Be brief in it, to the castle; for my writ 245
Is on the life of Lear and on Cordelia.
Nay, send in time.

Albany.   Run, run! O run!

Edgar. To whom, my lord? Who has the office? send
Thy token of reprieve.

Edmund. Well thought on: take my sword, 250
Give it the captain.

Albany.   Haste thee, for thy life. [*Exit* EDGAR.

Edmund. He hath commission from thy wife and me
To hang Cordelia in the prison, and
To lay the blame upon her own despair,
That she fordid herself. 255

Albany. The gods defend her! Bear him hence awhile.

[EDMUND *is borne off.*

Enter LEAR, *with* CORDELIA *dead in his arms;*
EDGAR, Officer, *and others.*

Lear. Howl, howl, howl, howl! O! you are men of
stones:
Had I your tongues and eyes, I'd use them so
That heaven's vaults should crack. She's gone for ever.
I know when one is dead, and when one lives; 260
She's dead as earth. Lend me a looking-glass;
If that her breath will mist or stain the stone,
Why, then she lives.

Kent.   Is this the promis'd end?

---

243 pant for life: struggle to live a little longer.   **245 writ:**
writing, the order given (l. 28 above).   **255 fordid:** destroyed
[*N*].   **257 men of stones:** unfeeling [*N*].   **262 stone:** a
mirror of polished stone.   **263 the promis'd end:** the end of
the world foretold (in biblical prophecy).

Edgar. Or image of that horror?

Albany.   Fall and cease!

Lear. This feather stirs; she lives! if it be so,   265
It is a chance which does redeem all sorrows
That ever I have felt.

Kent. [*Kneeling.*]   O, my good master!

Lear. Prithee, away.

Edgar.   'Tis noble Kent, your friend.

Lear. A plague upon you, murderers, traitors all!
I might have sav'd her; now, she's gone for ever!   270
Cordelia, Cordelia! stay a little. Ha!
What is't thou sayst? Her voice was ever soft,
Gentle and low, an excellent thing in woman.
I kill'd the slave that was a-hanging thee.

Officer. 'Tis true, my lord, he did.

Lear.   Did I not, fellow?   275
I have seen the day, with my good biting falchion
I would have made them skip: I am old now,
And these same crosses spoil me. Who are you?
Mine eyes are not o' the best: I'll tell you straight.

Kent. If fortune brag of two she lov'd and hated,   280
One of them we behold.

Lear. This is a dull sight. Are you not Kent?

Kent.   The same,
Your servant Kent. Where is your servant Caius?

Lear. He's a good fellow, I can tell you that;

---

264 **image:** copy, reproduction (cf. 'great doom's image', *Macbeth*
II. iii. 61).   **Fall and cease!:** (probably) let the heavens fall and
all things come to an end!   274 **the slave:** not literal, but
abusive.   276 **falchion:** a kind of light sword.   278
crosses: troubles.   **spoil me:** destroy me (as a fighter).   279
straight: straightway, in a moment.   280 **two . . . hated:**
one whom she raised up (to the highest) and one whom she put
down (to the lowest).   281 **One of them:** in Lear.   282
dull: melancholy [*N*].   283 **Where . . . Caius?:** probably Kent
is inviting Lear to recognize in him the former Caius.

He'll strike, and quickly too. He's dead and rotten.   285

Kent. No, my good lord; I am the very man—

Lear. I'll see that straight.

Kent. That, from your first of difference and decay,
Have follow'd your sad steps.

Lear.   You are welcome hither.

Kent. Nor no man else; all 's cheerless, dark, and deadly:
Your eldest daughters have fordone themselves,   291
And desperately are dead.

Lear.   Ay, so I think.

Albany. He knows not what he says, and vain it is
That we present us to him.

Edgar.   Very bootless.   294

Enter an Officer.

Officer. Edmund is dead, my lord.

Albany.   That's but a trifle here.
You lords and noble friends, know our intent;
What comfort to this great decay may come
Shall be applied: for us, we will resign,
During the life of this old majesty,
To him our absolute power:—[*To* EDGAR *and* KENT.] You,
    to your rights;   300
With boot and such addition as your honours
Have more than merited. All friends shall taste

285 **strike:** as he did Oswald (I. iv. 82).   287 **straight:** cf.
279. But Lear is only half conscious of what is going on.   288
your first of difference: the commencement of your change of fortunes.   290 **Nor . . . else:** *either* neither I nor anyone else can
be very welcome (well come?) to this scene (which suits what
follows), *or* a continuation of his words at 286.   292 **desperately:** in despair.   294 **us:** ourselves. **bootless:** useless.   296
our: the royal plural, since Albany represents those to whom Lear
surrendered power.   297 **great decay:** ruin of greatness (Lear).
300 **to your rights:** betake you to, enjoy your rights.   301
boot and such addition: the profit of such additions. **honours:**
honourable deeds.

The wages of their virtue, and all foes
The cup of their deservings. O! see, see!

Lear. And my poor fool is hang'd! No, no, no life!   305
Why should a dog, a horse, a rat, have life,
And thou no breath at all? Thou'lt come no more,
Never, never, never, never, never!
Pray you, undo this button: thank you, sir.
Do you see this? Look on her, look, her lips,   310
Look there, look there!   [*Dies.*

Edgar.   He faints!—my lord, my lord!

Kent. Break, heart; I prithee, break.

Edgar.   Look up, my lord.

Kent. Vex not his ghost: O! let him pass; he hates him
That would upon the rack of this tough world
Stretch him out longer.

Edgar.   He is gone, indeed.   315

Kent. The wonder is he hath endur'd so long:
He but usurp'd his life.

Albany. Bear them from hence. Our present business
Is general woe. [*To* KENT *and* EDGAR.] Friends of my soul,
    you twain
Rule in this realm, and the gor'd state sustain.   320

Kent. I have a journey, sir, shortly to go;
My master calls me, I must not say no.

Edgar. The weight of this sad time we must obey;
Speak what we feel, not what we ought to say.
The oldest hath borne most: we that are young   325
Shall never see so much, nor live so long.

                    [*Exeunt, with a dead march.*

303 wages: rewards.   **305 poor fool**: (term of endearment)
Cordelia [*N*].   **312 Break, heart**: *either* to his own heart *or* of
Lear's [*N*].   **313 ghost**: spirit.   **314 rack**: metaphor from an
instrument of torture ('racking' the limbs).   **317 usurp'd**: kept
what was due to death.   **320 this realm**: (probably) that half
of Britain which had been Regan's share.   **gor'd**: maimed, injured.
324 i.e. (probably) at present we can only speak from the heart,
not prudently as after reflection.   **325 The oldest**: especially Lear.

NOTES

s.d. = stage direction(s).

Q (or Q 1) = the first Quarto published in 1608.

F = the first Folio published in 1623.

O.E.D. = *Oxford English Dictionary.*

GB = H. Granville-Barker.

The *titles* of the books by critics quoted are only mentioned here (once) when they are *not* given later in the Select Criticism.

Textual notes and a few other more advanced notes are enclosed within square brackets thus [ ].

ACT I, SCENE I

The first scene of this play is unusually important since it not only introduces us to the main actors but also provides the cause of all the disaster which follows. Lear's plan to divide his kingdom is taken for granted as a 'datum' of the play, but we are shown his hasty and passionate character and the different character of his daughters. The subplot is also disclosed in the attitude of Gloucester to Edmund.

It should be noticed that Lear *has* already divided his kingdom into three parts, with the best for Cordelia, and that the trial of affection is therefore a sort of game to please his vanity. 'The play is primitive from its first origins. It is founded on an incident as childish as you will, a nursery story of early man. The oldest boy will give away his things: and who loves him most? Who is most friends with him? The shy little girl comes off badly' (G. Gordon).

The stage directions as to locality in this play are not in F or Q. Some modern critics prefer to omit the setting as the Shakespearean stage with its simpler scenery was less localized than the modern, but they have been retained in this edition. The list of characters present was inserted by Rowe, the first editor. In Q Edmund is called 'Bastard' whenever he speaks.

3. us. Gloucester cannot use a royal plural. Who then are the 'us'? Bradley suggested that there had been a division between Lear's councillors over the question of the abdication, which led to Kent's absence from some meetings.

15. smell. The word is used here quite lightly and naturally, but it starts one of the image patterns of the play; for it is a sense strongest in animals (cf. Select Criticism under Imagery). Cf. III. vii. 93 and Note.

18–24. Edmund may not be intended to hear this speech, but at least it shows his father's frivolous attitude to his moral laxity. He has also kept his illegitimate son away from home for many years and proposes to send him away again, which may be supposed to have a good deal to do with Edmund's attitude to his father.

35. our darker purpose may convey more than the surface meaning given in the footnote. 'The adjective is carefully chosen as a first indication of the obscure, unrealized sources of the emotions which are so soon to come to the surface in the form of uncontrolled passion' (Traversi).

36–53. The division of the kingdom has already been made (cf. 194 and 242), but the King suddenly takes the fancy to hear protestations of love from his daughters, perhaps hoping to confirm his preference for Cordelia. 'And then, so it naturally seemed to him, she put him to open shame' (Bradley).

39–44. [This is the first example of many where a few lines are omitted in Q, from 'while we' to 'prevented now' in 44. It could hardly be doubted that the words are part of the play as Shakespeare wrote it, and the rival theories to account for the omission are that Q omits passages to shorten the play for the stage *or* that the Q text was made up from what actors remembered of their parts.

The change of 'the princes' (44) to 'the two great princes' might have been designed to fill out a whole line after the cut (ignoring the incomplete line 39).]

44. We need not ask whether these titles correspond to the state of France when Lear ruled Britain. The dramatist will be thinking, in this and much else, of the fifteenth or sixteenth century.

48. divest. The metaphor is natural enough here, but it also happens to be the first of a whole series involving clothes that play an important part in the play (cf. 217–18 below). 'This undressing for easy sleep' (the source of the metaphor here) is also 'a removal of armour against the arrows of fortune' (Heilman). Cf. 'invest' at l. 129.

52. The exact construction is uncertain. 'nature' may *either* be challenging 'merit' or the deserts of her character, *or* combining with merit to claim her due reward.

61. [**Speak.** It is impossible, as often, to decide between F and Q, F's 'speak' and Q's 'do'. Perhaps 'speak' is the harder reading in view of 'be silent', and for that very reason the more likely one. Perhaps Shakespeare first wrote 'do', and later changed it to what was more difficult still for Cordelia. So in l. 77, where we keep the Q's 'more richer', Shakespeare may have substituted the more uncommon 'ponderous' (F); or it might be due to someone else disliking the double comparative, which, however, is common enough in Shakespeare.]

68. Regan speaks only too truly, as the audience will see—a sort of prospective dramatic irony. Note also that, like Goneril above, she uses rather stilted language, especially in 73–74, which may be intended to suggest insincerity, and anyhow makes the contrast with Cordelia's words more marked.

73. square. The word may be used simply in the plain sense of 'piece', or may have a more technical sense as in a carpenter's 'square', implying here the perfection of sense.

84–85. It was clear that Lear had already divided his realm when the scene opened. It is therefore only the whim of the moment that makes him promise the best third to the daughter who tickles his vanity best in the protestation of her love.

89. In the present tense a Latin proverb, *nihil ex nihilo fit*.

92. It may be a bit of Lear's own obstinacy that makes Cordelia define her love in semi-legal phraseology, provoked to understatement by her sisters' facile abstractions. In 105–6 below her short reply balances his exactly, with the addition of the respectful 'my lord'.

'Lear felt, and rightly felt, that Cordelia's attitude to his request was a rebuke to his vanity and to his craving for approbation, and Lear was not accustomed to rebuke' (Branson, *The Tragedy of King Lear*, 1934).

[Surely Shakespeare would not have given Cordelia language like this if he meant it to represent 'a norm, a plenitude', as Mr. Traversi argues (*Scrutiny* xix, 451).

And Mr. Danby seems also to be misapplying learning when he writes: 'For both the sixteenth century and for the romantic a "bond" is a potentially frigid thing. For the middle ages and for Cordelia, on the other hand, the word means "I love you as every normal girl loves her father—naturally"' (*Shakespeare and the Nature of Man*).]

106. 'Yes, "heavenly true". But truth is not the only good in the world, nor is the obligation to tell truth the only obligation. The matter here was to keep it inviolate, but also to preserve a father. And even if truth *were* the one and only obligation, to tell much less than truth is not to tell it' (Bradley).

This was 'one of those repartees in Shakespeare which always brought tears to my eyes', said Tennyson, who, even if his expression of his emotions is not in the mode of this century, had a fine taste in poetry.

108–19. In the violence of his oath and the cosmic imagery Lear already anticipates his curse on Goneril (I. 4) and the heath scenes.

109. **Hecate** was the Greek goddess of night and the lower world, connected with mysterious rites and witchcraft (cf. *Macbeth* II. i).

115–16. Scythia was in ancient times the district round the Black Sea, of which the inhabitants were to the Greeks and Romans barbarous.

generation *should* mean children, as it does elsewhere; but it seems quite likely that Shakespeare here uses it meaning 'parents', as he does the word 'progeny' in *Coriolanus*, since there appears to be no record of a tribe that ate its children (apart from Swift's satire *A Modest Proposal!*), whereas Herodotus recounts that the Scythians ate elderly relations, and Chapman in his play *Byron's Tragedy* (published 1608) refers to the same custom.

134–5. Lear wants the impossible—to have the honour and glory of power without its responsibilities; and in this desire lay part of the cause of his tragedy.

141. This suggests Christian intercessory prayer as contrasted with the pagan gods invoked by Lear above and 159 below, and at II. iv. 20. Kent's character of bravery and loyalty appears from the first, and is based, as we might expect, on firm piety.

145. Kent's bluntness assumes that by divesting himself of kingship Lear is merely an 'old man', and prophetically anticipates his later madness; while in 148 we may feel an anticipation of his coming equality with the Fool in his misery.

152–3. Cordelia's low voice (cf. v. iii. 272–3) could cause no echo, whereas the louder protestations of her sisters echo the more from the hollowness (metaphorical for the insincerity) of their hearts.

176. **tenth** may be understood as allowing Kent time to leave the country altogether.

[On the other hand 's'enth', as an abbreviated form of 'seventh', is an emendation which only involves a change of one letter.]

180–7. Notice the rhyming couplets used to finish off an episode, as often at the end of scenes. Cf. France's farewell speech, 254–61.

197. At 259 France proudly calls Cordelia an 'unpriz'd' maid. Ideas of value, and various expressions of it, form one of the recurrent themes of the play.

198. **[little-seeming substance.** In spite of much discussion the exact sense intended by Shakespeare must remain uncertain. The view taken in the footnote gives perhaps the strongest point. There is no hyphen between the first two words in F or Q, and 'seeming' may be taken by itself as meaning 'specious' or 'plausible', and the 'little' as a contemptuous reference to Cordelia's form; but it would not be just to conclude from this obscure phrase that Cordelia is to be considered as small.]

219–20. unnatural ... monsters. In Latin *monstrum* means a 'portent' or 'prodigy', and the English word retains about it a smack of the 'unnatural'. It might be claimed that Nature with its derivatives and their opposites is the dominant idea of the play. It is, of course, the conduct of Goneril and Regan that is 'unnatural', as is that of Gloucester's 'natural' son towards his parent.

[The word 'Nature' occurs forty times in this play—more frequently than in any other—while one-fifth of all Shakespeare's uses of the word 'unnatural' are in *Lear*. Two basic senses of the word may be distinguished: (1) the fundamental principle of order, almost corresponding to eternal law and justice, *lex*, νόμος; (2) the vital force, φύσις, individual will. When Lear calls on 'Nature' to avenge him (I. iv. 275), he is clearly using it in the first or normal sense. Edmund alone clearly uses it in the second sense (I. ii. 1) where the context gives it the flavour of lust (cf. Donne's 'golden law of nature' in *Elegy* XVII. 48). But Edmund rationalizes an outlook he shares with Goneril and Regan.]

238–40. The amount of dowry ('respects of fortune', 248) is quite irrelevant to genuine love. Shakespeare had already used the first words of this sentence in a sonnet (CXVI) which will come back to the mind of most lovers of poetry:

> Love is not love
> Which alters when it alteration finds,
> Or bends with the remover to remove:

268. The jewels of our father. There are other clear examples of the use of nominative for vocative in Shakespeare, e.g. the address of Brutus to the dead Cassius: 'The last of all the Romans, fare thee well' (*Julius Caesar*, v. iii. 99).

When Cordelia speaks of her eyes as 'wash'd' she means by tears, but we may well understand a secondary meaning of 'cleansed', so that she can see the true character of her sisters. The phrase in which she expresses this, 'I know you what you are', is one of Shakespeare's many reminiscences of the Bible, and it may be not insignificant, though not previously noted, that in Mark i. 24 the unclean spirit is *recognizing* who Jesus really is: 'I know thee who [so A.V.; earlier translators "what"] thou art, the Holy One of God.'

279. [The interpretation in the footnote takes 'the want' as a *cognate* accusative (in the phrase of the Latin grammars), that is simply carrying on, with sarcastic emphasis of repeated sound, the meaning of the verb. But it is possible to give a fuller meaning and to paraphrase 'you well deserve to lose your dowry in return for your unkindness to your father'.]

280. The word 'plighted' is another form of 'pleated' and is quite distinct in origin from the noun 'plight' of 100. Its use seems to have suggested to the poet the carrying on of the clothes imagery in the next line. 'Three acts, full of injury and suffering, must pass before the garments of the worldly begin to wear thin and betray the wearer' (Heilman).

283. Prose is introduced for the lower level of the sisters' scheming. In this it may be noted that Goneril takes the lead as the more active, though not more evil, partner.

288. One of the three notes left by Keats on the play which meant most to him is on this line:

'How finely is the brief of Lear's character sketched in this conference—from this point does Shakespeare spur him out to the mighty grapple—"The seeded pride that hath to this maturity blowne up" [*Troilus and Cressida*, I. iii] Shakespeare doth scatter abroad on the winds of passion, where the germs take buoyant root in stormy air, suck lightning sap, and become voiced dragons— self-will and pride and wrath are taken at a rebound by his giant hand and mounted to the Clouds there to remain and thunder evermore' (Keats's *Works*, ed. H. B. Forman, iii. 15, original punctuation).

292-5. The sisters have laid their fingers on their father's 'tragic fault', that flaw in character which is usually considered necessary for the hero of tragedy. So also in the subplot, Gloucester, though not of the calibre of a tragic hero, is shown as not guiltless in the matter of Edmund.

ACT I, Scene II

This scene does for the subplot what the previous scene had done for the main plot. The parallelism is close, since in both cases a parent is deceived by his children, or by a child, and in both cases the opportunity for the deceit comes, though in very different ways, from the fault of the parent. Prose is used for the intrigue, as in the later part of the former scene, whereas Edmund sets forth his philosophy of Nature at the beginning and end in verse. Here he proclaims, after the manner of villains in Renaissance tragedy, his self-justification for purely self-seeking conduct. 'Nature' is one of the most ambiguous words in the language, and Edmund here means by it the desires of our bodily nature (cf. 11). When Lear calls upon 'Nature' to hear him (I. iv. 269) the term includes something of what is natural to a rational and spiritual being, who may be expected to care for morality; and cf. II. iv. 178.

1. Edmund calls Nature his 'goddess' in the first place because he is a 'natural' son, illegitimate because not born within the status of wedlock but a child of nature. 'No mediaeval devil ever bounded on to the stage with a more scandalous self-announcement' (Danby).

6. **Bastard.** The pun on 'base' is obvious, although in fact that is not the derivation of the word. Edmund has some ground for his grievance that society visited the sins of the fathers so severely on the children. Illegitimacy is still a pretty severe handicap, although there has been some improvement.

11–15. The sense of these lines is that the passion felt for a mistress may cause more zest in the begetting of the illegitimate child than in the normal intercourse of husband and wife. There is, of course, no factual foundation for Edmund's inference that the bastard child will be endowed with better quality of body or mind.

21. [top is an eighteenth-century emendation of F and Q's 'to', which is just possible; but even Greg inclines to the change.]

22. Edmund is the only character to refer to the gods flippantly.

32. **Nothing:** one of the many echoes in which this play abounds. The words had proved disastrous already, I. i. 86.

36. Gloucester thinks he can see because his eyes are intact. Later on, when he is physically blind, his moral sight will be clearer. Thus these lightly spoken and easily intelligible words contribute to one of the underlying themes of the play, that of sight.

46–51. These lines and 71–74 below are also what Goneril and Regan think about *their* aged father, though they do not express it in quite the same way. The main and subplot are tied together by many such threads.

79–88. Edmund dares greatly here, but he is never one to shun risk.

103. The eclipses may be those of the autumn of 1605, but there had been others earlier, and the passage should not be made a certain criterion of the earliest possible date for the writing of the play. In what follows there may well be a reference to the Gunpowder Plot of November 1605. But the language may also be partly based on the prophecies about the end of the world in Matthew xxiv and Mark xiii.

104–6. Similarly, although scientists assured us that the bad summers of the early 1950's could not be caused by the explosion of atom bombs, many people noted the coincidence.

110. the prediction is surely that of Mark xiii. 12 : 'Now the brother shall betray the brother to death and the father the son: and children shall rise up against their parents, and shall cause them to be put to death.' (The present editor now finds the reference noted by K. Muir.)

116–17. Notice the irony. Gloucester will treat his true son as his master treated the loyal Kent.

118–33. Edmund is clear sighted and has no illusions as to his wickedness. Shakespeare, interested, like all men of his time, in the part played by destiny in human affairs, had already through Cassius in *Julius Caesar* asserted human freedom and responsibility :

> The fault, dear Brutus, is not in our stars,
> But in ourselves, that we are underlings (I. ii. 139–40).

Iago, the villain of the play before this, argues like Edmund: see *Othello*, I. iii. 322, &c.

['In Shakespeare's best plays, besides the vices that arise from the subject, there is generally some peculiar prevailing folly, principally ridiculed, that runs through the whole piece. Thus, in the *Tempest*, the lying disposition of travellers, and in *As You Like It* the fantastick humour of courtiers, is exposed and satirized with infinite pleasantry. In like manner, in his play of *Lear*, the dotages of judicial astrology are severely ridiculed.'—Johnson, who might have been a little surprised to find these 'dotages' on bookstall and in daily papers two hundred years later. But in Elizabethan days good ordinary men might have thought with Gloucester rather than with Edmund; cf. Kent at IV. iii. 32–35.]

134–5. It is a mark of crude construction in a play or novel if a disaster occurs too obviously just where it suits the plot.

136. Tom is an imaginary name taken by a vagabond. **Bedlam** is a contraction for Bethlehem, and the Royal Bethlehem Hospital in south London was the first asylum. The phrase anticipates the entry of Edgar in this disguise at II. iii (where see introductory note).

142–9. Edmund ironically parodies the ideas he had attributed to his father a few moments earlier.

148. [The phrase **dissipation of cohorts** has—not without reason—been felt to be corrupt, especially as here the Quarto is our only authority. Although Shakespeare does not use either word elsewhere, 'dissipation', like 'sectary' below and 'bastardizing' above, occurs in Florio's translation of Montaigne's *Essays*, published in 1603 and certainly read by Shakespeare.]

ACT I, Scene III

This short scene resumes the main plot from scene i, but after a certain interval of time; in fact Granville-Barker notes it as the only clearly indicated time-division in the play (cf. ll. 55–60 of the next scene). Goneril takes the initiative in forcing the issue with her father—an initiative that distinguishes her from her equally cruel sister.

8. The Middle-English poet Layamon in his *Brut* describes the provision made for Lear's hunting and his enjoyment of it, and this may somehow have reached Shakespeare's notice.

ACT I, Scene IV

In this scene Lear comes to life and begins to win our sympathy (e.g. 67–69). We are prepared for a Fool of special quality by the Knight's words about him, 71–72. The good and bad characters begin to divide more clearly, Kent in his loyalty to Lear, Goneril in her reprimands to her father (194, &c.), and in her contempt for her more scrupulous husband (308). Meanwhile the awful curse pronounced by Lear on Goneril, who had as yet done but little, strikes a new depth for Shakespearian tragedy.

84. In Elizabethan times football was a sport of low repute, played by idle boys who made themselves a nuisance to respectable citizens.

99. Lear had made Goneril and Regan independent of him and so, in a sense 'banished' them as daughters, while he had unwittingly blessed Cordelia by giving her to a man who loved her for herself alone.

105–6. The Fool first means that he would not have given away everything as Lear has done, but he goes on to hint that Lear is twice as much a fool as he is, and therefore needs a double coxcomb.

108–9. 'Truth' must represent Cordelia who is put outside in disgrace, while the more favoured bitch may pick out one of the other two—probably Goneril.

110. It is not easy to decide whether Lear is harking back to Oswald's insolence as having galled or irritated him, or the Fool's home truths, or his own folly, of which he is tasting the bitterness. 'He listens and finds cheer in the Fool's chatter and song, throws him

an answer or so to keep it alive, snarls now and then like an old
lion if a sting goes too deep; yet his thoughts, we can tell, are away'
(GB).

128. At i. i. 89 Lear used almost these words to Cordelia. Now that
he is brought to apply the thought to himself he may well call the
Fool 'bitter' or sarcastic.

135–145. This may be a reminiscence of the old play in which a
certain lord *did* counsel Lear about the division of his realm.

159. **Let him be whipped, &c.** The Fool may mean that anyone
who finds his remarks folly will be no friend of Lear, *or* that if the
King rejects the Fool's criticism he shows such folly as deserves
whipping.

168. This snatch of song, like some others in the play, is adapted
from sources known to us. Here the first two lines are derived and
the second two original.

211. The Fool's words are apparently nonsense in that they have no
connexion with what has immediately preceded. In 218 'Whoop,
Jug' half covers up a bitter saying. But here the words may
suggest the moral chaos of daughters teaching fathers. They may
have come into the poet's mind from Spenser, *F.Q.* ii. x. 30 about
Lear.

224. In the old play the King tells a lord to 'think me but the shadow
of myself'. Here Lear goes on to say that he must learn to think
of himself as but a shadow since his badges of rank, his memory, and
his reason tell him that he is Lear, the father of Goneril.

253–5. Shakespeare had already spoken strongly of ingratitude in
the song 'Blow, blow, thou winter wind' of *As You Like It*. Here
he connects it with the animal world, making the first of a number
of animal images hereabout, and probably only chooses the 'sea-
monster' as something far removed from humanity (cf. i. v. 36),
although it is just possible he is thinking of the hippopotamus (a
river beast) which was proverbial for such vices at that time, or
of the monsters of classical antiquity who came out of the sea
to devour Andromeda, &c. He then goes on to call Goneril a
kite, a bird of which the form suggests rapacity but which is asso-
ciated with other unpleasant things in Shakespeare (see a book
by an authority on birds, Armstrong, *Shakespeare's Imagination*,
ch. I).

269–83. This terrible curse—as terrible coming from a father as the
ingratitude of the daughter and a second example of Lear's

'hideous rashness'—may be uttered in a voice of deadly calm between two explosive speeches. This effect is enhanced by the short line 271, and it is not necessary to fill it up by separating the vowels of the first syllables of 'creature and fruitful'. Lear appears for the moment to make 'Nature' a goddess, as Edmund had done (I. ii. 1), and it is possibly in protest against this that Albany (284) speaks of the 'gods that we adore'.

287–8. Since Goneril refers to Lear still having a hundred knights in 317, I suggest that Lear is supposed to have been told off stage that he must be rid of fifty within the next fortnight (see also II. iv. 158). Thus J. S. H. Branson's complaint that 'Goneril had done nothing before the curse' is not quite true.

321. dotage. Goneril uses the same word at II. iv. 197, and it is revealing. The characters are divided by their attitude to 'age' and to 'nature'.

336. So a more imperial Goneril, Lady Macbeth, reproaches *her* husband:

> 'Yet do I fear thy nature:
> It is too full o' th' milk of human kindness,
> To catch the nearest way' (*Macbeth*, I. v. 16–18).

338. [attask'd. Following the textual arguments of W. W. Greg, the most recent editors (Duthie, Muir, and Alexander in the *Tudor Shakespeare*) print 'attax'd'; but the meaning is the same and the words 'tax' and 'task' are of the same derivation. In either case the word would be a Shakespearian coinage.]

ACT I, SCENE V

This short scene serves to increase our foreboding, through the Fool's fear of the treatment awaiting Lear at the hands of Regan and Cornwall, and through the King's own fear of madness. Lear only talks to the Fool with half his mind; with the other half he begins to see how he has wronged Cordelia (23), or possibly even Goneril, in his cursing of her, and to what the 'Monster ingratitude' (36) of the others may lead him (42–43).

1. Gloucester. The home of Cornwall and Regan is apparently conceived as being near the town of Gloucester and Gloucester's own home. But the difficulties as to place and movements are so great (see Note U in Bradley's *Shakespearean Tragedy*) that Granville-Barker conjectured Cornwall instead of 'Gloucester' here.

10–11. The Fool appears to mean that Lear would have no chilblains because his heels would be brainless in going such a journey as that

to Regan. The talk about brains in the heels was proverbial at the
time. Slippers were sometimes called 'slipshoes', and a line in
Jonson's *Alchemist* nicely illustrates the idea:

> Your feet in mouldy slippers for your kibes.

21–22. Once more, amid his nonsense, the Fool hints a bitter truth—
that Lear had not been circumspect in giving away his crown
('house', 25).

25. [This question and that as to the seven stars being seven (32–33) have
been traced by G. S. Gordon to a medieval catechism of instructive
knowledge which was translated in the sixteenth century. In Act III,
scene iv another much discussed question is raised, 'What is the
cause of thunder?' (149), and there Lear calls Edgar a philosopher,
mistaking him for the professional wise man who like the Fool
was retained by some kings (see Gordon, *Shakespearean Comedy*, pp.
126–8).]

46–47. The paraphrase quoted in the footnote from the new *Arden*
edition is the best attempt to make these two lines relevant to their
context. They have usually been regarded as irrelevant, as well as
indecent, and perhaps an actor's gagging. But the mental vigour
and fertility of Shakespeare often expressed itself in puns or
innuendo involving sex. The Fool may also be anticipating his
own speedy return from the fruitless mission to Regan.

ACT II, SCENE I

In this scene the subplot is brought into connexion with the main
plot: Edmund, having caused his brother to flee, allies himself with
Cornwall. We begin to see that the Fool was right in likening Regan
to Goneril, though possibly she has more spite and less imperiousness.

1. Curan, who does not appear in Shakespeare's sources, seems to be
a confidential servant of Gloucester.

15. Here, as at II. iv. 187, I have moved back the entry to where
F and Q put it. Time had to be allowed for a character to move
forward on the deep Elizabethan stages.

24. Note how the trisyllabic feet give the idea of urgency, and also
how the mention of night suits the character of Regan and the dark
deeds that are to ensue. Cf. 119 below and in II. iv and III. i and vi.

25–26. [The interpretation in the footnote fits the context best. The more
natural meaning of the words in themselves would be 'have you said
nothing on Cornwall's side against Albany ?', the exact opposite of l. 24,
the only explanation of which offered is that they may be meant to
confuse Edgar.]

34–35. Young men in their cups would mix some of their own blood in drinking toasts to their ladies.

55. This word, which is not connected with 'ghost', is nicely illustrated by *Piers Plowman* (A) vii. 29: 'Gast crowen (scare crows) from his corn and keepen his beestes.'

106. This acme of hypocrisy may remind us of Richard III between two bishops (*Richard III*, III. vii).

ACT II, SCENE II

This scene is not very important for the plot. The quarrel between Kent and Oswald reflects that of their masters, and reveals that the former's loyalty outweighs his good sense. 'The exasperation of Kent is a fine touch. Like the King, he did not find it easy to play his new part. The great nobleman will peep out in unguarded moments' (Branson).

8. Lipsbury is not known as a place name, though **pinfold** usually means a pound, or enclosure, for straying beasts. There may be some allusion lost to us, or Shakespeare may be coining a phrase to suggest within the lips (mouth) *or* that Oswald used his lips too loosely.

13. In this and the following speeches of Kent Oswald is attacked both as being a mere servant, and at the same time as apeing the gentleman, as poor and yet a bit of a dandy (e.g. 30).

28–29. If we want to pry beyond the good, mouth-filling abuse, we must say *either* that Kent would soak Oswald in moonlit puddles, after knocking him down, *or* that he would make him full of holes for the moon to shine through.

33. Vanity was a common character in the old Morality plays. **Puppet** may refer to the acting of similar play by puppets, or merely be a term of contempt for a woman, in this case for Goneril.

60. The letter *Z* was not given in most early dictionaries, its work being done by *S*.

68–69. wear anticipates the clothes imagery which is to be so prominent later on. 'In contrast with the physically naked, Oswald is morally naked' (Heilman).

74. halcyon. 'A little byrde called the King's Fisher, being hanged up in the ayre by the neck his nebbe, or bill, will be always direct or straight against the wind' (T. Lupton, *c.* 1580). Sir Thomas Browne attacked this popular belief in his *Vulgar Errors*.

76. Dogs are nearly always mentioned by Shakespeare either for their fawning, as here, or for their messiness.

79-80. All the picture we need is of Kent whipping the cackling goose Oswald before him over the plain. Camelot, the residence of Arthur and his knights, was placed by Malory and the Elizabethans at Winchester. A 'Winchester goose' was the nickname for a nasty disease.

101-4. Kent adopts an inflated style since Cornwall did not like his homely speech. Cf. the Players' speeches in *Hamlet*.

106-9. The exact force still seems doubtful. 'Your displeasure' may be a sort of parody of 'your grace', since Kent hates Cornwall. The 'it' of the last phrase would naturally mean 'to be a plain knave', which he would be, in his own opinion, if he flattered Cornwall.

121. Ajax was one of the most famous of the Greeks at the siege of Troy, and the subject of a play by Sophocles. Shakespeare often refers to him, most frequently in the recently written *Troilus and Cressida*, where 'he is treated as a fool by the rogue and coward, Thersites' (Muir).

147. [F, omitting 'good', assigns the words 'Come, my lord, away' to Cornwall. This would give the nice point that Gloucester, before obeying, stops to sympathize with Kent.]

161-6. Kent means that the letter has come when comfort is most needed. Cf. 'When bale (woe) is att hyest boot is att next (healing is nearest)' from the old ballad of *Sir Aldingar*.

Shakespeare at once draws attention to *and* excuses the coincidence. We may conclude from III. i. 30 what the letter contained.

[After 164 a line may have dropped out. Most editors see corruption. GB would omit in acting 161-2 and 164-6. The 'enormous state' of 165 might, less probably, be the cares of the French kingdom.]

169. The wheel of Fortune, which, by her revolutions, gives man good or bad luck, was a medieval commonplace inherited by Shakespeare.

ACT II, SCENE III

This little scene, which is not separated from the preceding in the Folio, shows us Edgar assuming madness in order to remain undetected, just as Kent had had to assume the disguise of a serving man. Bedlam asylum allowed its less violent patients to go out and beg under the name of Abraham-men, and here is part of an account of them from Dekker's *Bell-man of London* (1608):

'He sweares he hath been in Bedlam and will talk franctickely of purpose: you see pins stuck in sundry places of his naked flesh, especially in his arms, which paine he gladly puts himself to, only to make you believe he is out of his wits. He calls himself by the name of *Poore Tom*, and coming near anybody cries out, *Poore Tom is a-cold.*'

Thus Shakespeare uses a familiar contemporary figure to give the primitive atmosphere he desires.

11. **nakedness.** 'Edgar's nakedness . . . becomes a symbol of that defencelessness in the world which Edgar has already shown, and indeed of the situation of innocent people generally' (Heilman).

ACT II, SCENE IV

This long closing scene of the second act is the first of those very great scenes that have made *King Lear* supreme even among Shakespeare's tragedies for depth and width. It describes what happened at Gloucester's house, and by the end we know the full measure of the two daughters' harshness, while Lear has learned that he was wrong in thinking Regan any better than her sister. Cornwall's final remark well registers the climax. Lear's final speech ('O! reason not the need', &c.) may be considered as dramatic poetry to achieve a height even beyond the soliloquies of *Hamlet*, although, and partly because, it cannot be separated from its context.

55–56. Lear has a feeling of strangulation which he bids return to the belly in which it was supposed to originate. A book published in 1605 was called *A Brief Discourse of a Disease called the Suffocation of the Mother*, and contained these words: 'most commonly it takes them with choking in the throat; and it is an effect of the mother or wombe.'

67–76. The Fool says that most men can see that Lear's fortunes are in decline, and that from the ordinary point of view that is the moment to desert his cause, just as it is worldly wisdom to attach oneself to a rising fortune. This is the counsel for knaves, but he himself will not follow it (81–84).

121–5. The three words 'cockney', 'coxcomb', and 'wanton' occur together in a passage of Lyly's *Euphues*, and that probably accounts for the association here. Point is added to the next remark if we know that in fact ostlers *did* put grease on hay, because then a horse would not touch it and the ostler had it to dispose of to his own profit.

134. Lear imagines Goneril's ingratitude as a vulture gnawing at his heart, just as in the *Prometheus* of Aeschylus a vulture gnawed at the heart of Prometheus, a punishment inflicted by Zeus. The bird of prey reminds us of 'detested kite' in I. iv. 256; cf. also III. iv. 73. The animal imagery or references usually concern Goneril, Regan, or Oswald.

137–9. Editors, including Johnson and Greg, have found difficulty here, but surely unnecessarily. Regan piously hopes that it is not so much a case of Goneril neglecting her duty as of Lear misjudging her.

154. Lear ironically adopts the view of age which younger people, not only Gonerils and Regans, often adopt—that the old are just a burden on the young. This is to look at things from the purely economic point of view, at which he again protests in the famous 'O! reason not the need', &c. (264 below). 'Shakespeare with a true instinct and with consummate art makes the heartlessness of youth to age the most bitter and fatal quality of the primitive world which he depicts' (G. Gordon).

   Johnson for once erred when he paraphrased as 'old age has few wants'.

162–3. This curse is quite intelligible as directed simply at Goneril, young at any rate compared to her father. But it is to be feared that the curse is still more dreadful, being directed at her unborn children. In the old play Lear uses the phrase 'young bones' unmistakably in that sense; and so do other Elizabethan writers.

187. Goneril may be supposed to have come to Gloucester's castle in order to prevent a possible pact between Regan and Lear. Her conduct may be dictated less by wanton cruelty than by her ambition to rule the country; and she succeeds in imposing her will on Regan.

189–92. Lamb instanced these lines as beyond acting (cf. Select Criticism). This is not, of course, to deny—what is only too much insisted on in these days—that Shakespeare was a man of the theatre and wrote for it, but to insist that there are depths of poetry which can scarcely be fully appreciated in the theatre, and situations where the physical presence may hinder rather than help our imaginations. Hazlitt speaks of Lear's 'sublime identification of his age with that of the heavens; for there is no other image which could do justice to the agonising sense of his wrongs and despair'. But Lamb speaks only of 'seeing' and ignores hearing in the theatre.

218–21. Lear is struggling to be patient and conciliatory.

227–8. Shakespeare regularly puts the play in a pagan religious setting. In 20–21 Lear had called on Jupiter and Kent had replied
with Juno. Here we are reminded of classical stories of the vengeance of heaven on impious men. But in itself this tells us
nothing as to Shakespeare's own beliefs. Even Milton calls God
'the thunderer' in *Paradise Lost*.

235. Regan, somewhat less outspoken than Goneril, refrains from an
ending that could only serve to exasperate Lear more.

264–86. This great speech shows 'the nadir of Lear's fortunes'. It
is significant of eighteenth-century taste in Shakespeare that Tate
cut it out of his acting version. Granville-Barker discusses its very
marked use of repetition (op. cit., pp. 160–2).

For the idea in the opening lines that it is the possession of something more than is necessary to keep our body alive that makes
human dignity, cf. Wordsworth's poem in *Lyrical Ballads* called
'The Last of the Flock', to which he was prompted by the dogma
of Godwin that property was a bad thing. Lear's knights are to
him what his sheep were to the old man, a mark of human dignity.

The hit at the chilliness of fashionable dress (270) is sometimes
as applicable now as to the extravagant costumes of the reign of
James I.

280. The incomplete sentence represents the incoherence of passion.
Note also that at one moment Lear is humble, at another furious
with anger.

287. At first hearing Cornwall's line is merely commonplace; but the
'storm' may be applied to Lear's mind as well as to the elements.
In the last two lines of the scene Cornwall gives the same warning,
and there he identifies himself with the brutality of his wife; whereas Albany has already begun to dissociate himself from Goneril's
behaviour.

300–2. 'The bareness of the heath itself reinforces and reflects what
the king discovers there that "unaccommodated man is no more
but such a poor, bare, forked animal"' (T. Spencer, *Shakespeare
and the Nature of Man*).

305. Lear had apparently not brought his train with him (the s.d. at
the beginning of this scene is from F). Unless, therefore, they are
supposed to have followed him, Regan is not strictly accurate.

307. Irony again! Lear had indeed had his ear 'abused' by the protestations of love that Goneril and Regan had given him. Hypo-

crisy or 'seeming' is a constantly recurring thought in Shakespeare. Lear had accepted at face value the appearance of hardness in Cordelia and of love in her sisters.

'If the play with the invocation of the curse upon Goneril entered an arena of anarchy and darkness, Lear himself is now to pass from personal grievance to the taking upon him, as great natures may, of the imagined burden of the whole world's sorrow—and if his nature breaks under it, what wonder!' (GB).

ACT III, Scene I

Hitherto everything has gone easily for the cruel sisters. Now we hear both of dissension between their husbands and of a move from Cordelia's side. For this some lapse of time would naturally be supposed, but Shakespeare is deliberately vague, so that the picture of Lear driven straight out into the storm may not be impaired. In fact there is a double time scheme, though not so marked as in *Othello*. In the old play there was no storm. Shakespeare would have noticed it in the context from which he took the story of Gloucester in Sidney's *Arcadia*; but, even if he had not, he would doubtless have added it, for its superb fitness to symbolize the storm in Lear's mind.

The poetic speech of the Gentleman is very effective in arousing our full sympathy for the King and preparing for his entry in the next scene. 'Lear now clearly assumes a stature that is more than merely personal, becomes man . . . exposed to a suffering to which the frame of things itself contributes' (Traversi).

2. The Gentleman may be supposed to be one of Lear's followers, now arrived, or someone Kent had known at court in old days.

10. It was common in those days to speak of man as a 'microcosm' (Gk. for 'little world') as compared with the great world, or 'macrocosm'. For 'out-scorn' Steevens made the very attractive conjecture 'out-storm'; but the emendation is not *necessary* since 'out-scorn' suggests that Lear is as contemptuous of, indifferent to, the elements as they are of him (see 9 and 15).

22–42. All this is omitted by *either* F *or* Q—possibly alternative cuts to shorten the play for acting—which is enough to show how much we should lose if we attempted to follow either exclusively as our authority for the text of the play.

ACT III, Scene II

This scene with iv and vi is really one very long scene broken by brief interludes, iii and v. This part of the storm on the heath contains four speeches from Lear which draw forth Shakespeare's highest powers. 'Any actor who should try to speak these lines realistically in the character of a feeble old man would be a fool' (GB). Lear begins to learn from his sufferings sympathy for others (72–73).

1–9. There is almost 'a new element of cosmic force' in the verse here, partly produced by the predominance of spondees. In the first line only 'and' and 'your' are unaccented.

4–5. Cf. *The Tempest*, i. ii. 201–3:

> Jove's lightnings, the precursors
> O' the dreadful thunderclaps, more momentary
> And sight-outrunning were not.

7–8. Although Lear calls upon the thunder to destroy the fertility of the *world*, he uses language suggested by the sexual organs of men and women; for he wishes the human race to be abolished.

20. Notice the slowing down of the rhythm which helps to accomplish the transition from passion to pleading.

35–36. As usual, after he has said something bitter the Fool turns to a piece of irrelevance. He may be glancing at the vanity of a Goneril and Regan.

59–60. **I am a man.** . . . i.e. it is not upon me that the thunder should be directed. The sentence, which has become one of those most commonly quoted or adapted from Shakespeare, is close to some words of the aged and suffering Oedipus in the *Oedipus at Colonus* of Sophocles:

$$τά γ' ἔργα μου$$
$$πεπονθότ' ἐστὶ μᾶλλον ἢ δεδρακότα \ (266–7)$$

'my deeds are rather deeds of suffering than doing.' Shakespeare did not know Sophocles, but the two plays have not a little in common.

74–77. This song is an adaptation of that in *Twelfth Night* (end), perhaps sung by the same actor.

79–end. These lines, which are omitted in Q, are the only lines present in either F or Q that that cautious scholar E. K. Chambers regarded as certainly spurious. Granville-Barker, writing as a producer, held that the King could not have left the Fool behind him. They are certainly not of much value. The first four lines refer to present conditions, the next six (85–91) to what is by no means the case, to an ideal state of affairs. The last four lines (91–94) do not logically follow from what has preceded.

95. **Merlin** was a wizard of Arthurian legend, and the Fool says that
he lives before Merlin's time because the story of the play comes
from the legends of early British history, long before the supposed
time of Arthur (fifth century A.D.).

ACT III, Scene III

A short piece of the subplot serves to separate two 'heath' scenes.
Gloucester appears in a *more* favourable light than hitherto from his
willingness to endanger himself for Lear, and Edmund in an even *less*
favourable light than before, notably in the callousness of the closing
couplet.

2. **unnatural.** Shakespeare had read the word in the passage of
Sidney from which he took the subplot, but he makes a great deal
of the words 'natural' and 'unnatural' throughout the play. We
are continually brought up against the question, what is natural
for man? Is it the same as what is 'natural' for beasts? (cf. note
to I. i. 219–20).

ACT III, Scene IV

This great scene may be called the climax of the play. The plot and
the subplot are brought together when Gloucester and Edgar are
joined to Lear and Kent. The proud and fiery king becomes humble,
first in his thought for the Fool and then for other unfortunate men
(cf. 32–33 here with 59–60 of scene ii). An editor who is compelled
to explain or paraphrase any part of the King's 'prayer' (28–36) may
be permitted to insist how much of the effect of these lines, as of
many another crucial passage in the plays, depends on Shakespeare's
power as a poet as well as a dramatist. We shall only get the right
impression in so far as we are moved by the expression. How much
evaporates in a prose paraphrase! We shall get nearer to Shakespeare's
meaning if we learn the lines by heart.

27. 'The prayer', says Kenneth Muir (in a note added in the revised
Arden edition of the play), 'is not to the gods but to the poor'. The
point does not seem to have been raised by earlier editors. It is
true that Lear addresses the poor at first, as he does 'pomp' later,
but perhaps the prayer is no more to them than to himself. May
not the prayer consist in just that self-humbling in which all true
religion begins (cf. Isaiah vi. 5 and Peter's 'Depart from me, for
I am a sinful man, O Lord'). The feeling of creatureliness leads to
a fellow-feeling for other creatures. And it is this feeling of abase-

ment, not expressed in words here, in which the prayer consisted.
We hear its results. Perhaps the point is not negligible.

45–46. Both sentences are found in very similar forms before Shakespeare.

49. [Keats in his copy of the Folio underlined 'Poor Tom' and wrote in the
date, 'Sunday evening Oct. 4, 1818'. He was then in constant atten-
dance by the bedside of his brother Tom, who died in the first week of
December.]

52–53. The idea of the knives and halters, the devil's encouragement
to suicide, comes from Harsnett's *A Declaration of Egregious
Popishe Impostures* of 1603, from which Shakespeare took a good
deal for this play, e.g. the name 'Flibbertigibbet' in 111 below.
(See K. Muir, 'S. Harsnett and King Lear' in *R.E.S.* 1951.)

56. The **five wits** were not the same as the five senses, but mental
qualities like imagination and memory.

60–62. Lear thinks that anyone brought as low as he is must have
owed it to his daughters. Bradley marked 47–48 as the point of
Lear's becoming mad.

82–97. It is part of Edgar's assumed madness to accuse himself of
numerous vices, and also to warn others against them. It was a
medieval commonplace to connect the Seven Deadly Sins with
specific animals (90–91). The following lines (91–93) seem to mean:
'if you must have creaking shoes (accounted fashionable!) and
rustling silks, to impress women, at any rate don't trust them.'
Donne had written in Elegy iv:

> I taught my silkes their whistling to forbeare,
> Even my oppresst shoes dumbe and speechlesse were.

But all previous editors appear to ignore the sentence, and it may
be hardly worth while to look for logic in what Edgar says.

98–106. The thought of this passage has been traced to Montaigne's
Essais; and, since the words 'adulterated' and 'sophisticated'
occur in Florio's translation of the passage, there is no doubt that
Shakespeare *was* using it for his general purpose of inquiring into
the fundamental nature of man. The almost naked Edgar causes
Lear to desire to imitate him and to rid himself of all the decencies
of civilized life of which his daughters had robbed him. So the
clothes imagery, begun with 'divest' in i. i. 49, reaches a climax,
and is united with the imagery from wild animals and the thought
of nature in the raw. When our text, that of F, concludes with
'Come; unbutton here' the Q reads 'Come on, be true'—a variant

giving a good sense in the context, and perhaps equally Shakespearian.

107–10. I have restored the entry of Gloucester to the place where it occurs in F (cf. II. i. 15 and note). This makes it easier to see what makes the Fool speak of an 'old lecher', though it would still have been more natural if he had said that 'an old lecher's heart is like a little fire in a wide field', &c. His lustful feeling is the only warm thing about him.

113. [squinies. This rare word probably underlies the Q reading, as Greg argued, while F's 'squints' is an obvious substitution of a commoner form. The verb occurs again at IV. vi. 138. It is confirmed in a very interesting way: Armin uses it in a book published in 1608, and he is probably the man who acted the part of the Fool when Lear was first produced.]

115–17. These words, reciting how St. Withold subdued a demon, may have been used as a charm.

133–4. These two lines are slightly changed from a couplet in an old romance, *Bevis of Hampton*, possibly suggested here by the rhyme with 'wear'. The name **Smulkin**, together with **Modo** and **Maho** (137–8), come from Harsnett (see note to 52–53)

139–40. It was first suggested by Cowden Clarke, Keats's friend, that something in Edgar's voice reminds Gloucester of his son and so prompts this remark (cf. IV. i. 32–34). When he takes up the subject again in 160–4 he would have made it difficult for Edgar not to disclose himself.

148. Lear calls Edgar first a 'philosopher' (cf. I. v. 25 note), then a 'learned Theban' (151), and finally an 'Athenian' (174). The allusions have not been certainly explained. Blunden would connect them with Horace, *Epistles* II. i, where Thebes and Athens occur in the same line as 'modo', but the last is not a name there as in 137 here, and the context in Horace shows little connexion with that here. Edith Sitwell thinks the 'learned Theban' was Oedipus, who solved the riddle of the Sphinx at Thebes.

157. Notice the dramatic irony; for the case is applicable to the speaker. On what Kent had said to Gloucester cf. Bradley, *Shakespearean Tragedy*, p. 447.

176–8. The first line may well have come from a lost ballad or romance, Roland being famous especially in the *La Chanson de Roland*. The last line and a half come from the story of Jack the Giant Killer with the change of English to British, perhaps to suit ancient Britain, perhaps James I's uniting of the crowns.

'So they reach the outhouse, all of his own castle that Gloucester
dare offer. What a group! Kent, sturdy and thrifty of words;
Gloucester tremulous; the bedraggled and exhausted Fool; and
Lear magnificently courteous and deliberately keeping close company with his gibbering fellow-man' (GB).

ACT III, Scene V

This short scene provides a respite between two stages of Lear's madness. It shows Edmund at the height of his villainy and hypocrisy;
he disguises naked self-interest under the word 'loyalty'.

19. **comforting.** The modern legal language for treason still includes the words 'comforting the King's enemies'. There are many
examples of words used in their legal sense in Shakespeare, not
least in the Sonnets.

ACT III, Scene VI

Gloucester has now brought them in from the storm (cf. III. iv. 147).
Otherwise all the rest of Coleridge's comment stands: 'O, what a
world's convention of agonies is here! All external nature in a storm,
all moral nature convulsed—the real madness of Lear, the feigned
madness of Edgar, the babbling of the Fool, the desperate fidelity of
Kent—surely such a picture was never conceived before or since!'

6–8. We must not expect logical sequence nor relevance to the other
speakers in Edgar's remarks in this scene; and we shall not miss
much of the effect of this phrase provided we know something of
the reputation of the Emperor Nero (A.D. 54–68) for wickedness.

[The source for this remark used to be found in Rabelais, but the parallel
was not close. In fact Shakespeare may well have read in Chaucer
(*Monk's Tale*, 3665–6) that Nero was said to have fished with gold nets
in the Tiber, and perhaps he had somehow heard that the Greek writer
Pausanias records that Nero tried to fathom a certain lake—unsuccess-
fully. Shakespeare therefore pictures him angling in hell, in the 'dark-
some Stygian lake', as a contemporary writer had it. Edith Sitwell
takes the lake to stand for 'the bottomless pit of human nature'
(*A Notebook on William Shakespeare*, p. 48).]

20–23. Lear now stages a mock trial which he continues to l. 54. We
are to imagine a bench of several judges, as with Justices of the
Peace or with the High Court of Appeal. 'At the moment of
greatest breakdown we are given a judgment that represents
amidst chaos the memory of civilisation' (R. Peacock, quoted K.
Muir). Justice and injustice are prominent ideas of the play, e.g.
concerning the 'stocking' of Kent (II. iv. and IV. ii. 79).

41. Most children know the line 'The sheep's in the corn' from the nursery rhyme of *Little Boy Blue*. It may be assumed that all the verse quotations in these scenes are more or less closely derived from older material, even where we do not know it.

60–61. Lear imagines that even the pet household dogs, implied by the names, had turned against him.

67. [**brach**, which in I. iv. 109 ('Lady the Brach') only meant 'bitch', seems here to mean a type of dog, one hunting by scent; but even so it does not fit too well with a more specialized name, a lymmer. 'lym' is, in fact, a correction of F's 'Hym' and Q's 'him'. This is retained by the *Yale* edition, and the meaning would then be 'female or male'.]

70. Edgar makes a sudden motion of his head. More elaborate actions have been suggested but are not necessary.

82–83. Lear sees no supper in prospect; or, if we press Gloucester's assurance in scene iv that there will be food, he feels disinclined for it yet. The Fool takes up the idea of doing things at the wrong time. Many deeper significances may be read into his words, as in the seven listed by Blunden in his essay 'Shakespeare's Significances' (reprinted in *The Mind's Eye* and in *Shakespearean Criticism 1919–25*, in World's Classics Series, p. 336). To those there may be added that the actor of the part will not appear any more in that role in the play.

79. **Persian attire.** Lear does not like Persian fashions any more than Horace: 'Persicos odi, puer, apparatus'—the beginning of the last ode of the first book of Horace, which Shakespeare might have read at school, as he almost certainly read some Virgil. But a Persian embassy had recently come to the court of James I.

99–100. [The speech of Kent containing this last reference to the Fool is in Q, not in F; whereas the Fool's last words in 83 were in F, not Q. They may well be alternative, the second being dropped when the first was added.]

101–14. [These lines are not in F. Aldis Wright thought them quite un-Shakespearian and Granville-Barker would omit them. But there are passages like this of explanation to the audience, and even in this style, elsewhere (cf. Cordelia at v. iii. 3–7), and there is one phrase 'he childed as I father'd'—which we could hardly deny to Shakespeare.]

ACT III, Scene VII

The subplot reaches its climax in the blinding of Gloucester, a physical horror to balance the spiritual agony of the King. As Gloucester had sinned in the flesh, he is punished in the flesh; and it is only when he is physically blinded that he becomes morally clear-sighted (91).

The actual blinding of Gloucester has been judged an artistic mistake by many from Coleridge to Bridges, and it is a clear breach of the canons of classical drama. On the other hand, it may be doubted whether the full horror and cruelty of the deed would have been adequately conveyed by a messenger, and it is not necessary that Gloucester's face should be visible to the audience while the deed is being done on the stage. For a detailed defence see J. I. M. Stewart in *Review of English Studies* for 1945. The reaction of the two servants (not in Sidney's narrative) shows that a sound moral sense still survives among ordinary people; so that the dramatist is not entirely pessimistic even here.

23-27. The language makes us think of a trial at law, thus providing a parallel with Lear's mock trial of the 'she-foxes'. Cornwall should in strict logic have said that strict right required a formal trial with which he was going to dispense as his power enabled him to do; and it was no doubt because he saw this that Johnson explained 'do a courtesy to' as 'indulge, gratify'. But the natural meaning of the phrase is nicely illustrated by Henry V when, wooing Kate, he says 'nice customs curtsy to great kings' (*Henry V*, v. ii. 293).

54. The metaphor is set out more fully in what was probably the next play to be written:

> They have tied me to the stake; I cannot fly,
> But bear-like, I must fight the course (*Macbeth*, v. vii. 2).

56-58. Gloucester speaks metaphorically; but with striking irony anticipates, if he does not actually suggest, his own fate.

['stick' is the F word, but the rarer 'rash' of Q, which is a verb specially used of a boar's attack, is more likely to be the original. Similarly in 63 F has 'stern' for the rare 'dern'.]

65. [This is possibly the phrase most disputed and least certain of interpretation in the whole play. I have adopted in the footnotes the explanation that Case, the general editor of the old *Arden* edition, gave in a supplementary note to Craig. (This reading is also taken to mean 'All other cruel creatures yielded to feelings of compassion'.) But one of the best solutions seems to be to read 'subscribe' of F instead of 'subscrib'd' of Q, put a full stop at 'key', and interpret with Tucker Brooke 'Give sanction and formal allowance, if you like, to all other cruel creatures, yet I shall see', &c.]

77. **What do you mean?** seems rather pointless coming from the first Servant. I have followed a suggestion of the old *Arden* editor, adopted by the new, of assigning it to Regan.

85-87. After the dreadful irony of this appeal Gloucester never refers to Edmund again—only obliquely in 91.

93. Smell, as Edith Sitwell pointed out, is the most animal of the senses; and it is to animals, or rather below them, that Goneril and Regan reduce man. But this taunt, like 71 and some other remarks, go far to justify Bradley in seeing Regan as the vilest human being, 'if indeed she is human', created by Shakespeare.

99-100. In fact Cornwall dies from this wound, IV. ii. 70-72. He had shown himself cowed in the presence of the King (II. iv), but grossly cruel to a weaker man.

ACT IV, SCENE I

This scene continues the subplot without any interval of time from the last. In it Edgar displays a true filial love for the father who has wronged him, as Cordelia does for Lear; and Gloucester, like Lear, has begun to learn sympathy for others through his misfortunes (44-45). 'The old peasant, too old himself to go far with his lord . . . will risk his fortunes to do Gloucester a last, simple service' (GB). 2-4. Cf. *Paradise Regained*, iii. 206: 'For where no hope is left, is left no fear.'

10. The Old Man is to Gloucester as Kent is to Lear.

[**poorly led.** K. Muir suggests that Shakespeare wrote 'poorly rayed', i.e. arrayed, which is the phrase in Sidney's narrative about the Paphlagonian king and his son—an attractive conjecture, as F is rather weak and Quartos show confusion.]

10-12. The same thought, quite independent in expression, comes in Arnold's *The Scholar Gipsy*, 142-50:

> For what wears out the life of mortal men?
> 'Tis that from change to change their being rolls:
> 'Tis that repeated shocks, again, again,
>   Exhaust the energy of strongest souls,
>   And numb the elastic powers.
> Till having us'd our nerves with bliss and teen,
>   And tir'd upon a thousand schemes our wit,
>   To the just-pausing Genius we remit
> Our worn-out life, and are—what we have been.

19-21. Three of the most haunting and significant lines in the play! 'The whole play is built on this double paradox' (K. Muir). The paradox is strikingly paralleled in the *Oedipus Tyrannus* of Sophocles when the blind prophet Teiresias sees the truth while the King says to his eyes 'Long enough have ye failed in knowledge', and, when he knows the full truth, blinds himself.

23. to see thee in my touch is a phrase of genius. It is the only way a blind man can see, but for Gloucester, in his agonized sense of having wronged his son, the sense of touch would be worth all the rest. He would have eyes again in knowing the truth about his son.

32-33. Cf. Lear's estimate at III. iv. 101, &c. The actual comparison of man to a worm is probably due to Job xxv. 6.

36-37. The first thing to notice about these famous lines is that they are said by a particular man at a particular moment—before he yet knows all that shall be—and it is quite unjustifiable to take them as Shakespeare's final philosophy. We must weigh with them Edgar's answer at v. iii. 170-3 and Albany's words at IV. ii. 78-80.

58-63. As before, most of this material about evil spirits comes from Harsnett's book (cf. note to III. iv. 52-53), including the 'possession' of three chambermaids.

66-69. In view of the vague 'heavens' the injunction to sympathy and charity may be taken as inherent in true humanity; or Shakespeare may be thinking of specific teaching in the N.T., but deliberately keeping out Christian terms from this pagan story.
The corresponding passage for Lear himself is III. iv. 28-36.

74. confined *might*, however (cf. footnote), refer to the narrow straits of Dover.

ACT IV, Scene II

The early part of this scene shows that the adulterous love of Goneril and Edmund has made considerable progress on the journey from Gloucester's castle to Albany's, wherever that may be. Albany now for the first time reveals himself to be a man of character and honesty who has made up his mind to break with his wife.

12. [The emendation 'currish' for 'cowish' explains some corruption in Q here, and is quite attractice, but it cannot be regarded as necessary. 'Currish' is used by Gratiano of Shylock's spirit (*M. of V.*, IV. i. 124).]

21-25. Granville-Barker nicely speaks of 'the regal impudence of the woman' and 'the falsely chivalrous flourish of the man's reply'. The word 'mistress' may carry as full a sense as we like to give it, possibly including the suggestion that she will be queen one day and Edmund her royal consort (cf. 85). The 'wrongs' which Albany's head is made to 'bear' (51) may well include the horns of the cuckold.

38. [The reading of the Oxford text, which is a mixture of a corrected Q 'A foole usurps my bed', and the F 'My fool usurps my body', first adopted by Malone, is also favoured by Greg.]

48. It will come. 'An irregular line of three monosyllables introduces with particular solemnity the doom upon humanity left to
itself' (Bethell, *Shakespeare and the Popular Dramatic Tradition*).

49–50. Once more but this time from Albany, we have the idea that
this unfilial behaviour is 'monstrous'; cf. I. i. 220 (France), I. iv.
255, and I. v. 36 (Lear). Human beings in sinning fall to the level
of beasts. It is often thought that Darwin first revealed the preying
of beast upon beast, but in fact the observation is as old as Hesiod,
and there are many Elizabethan and earlier English parallels. In
the famous speech of Ulysses in *Troilus and Cressida* (I. iii) one
of the consequences of taking 'degree' away would be that

> Appetite, an universal wolf, . . .
> Must make perforce an universal prey,
> And last eat up himself.

57. [Our only authority for these lines from 43 to the end of the speech lies
in the Quartos and they do not agree among themselves. Q 1 'Thy
slayer begins threats', i.e. thy would-be slayer, is barely possible.]

62–63. [An alternative to the footnote explanation is 'having assumed the
appearance of a fiend, so concealing your woman's self', and this fits
a little more easily with the next line, making your expression devilish.]

68. Mew is explained as the cat's noise suggesting effeminacy, *or* a
catcall of an Elizabethan audience. In any case contempt is the
main point, so that we may compare Goneril's words with the
taunts levelled by Lady Macbeth at her husband: 'A soldier and
afeard!' But Albany is sounder stuff than to allow taunts to blind
his sense of right and wrong.

[Some copies of Q 1 read 'manhood now', which could be understood as
'we see what your courage is by your threatening a woman'.]

ACT IV, Scene III

This scene is not in F, and may have been dropped on revision,
perhaps because it proved too sentimental in presentation. Its purpose is to bring Cordelia back to our minds.

1–4. It would be natural for the King of France to come with his
wife, but it was a delicate matter to show a foreigner invading
England; so Cordelia is left as the bringer of aid to her father, even
though it must be martial aid (cf. IV. iv. 23–29).

16–24. The comparison of tears to sunshine and rain occurs in Sidney's *Arcadia*, but the style in which it is expressed is Shakespeare's,
and would be almost enough to prove this scene his writing. Pro-

bably 'sunshine' and 'rain', suggesting good crops, prompted the
adjective 'ripe'.

31. [clamour-moisten'd. The hyphen is a conjecture of editors. Without it we can take 'moisten'd' as a main verb, she moistened her
clamour, i.e. drowned her exclamations with tears. Q inserts 'her' after
moisten'd, which destroys metre and gives a difficult sense.]

45. dog-hearted. Notice the animal imagery once more! Dogs for
Shakespeare are usually either fierce, or fawning (e.g. IV. vi. 98) and
messy.

51. We are never told what the 'dear cause' is.

ACT IV, Scene IV

Cordelia is now brought before us in person for the first time since
Act I. We find her entirely concerned with her father's state of mind.

4. [cuckoo-flowers. There are almost as many identifications of this
flower as there are editors of the play. The name implies a flower that
comes with the cuckoo; and if the name is the same as the 'cuckoo-buds
of yellow hue' of *Love's Labour's Lost*, the cowslip is likely enough.
Wright's *Dialect Dictionary* records no less than eleven different
flowers to which the name has been applied in different parts, to which
can be added its use for the 'cuckoo-pint' in the Forest of Dean,
according to information from a friend of the editor's; but this is a
lilac, not a yellow flower.]

6. A century is strictly only a division of the Roman army, and so the
word is naturally used in *Coriolanus*; but Shakespeare may here
have imported it into a pre-Roman Britain to signify a troop sent
out on search (cf. 'cohorts', I. ii. 148).

[Others take the 'centery' of F as the older form of 'sentry'—but one
man seems inadequate for the task.]

ACT IV, Scene V

It becomes clearer that the sisters will fall foul of one another over
Edmund. Regan shows (12) an hypocrisy only equalled by that of
Edmund in II. i and III. v, and Oswald one slightly redeeming feature,
in his loyalty to his mistress.

21–22. The broken sentences are deliberate, where one party asks to
be allowed the unladylike action of reading a private letter and the
other—a servant—does not like to refuse rudely.

29. this note. The word could be used for a short letter by that date
(*O.E.D.*), but makes better sense with what follows when taken as
in the footnote. In 248 of the next scene Oswald has 'letters' for
Edmund, but Regan may refer to a letter in the 'this' of 33.

ACT IV, Scene VI

This scene, one of the highlights of the play, follows on the first of this act, where Edgar had undertaken to lead Gloucester to Dover. The scene falls into three parts: (1) Gloucester and Edgar at Dover; (2) Lear, Edgar, and Gloucester from 82; (3) development of the plot from 188 or 204 (Lear's exit). Lear and Gloucester have been separated since III. vi.

Shakespeare's company visited Dover in 1605–6 (E. K. Chambers, *W. Shakespeare*, ii. 333), and this might account for the vivid details with which Edgar describes the cliff still called 'Shakespeare's'. But such pictures, bringing the setting before the mind's eye, are an essential part of romantic poetry, as opposed to the merely general description which Johnson's more classical taste would have preferred here.

8. In this part of the scene Edgar speaks in verse, whereas in IV. i he spoke in prose.

16. Cf. Drayton's *Polyolbion* (1622) xvii. 764:

> Rob Dover's neighbouring cliffs of samphire, to excite
> His dull and sickly taste, and stir up appetite.

56. Sir Thomas Browne in *Religio Medici* said that his life was 'a miracle of thirty years'. He shared with the character created for Edgar by Shakespeare a sort of natural piety and reverence; cf. 73–75 below, and the last scene of the play.

70–73. Edgar plays on Gloucester's superstition, as Edmund had in II. i. The temptation to suicide was supposed to be specially the work of fiends. Edgar wants his father to feel that he has been delivered by the favour of heaven and hence to regain hope and trust in God. Shakespeare, following the conventions he uses almost throughout the play, speaks of 'the gods', but 74–75 is surely a reminiscence, perhaps unconscious, of 'With God all things are possible' in Matthew xix. 26.

76–78 Cf. Lear at III. iv. 18: 'I will endure.'

84–93. Lear's remarks are not in full logical connexion with one another, but neither are they sheer nonsense. First he reverts to the idea of a trial and asserts his acquittal on a charge of forgery. 'Coining' suggests (press-)money. Next he imagines he has the recruits in front of him and criticizes their archery After the mouse interlude (an imagined enemy?) we return to war, halberdiers, archery, and a password.

[Mr. Norrington suggests to me that 'Lear comes in fingering his
flowers and fancying them money. "Nature, above art" might then
mean these natural coins are better than the coiner's counterfeits.'
Then Lear's mind all the time from his entry to 187 will be running on
the means of raising forces to fight Goneril and Regan.]

108–32. [It is not possible to decide how much of Lear's speech should be
treated as verse. Editors differ in the matter, as had F and Q. If it be
intended as verse there are a quite unusual number of incomplete lines.]

120. There is contemporary authority for 'forks' as a support for the
hair. On the other hand, we should more naturally take 'forks' as
legs (comparing Falstaff's description of Shallow as a 'forked
radish'), in which case the words 'between her forks' should be
taken after 'snow', where we should have expected to find
them. We may be reminded of Goneril's affected virtue in I. iv.
241–4.

149. This line is capable of deep application : now he no longer has
his eyes he sees more truly. Cf. 'I stumbled when I saw' (IV. i. 19)
and also IV. i. 67–69.

160–72. This great speech brings together many of the leading themes
and images of the play, and, indeed, of Shakespeare's mind at
this time—hypocrisy, the abuse of authority (cf. *Measure for Measure* and *Timon of Athens*, especially IV. i and iii), disgust with sex
and lust, and pity for the underdog. The last theme continues the
redemption of Lear from the 'naked wretches' speech of III. iv. 28,
&c.; but Lear now has compassion for the sinner as well as for the
poor.

160–3. Cf. 'He that is without sin among you, let him first cast a stone
at her' and the whole story of Christ's treatment of the woman
taken in adultery, John, viii. 1–11.

162. [lusts need not be emended to the cacophonous 'lust'st'. Elizabethan
usage allowed the simpler form.]

165. [Plate sin (Theobald) is one of the comparatively rare convincing
emendations of Shakespeare's text. F has 'Place sinnes', and there is
no Q.]

173. The line may suggest the 'impertinency' of Edgar's comment;
but it is permissible to see in it also the thought that Lear is nearing
the end of his mortal journey. So also the following phrase 'Reason
in madness' can be widely applied; for it is the fools and tem-
porarily mad who discern the true values. The mad Lear, released
from logic, shows an imaginative understanding of the world,
expressing himself in image patterns of sight, smell, clothes, sex,
animals, and justice (cf. Heilman's ch. VIII).

178. For Lear preaching patience cf. Edgar at 81. But the other Lear reasserts himself at 187.

183. **block.** It has usually been thought that Lear sees a hat of Elizabethan type, applies to it the word that properly meant a wooden block on which hats were shaped, but goes on to think of another use to which felt could be put. Perhaps, however, he mistakes something wooden for a mounting-block, which suggests horse-soldiers. The sequence of thought in 'stage of fools' . . . 'block' may have lingered in Shakespeare's mind from some verse in Sidney's *Arcadia* where we get 'stage . . . fools . . . blockish'; and the words that follow here may be due to the three kinds of block—boot-block, mounting block, hat-block.

205-7. Although the primary reference is to the evil sisters a Christian hearer could hardly avoid thinking of the 'original sin' of Adam and Eve. The lines therefore 'put Cordelia's goodness in the spiritual context of redemption' (Traversi). It has also been noted that the 'holy water' in her eyes (IV. iii. 30) usually has ecclesiastical associations, and that the words used by Cordelia herself at IV. iv. 23-24 recall the words of Christ when he was found in the Temple (Luke ii. 49).

> [Another modern writer would go even further: 'Cordelia is the other Nature Edmund, Goneril, and Regan ignore. In our view she is a figure comparable with that of Griselda and Beatrice: literally a woman: allegorically the root of individual and social sanity; tropologically Charity . . . anagogically the redemptive principle itself.' But the present editor does not share Mr. Danby's fondness for reducing Shakespeare's characters to symbols and his plots to type-stories like 'Killing the King'!]

217. **You ever-gentle gods.** In 35 it was 'O you mighty gods'. Perhaps the change is deliberate, intended to show that Gloucester is learning to 'bear free and patient thoughts' (81).

235. Edgar, pretending to be a peasant, speaks in a south-west dialect more or less current from the Cotswolds (below which lies Stratford) and Gloucestershire (where Edgar's home had been) to Somerset and Devon.

245. [The s.d. is that of Rowe, the first editor, and suggests that Edgar uses his 'cudgel'. Q has 'they fight', F nothing. Granville-Barker suggests that Edgar may have wrested a knife or dagger from Oswald.]

248-50. Oswald is still loyal to the interests of his mistress.

250. [**English** (F). Either Shakespeare or a corrector seems to have been thinking of the conditions of recent centuries, the English wars with France. Q has 'British', which would be more consistent.]

251–3. Edgar reverts to educated language and this time Gloucester makes no comment. We may suppose him to be too preoccupied with thoughts about the King, to which he reverts in 279, ignoring all that has intervened since 203.

ACT IV, Scene VII

This scene is as moving as any reconciliation scene in Shakespeare and more so than those in the late Romances, in proportion as tragic feeling has been deeper. Cordelia's words 'And so I am, I am' (70) seem to heave her heart into her mouth, while the repetition (cf. 75) may remind us of its effectiveness at the conclusion of David's lament over Absalom (2 Samuel xviii. 33).

We last saw Cordelia at the end of scene iv, since when she has met Kent, whom we last saw in scene iii. But she has not seen her father since I. i.

6–7. Cordelia is asking Kent to put off the humble clothes he had assumed for disguise, and to dress according to his rank; but, in view of the frequent reference to clothes in this play, a change of clothes may symbolize, as well as actually proceed from, a change of fortune. So, in l. 20 below: 'Is he array'd?' may suggest also restoration to full human consciousness, or even to a purified state. It is in ways like this that *King Lear* is nearer than the other tragedies to the close of *The Winter's Tale* (see Bethell's edition in this series).

14. **O you kind gods.** The tone of the scene and Cordelia's deeply forgiving spirit would have led us to expect an invocation of the Christian God; but, as we have seen earlier, Shakespeare has in this respect shown an unusual care to avoid anachronism and to preserve a pagan atmosphere.

20. The s.d. following this line (in F only) suits what follows. 'For when he comes to himself it is to find that he is royally attired and as if seated on his throne. It is from this throne that he totters to kneel at Cordelia's feet' (GB). By 25 the attendants have brought Lear far enough on to the deep Elizabethan stage for the doctor to address them. Perhaps no inner stage was being used for this representation, since, if it were, it would have probably been used for the King's disclosure.

[Many older editions made Lear present, asleep, from the beginning of the scene. Bradley (note W) showed how wrong this was.]

35. **perdu.** The word 'watch' (be awake and out in the open at night)

probably made the poet think of a sentry, and the phrase 'sentinelle perdue' was an old one for a sentry in an advanced and dangerous position. But 'perdu' itself means 'lost one', and that is the primary meaning here. Such ambiguities of language are a common feature of Shakespeare's later style and link him to the metaphysical wit writers, also of the early seventeenth century.

47. Lear imagines himself in Hell. The torment of a wheel of fire is not from the Bible but from Apocryphal (not *the* Apocrypha) books which were much drawn upon in the middle ages but are now little known. They are conveniently collected by M. R. James, *The Apocryphal New Testament.*

59. We must imagine a stage direction 'Lear makes to kneel'. But Cordelia will already have knelt to *him* for his blessing. We may remember and contrast the two chief characters kneeling to make their awful vow of vengeance in the tragedy that preceded this one, *Othello,* III. iii. 461.

78–82. 'There is a lull before the end, a hesitation on the brink of severity that reminds us of Hamlet when he returns from England and talks with Horatio in the churchyard, or even of Othello when Emilia says "he looks gentler than he did" ' (M. Van Doren, *Shakespeare*).

85. [From here to the end is absent in F, a natural cut to shorten the play for acting, and therefore, with similar passages, evidence that F is derived from an acting version.

ACT V, Scene I

This slight pause before the climax reveals the rising discord on the side opposed to Lear. Edmund makes his first long speech since III. v (if we can call those long), revealing that he has no more love for one sister than the other, and seeks only the fulfilment of ambition.

21. This line can be reduced to the normal metre, apart from the extra syllable at the end, if 'to his' is read as one syllable.

24–27. Albany, and Shakespeare, are on ticklish ground here, which may account for some obscurity of language, though corruption is not improbable. Albany is in the position of commanding where he has much sympathy with the other side, while the dramatist has to show before an audience that had not forgotten either the Armada or the traditional enmity with France an invader landed to vindicate the right of the abused king. The 'others' of 26 may include Edgar.

37. The easiest explanation of this passage seems to be as follows: Regan observes that Goneril shows no sign of going away and suspects her of trying to go to the Council of War in order to take the opportunity of private communication with Edmund. Goneril sees her suspicions and comments on it (not necessarily 'aside', as editors have it), but for the moment humours Regan by agreeing to go with her. This explanation would still hold if Regan were herself attending the Council of War (in her deceased husband's place) and did not want to leave Goneril behind with Edmund even for a moment or two.

56–57. This and v. iii. 85 'This gilded serpent' round off the animal imagery used of the two sisters. Here, of course, it is quite indirect since the simile simply illustrates the idea of 'once bitten twice shy', but the choice of a snake for this purpose has the effect of associating the image of an adder with the sisters, whether the hearer or reader is conscious of it or not; and it is in the noting of such effects that modern discussion of Shakespearian Imagery largely consists.

61. **carry out my side** might mean 'repay her affection', 'satisfy her lust', in which case the words would be used in their ordinary sense today, and not in a metaphor from card-playing, which probably underlies the other explanation given in the footnote. Nor is deliberate *double entendre* to be ruled out.

ACT V, Scene II

The slightness of this account of the crucial battle may be partly accounted for by the awkward division of sympathy which an audience, particularly an Elizabethan audience (cf. note to 24–27 of previous scene), might suffer; but also from the amount of material already in the play. Nor was Lear a soldier, like Macbeth or Antony, to lead his own army.

Q begins with a stage direction which is too good to lose: 'Enter the powers of France over the stage, Cordelia with her father in her hand' (i.e. holding his hand in hers).

9. **in ill thoughts again.** In IV. vi Edgar had diverted his father from suicide, and this is the force of the famous lines that follow, *not*, as taken out of their context they might suggest, that men must put up with death as with birth. There is a close parallel in *Hamlet*, v. ii. 233, 'the readiness is all', where Hamlet is discussing with Horatio his forthcoming duel with Laertes and its possible result.

11. Gloucester's last words express acquiescence in the will of heaven.

ACT V, Scene III

The play ends with a crowded denouement involving the death of the
three worst sinners, but also of three of those most sinned against
(Kent's death being anticipated). Cordelia, as usual, says little, but
we remember her almost as much as we do her father. The scene
may be compared with that which closes *Hamlet*, where Horatio and
Fortinbras correspond roughly to Albany and Edgar here.

3–6. Note the rhyme which gives a kind of formality to Cordelia's
words, as if she dared not let herself go.

8. The fourfold 'No' with which Lear refuses to see 'these daughters'
seems to repudiate the whole circle of their cruelty and his misery
as he looks only to the future; and in that he does not even mind
prison, provided he has Cordelia. 'The whole episode (8–25)
creates as it were an island of peace, precariously isolated, in a
world of ruin' (Traversi).

10–11. Cf. iv. vii. 57–59. This is the climax of Lear's humility, cf.
ii. iv. 280 note.

13–17. The new *Arden* edition would take the butterflies literally,
but I cannot regard this as probable. The 'poor rogues' may be
fellow prisoners, but I suspect that the 'poor' refers less to their
condition than to the state of mind of anyone who should take
these ups and downs in worldly fortune seriously. Lear almost
imagines himself and Cordelia seeing things *sub specie aeternitatis*,
with God's view. K. Muir prints 'Gods'' with an apostrophe after
the s (F and Q having no apostrophe at all), but this would be indistinguishable to the ear from the singular and would be an unnatural
substitute for 'spies of the gods'. It is true that here alone in the
play God in the singular is mentioned, but that would seem to be
dictated by the atmosphere of the speech, which breathes forgiveness and trust.

20–21. The footnote interprets 'such sacrifices' as the imprisonment
referred to in the lines immediately preceding, which would
include, of course, the patience with which it was to be borne. This
is therefore, in effect, their renunciation of the world. But Cordelia has already made the sacrifice of her freedom in trying to
vindicate her father and is shortly to sacrifice her life as well. In
spite of the plural 'gods' we should see the basis of the phrase in
the Bible (Psalm li. 17 and Hebrews xiii. 16: 'With such sacrifices

God is well pleased'), and in the Apocrypha (Wisdom iii. 5–6: 'God made trial of them . . . and as a whole burnt-offering he accepted them'). There may even be at the back of Shakespeare's mind some thought of Calvary, the supreme example of undeserved suffering willingly endured.

24. **The good years.** There is no authority for any other reading, and the explanation of the *O.E.D.* is now usually accepted that the word(s) 'goodyear' had come to be used as a vague imprecation 'as denoting some undefined malefic power or agency'; hence footnote. It is, however, possible that the words should be given their ordinary sense with the meaning that even their present prosperity will bring Goneril and Regan to ruin. Once more biblical language may be at the back of Shakespeare's mind, this time Pharaoh's dream about the ears of corn (Genesis xli), including the words 'devour' and 'starve'.

57–60. Edmund implies that if they judged their late enemies in the moment when they were smarting from the losses of the battle they might deal too harshly with them. In reality he desires to postpone consideration of Cordelia and Lear till his servant has murdered them. He remains constant to his hypocrisy.

73. There was an old proverb 'Love, being jealous, makes a good eye look a-squint'; so Goneril says 'you must be in love with him'.

122. Shakespeare can coin compound epithets in which the two words may be in various differing relationship to one another, as is well illustrated by this line and 132, 138, and 147 in close proximity.

134. **False to thy gods.** Whatever gods Edmund acknowledged, he was false to them by his perjury in the plot against Edgar and his father.

151. **Save him.** Presumably Albany wants Edmund to live long enough for his acts of treachery to be examined and cleared up. But many editors have transferred the words to Goneril.

155. [Q has 'stople', which is more likely to be the original, as the rarer, word. Q also omits 'Hold, sir' and the line scans without it, while the difficulty of explaining these words is removed. If they are retained, as they are even by those editors who print 'stople', it is possible to take 'Thou' as Edmund, and to insert the s.d. after 157 'gives the letter to Edmund'. I prefer on the whole to suppose that (with the exception of 'Hold sir', if it be retained) Albany speaks to Goneril right down to her frantic exit. We then assign the second part of 160 to Goneril with Q, not to Edmund with F.]

158. Goneril means that she is the King's daughter, and, she hopes, queen-to-be, Albany only her consort.

170–1. These lines may be taken as a formal answer to Gloucester's accusations in IV. i. 36–37. But, as Bradley says, 'there never was vainer labour than that of critics who try to make out that the persons in these dramas meet with "justice" or their "desert"' (see the whole passage, *Shakespearean Tragedy*, 279).

174. Edmund is thinking of the wheel of fortune. He is back again at the bottom where he started, and the last three words seem fatalistically, if not humbly, to accept that position.

196–9. The description of Gloucester's death prepares the way for a similar death of Lear before our eyes. Thus the parallelism is preserved to the end.

231. Albany recognizes the justice of the doom that has befallen the sisters, but feels awe before this signal vindication of the punishment awaiting wickedness.

236. Albany had no special reason to be anxious about the fate of Lear and Cordelia. But Edmund had; and Bradley objected that no sufficiently clear reason is supplied for Edmund's delay in attempting to save Cordelia and Lear (244–6). But, as he finally answers, 'the real cause lies outside the dramatic *nexus*. It is Shakespeare's wish to deliver a sudden and crushing blow to the hopes which he has excited'. Shakespeare can rely on stage presentation to cover difficulties that careful reading discloses.

239. Yet. Edmund remarks to himself, with surprise, that here at least were two women who loved him. Perhaps we may see here that Shakespeare had pierced to what modern psychologists find to be the basis of most juvenile delinquency, the lack of the feeling of security and being loved. Edmund was not wanted at home (cf. I. i. 31–32).

242. Webster, consciously or unconsciously, remembered this to good effect in his famous: 'Cover her face; mine eyes dazzle; she died young' (*Duchess of Malfi*, IV. ii. 262).

251. [**Haste thee, for thy life.** F gives this speech to Edgar, and then another person must be found for the message, i.e. Exit Messenger or Captain. If we keep Q's assignment of the speech to Albany it is natural to make Edgar carry the message; and this suits 248.]

255. In the chroniclers Cordelia *did* commit suicide 'being a woman of a manlie courage, and despairing to recover libertie' (Holinshed). Cordelia's murder is the climax of cruelty in Shakespeare's exploration of evil in this play. Johnson could not bear to re-read it (see Select Criticism), and before we smile at him let us be sure we *feel* as much as he did from our reading!

256–7. After the s.d. 'Enter Lear with Cordelia in his arms' 'There should be a long, still pause, while Lear passes slowly in with his burden, while they all stand, respectful as of old to his majesty. . . . The same company are here, or all but the same, as in the first scene, and they await his pleasure. Even Regan and Goneril are here to pay him a ghastly homage. And this must not be counted as chance, for the bodies of Goneril and Regan are brought on— why else ?—and the dying Edmund, who might as well be dead and no great inconvenience, is removed' (GB).

257. **You are men of stones.** The modern idiom would require 'stone', but the use of the plural may arise from such an expression as *Julius Caesar*, I. i. 38–39:

> You blocks, you stones, you worse than senseless things!

In the next two lines Lear reverts to something of his language in the storm scene.

274. Lear retains his physical strength even in old age and mental weakness. In this the hero of *A Lear of the Steppes*, a short novel by Turgenev, most resembles his prototype, tearing off the roof of a house with his own hands; but the resemblance does not go much farther than the strength, the madness, and the ingratitude of daughters. A reading of the tale is as helpful as a reading of the old play of *Leir* to the appreciation of Shakespeare's achievement.

282. It is also possible (cf. footnote) that Lear is referring, as in 279, to his own failing sight, the result of his state of mind as much as of physical failing. In I. i his misjudgement of Kent was entirely due to moral blindness. So another of the chief image patterns of this play, sight and insight, is kept before us to the end, just as are those of clothes and animals by 306–9.

305–11. It is almost an impertinence to comment on one of the most moving passages in Shakespeare, especially when part of the power comes from the very simplicity of the fivefold repetition of the simple word 'never'. It is, however, necessary to point out that the 'poor fool' must in this context refer primarily to Cordelia, who has just been hanged. It may well be that Lear has also a confused remembrance of another 'fool' who was loyal to him although he was not hanged. It is part of Shakespeare's genius that he, unlike a classical tragedian, a Sophocles, or a Racine, will at such a moment bring in such homely ideas as 309 (cf. III. iv. 106: 'Unbutton here'. Lear feels a feeling of suffocation, preparatory to his heart bursting with grief. Then, for a moment, he thinks he sees breath rising from Cordelia's lips, or staining the mirror (262), and dies in an ecstasy of joy. 'Though he is killed by an agony of pain, the agony in which he actually dies is one not of pain but of ecstasy. . . . It seems almost beyond question that any actor is false to the text who does not attempt to express in Lear's last accents and gestures and look an unbearable *joy*.' Bradley (whose interpretation is endorsed by Granville-Barker as 'just such a fine piece of perception as we expect from him' and by R. W. Chambers in *King Lear*, 1942, a notable essay) compares the transition at 310 to that at the word 'Ha' in 271. In Sidney's *Arcadia* the Paphlagonian King died of 'excess of comfort' after his heart had been 'broken with unkindness and affliction' (Book ii, c. x of 1590 *Arcadia*, p. 212, ed. Feuillerat).

312. **Look up.** Edgar had used the words literally to his father at iv. vi. 59; taken in a more metaphorical sense they seem to suit the character that is gradually developed for him.

321. Kent's journey, of course, is to:

> The undiscover'd country from whose bourn
> No traveller returns

though the 'master' of 322 is Lear, not God or Christ.

Lamb, after quoting parts of 278-315, comments thus:

'So ends *King Lear*, the most stupendous of Shakespeare's dramas; and Kent, the noblest feature of the conceptions of his divine mind. This is the magnanimity of authorship, when a writer, having a topic presented to him fruitful of beauties for common minds, waives his privileges, and trusts to the judicious few for understanding the reason of his abstinence. What a pudder would a common dramatist have raised here of a reconciliation scene, a perfect recognition, between the assumed Caius and his master!— to the suffusing of many fair eyes, and the moistening of cambric handkerchiefs. The old dying king partially catching at the truth, and immediately lapsing into obliviousness, with the high-minded carelessness of the other to have his services appreciated, as one that

> served not for gain,
> Or followed out of form,

are among the most judicious, not to say heart-touching, strokes in Shakespeare' ('Table Talk by the late Elia' in the *Athenaeum*, 1834).

323-6. The rhyming couplets (from 319) give a kind of proverbial ring which prelude the end and make it unnecessary to attach too precise a meaning to 324, which commentators appear to have ignored.

Many editors give this last speech to Albany following F, partly on the ground that the final words should be in the mouth of one of the more important characters. But the Q attribution to Edgar enables him to answer Albany's invitation, while the reference to his youth seems more appropriate to Edgar. In fact if we consider the part taken by Edgar, particularly his words in the course of this act, we may find a ray of hope in that the last word lies with this 'very Christian gentleman' (GB).

SELECT LITERARY CRITICISM

The Play in General

(The extracts here are in chronological order)

ONE of the most remarkable differences betwixt ancient and modern tragedy, arises from the prevailing custom of describing only those distresses that are occasioned by the passion of love; a passion which, from the universality of its dominion, may doubtless justly claim a large share in representations of human life; but which, by totally engrossing the theatre, hath contributed to degrade that noble school of virtue into an academy of effeminacy. . . .

Shakespeare has shewn us, by his *Hamlet*, *Macbeth*, and *Caesar*, and above all by his *Lear*, that very interesting tragedies may be written, that are not founded on gallantry and love. . . . The distresses in this tragedy are of a very uncommon nature, and are not touched upon by any other dramatic author. . . . I shall confine myself at present to consider singly the judgment and art of the poet, in describing the origin and progress of the distraction of Lear; in which, I think, he has succeeded better than any other writer; even than Euripides himself, whom Longinus so highly commends for his representation of the madness of Orestes.

It is well contrived, that the first affront that is offered Lear, should be a proposal from Gonerill, his eldest daughter, to lessen the number of his knights, which must needs affect and irritate a person so jealous of his rank and the respect due to it. He is at first astonished at the complicated impudence and ingratitude of this design; but quickly kindles into rage, and resolves to depart instantly:

> —Darkness and devils!—
> Saddle my horses, call my train together—
> Degen'rate bastard, I'll not trouble thee.—

This is followed by a severe reflection upon his own folly for resigning his crown; and a solemn invocation to Nature, to heap the most horrible curses on the head of Gonerill, that her own offspring may prove equally cruel and unnatural;

> —That she may feel,
> How sharper than a serpent's tooth it is,
> To have a thankless child!—

When Albany demands the cause of this passion, Lear answers, 'I'll tell thee!', but immediately cries out to Gonerill,

> —Life and death! I am asham'd,
> That thou hast power to shake my manhood thus.
> —Blasts and fogs upon thee!
> Th' untented woundings of a father's curse
> Pierce every sense about thee!

He stops a little and reflects:

> Ha! is it come to this?
> Let it be so! I have another daughter,
> Who, I am sure, is kind and comfortable.
> When she shall hear this of thee, with her nails
> She'll flea thy wolfish visage—

He was, however, mistaken; for the first object he encounters in the castle of the Earl of Gloucester, whither he fled to meet his other daughter, was his servant in the stocks; from whence he may easily conjecture what reception he is to meet with:

> —Death on my state! Wherefore
> Should he sit here?

He adds immediately afterwards,

> O me, my heart! my rising heart!—but down.

By which single line, the inexpressible anguish of his mind, and the dreadful conflict of opposite passions with which it is agitated, are more forcibly expressed, than by the long and laboured speech, enumerating the causes of his anguish, that Rowe and other modern tragic writers would certainly have put into his mouth. But Nature, Sophocles, and Shakespeare, represent the feelings of the heart in a different manner; by a broken hint, a short exclamation, a word, or a look.

J. WARTON, from The *Adventurer*, Dec. 4th 1753

THE Tragedy of *Lear* is deservedly celebrated among the dramas of Shakespeare. There is perhaps no play which keeps the attention so strongly fixed; which so much agitates our passions and interests our curiosity. The artful involutions of distinct interests, the striking opposition of contrary characters, the sudden changes of fortune, and the quick succession of events, fill the mind with a perpetual tumult of indignation, pity, and hope. There is no scene which does not contribute to the aggravation of the distress or conduct of the action, and scarce a line which does not conduce to the progress of the scene. So powerful is the current of the poet's imagination, that the mind, which once ventures within it, is hurried irresistibly along. . . .

My learned friend Mr. Warton, who has in the *Adventurer* very minutely criticised this play, remarks, that the instances of cruelty are too savage and shocking, and that the intervention of Edmund destroys the simplicity of the story. These objections may, I think, be answered, by repeating, that the cruelty of the daughters is an historical fact, to which the poet has added little, having only drawn it into a series by dialogue and action. But I am not able to apologise with equal plausibility for the extrusion of Gloucester's eyes, which seems an act too horrid to be endured in dramatick exhibition, and such as must always compel the mind to relieve its distress by incredulity. Yet let it be remembered that our authour well knew what would please the audience for which he wrote.

The injury done by Edmund to the simplicity of the action is abundantly recompensed by the addition of variety, by the art with which he is made to co-operate with the chief design and the opportunity which he gives the poet of combining perfidy with perfidy, and connecting the wicked son with the wicked daughters, to impress this important moral, that villainy is never at a stop, that crimes lead to crimes, and at last terminate in ruin.

But though this moral be incidentally exposed, Shakespeare has suffered the virtue of Cordelia to perish in a just cause, contrary to the natural ideas of justice, to the hope of the reader, and, what is yet more strange, to the faith of chronicles. Yet this conduct is justified by the *Spectator*, who blames Tate for giving Cordelia success and happiness in his alteration, and declares, that, in his opinion, 'the tragedy has lost half its beauty'. Dennis has remarked, whether justly or not, that, to secure the favourable reception of Cato, 'the town was poisoned with much false and abominable criticism', and that endeavours had been used to discredit and decry poetical justice. A play in which the wicked prosper, and the virtuous miscarry, may doubtless be good, because it is a just representation of the common events of human life: but since all reasonable beings naturally love justice, I cannot easily be persuaded, that the observation of justice makes a play worse; or, that if other excellencies are equal, the audience will not always rise better pleased from the final triumph of persecuted virtue.

In the present case the publick has decided. Cordelia, from the time of Tate, has always retired with victory and felicity. And, if my sensations could add any thing to the general suffrage, I might relate, that I was many years ago so shocked by Cordelia's death, that I know not whether I ever endured to read again the last scenes of the play till I undertook to revise them as an editor.

s. JOHNSON, edition of Shakespeare, 1765

It is then the best of all Shakespear's plays, for it is the one in which he was the most in earnest. He was here fairly caught in the web of his own imagination. The passion which he has taken as his subject is that which strikes its root deepest into the human heart; of which the bond is the hardest to be unloosed; and the cancelling and tearing to pieces of which gives the greatest revulsion to the frame. This depth of nature, this force of passion, this tug and war of the elements of our being, this firm faith in filial piety, and the giddy anarchy and whirling tumult of the thoughts at finding this prop failing it, the contrast between the fixed, immoveable basis of natural affection, and the rapid, irregular starts of imagination, suddenly wrenched from all its accustomed holds and resting-places in the soul, this is what Shakespear has given, and what nobody else but he could give. So we believe.—The mind of Lear, staggering between the weight of attachment and the hurried movements of passion, is like a tall ship driven about by the winds, buffeted by the furious waves, but that still rides above the storm, having its anchor fixed in the bottom of the sea; or it is like the sharp rock circled by the eddying whirlpool that foams and beats against it, or like the solid promontory pushed from its basis by the force of an earthquake. . . . It has been said, and we think justly, that the third act of *Othello* and the three first acts of *Lear*, are Shakespear's great master-pieces in the logic of passion: that they contain the highest examples not only of the force of individual passion, but of its dramatic vicissitudes and striking effects arising from the different circumstances and characters of the persons speaking.

W. HAZLITT, *Characters of Shakespear's Plays*, 1817

FROM want of regular rest I have been rather *narvus*—and the passage in *Lear*—'Do you not hear the sea' [IV, vi] has haunted me intensely. . . . Whenever you write say a word or two on some new Passage in Shakespear that may have come rather new to you, which must be continually happening, notwithstanding that we read the same Play forty times. . . . I find I cannot exist without Poetry—without eternal Poetry . . .

KEATS, Letter to Reynolds, April 17th–18th, 1817

THE excellence of every art is its intensity, capable of making all disagreeables evaporate from their being in close relationship with Beauty and Truth. Examine *King Lear*, and you will find this exemplified throughout.

KEATS, Letter to George and Thomas Keats, Dec. 1817

I SAT down to read *King Lear* yesterday and felt the greatness of the thing up to the writing of a Sonnet preparatory thereto . . .

KEATS, Letter to Bailey, Jan. 1818

I SAT down yesterday to read *King Lear* once again: the thing appeared to demand the prologue of a sonnet, I wrote it, and began to read—I know you would like to see it.

O golden tongued Romance, with serene lute!
Fair plumed Syren, Queen of far-away!

Leave melodizing on this wintry day,
Shut up thine olden pages, and be mute:
Adieu! for, once again, the fierce dispute
    Betwixt damnation and impassion'd clay
    Must I burn through; once more humbly assay
The bitter-sweet of this Shakespearian fruit:
Chief Poet! and ye clouds of Albion,
    Begetters of our deep eternal theme!
When through the old oak Forest I am gone,
    Let me not wander in a barren dream,
    But, when I am consumed in the fire,
Give me new Phoenix wings to fly at my desire.

KEATS, *Letter to George and Thomas Keats*, Jan. 1818

THE modern practice of blending comedy with tragedy, though liable to great abuse in point of practice, is undoubtedly an extension of the dramatic circle; but the comedy should be as in *King Lear*, universal, ideal, and sublime. It is perhaps the intervention of this principle which determines the balance in favour of *King Lear* against the *Oedipus Tyrannus* or the *Agamemnon*, or, if you will, the tragedies with which they are connected; unless the intense power of the choral poetry, especially that of the latter, should be considered as restoring the equilibrium. *King Lear*, if it can sustain this comparison, may be judged to be the most perfect specimen of the dramatic art existing in the world.

SHELLEY, *A Defence of Poetry*, 1821

SAVE for a few beauties of lyrical eloquence in the famous tenth scene, and some fairly profound philosophical reflections (if we take the trouble to fathom them) in the mad scene proper—all of which is quickly told—with these exceptions, all the rest is no more than a heap of stupid crimes, foolish horrors, and idiotic vices. It is what I call, using a perhaps unjust and undoubtedly hybrid term, *bruto-tragedy* or *bruto-drama*. . . . With the exception of the short portions which I have reserved nothing is easier to put together. There is not a man in Europe at the present time (and I would even include the last 100 years) who would be capable of writing *Hamlet*, or *Othello*, or even *The*

Tempest. But almost anybody, no matter who, could write *King Lear*, with the exception of a few passages, which, all taken together, would barely fill a page. The characters, with their summary and almost childish psychology, all of a piece in their ignominious brutality, do not even arouse our curiosity.

E. FAGUET, *Journal des Débats*, 1905
(Quoted by M. Maeterlinck, trans. A. T. de Mattos.)

IT is safe to declare, after surveying the literature of every period and of every country, that the tragedy of the old king constitutes the mightiest, the vastest, the most stirring, the most intense dramatic poem that has ever been written. Were we to be asked from the height of another planet which is the synthetic play representative and archetypal of the human stage, the play in which the ideal of the loftiest scenic poetry is most fully realized, it seems to me certain that, after due deliberation, all the poets of our earth, the best judges in this exigency, would with one voice name *King Lear*. They could only for a moment weigh the claims of two or three masterpieces of the Greek stage, or else—for virtually Shakespeare can be compared with none save himself—of that other miracle of his genius, the tragic story of Hamlet, Prince of Denmark.

Prometheus, the *Orestes*, *Oedipus Tyrannus* are wonderful but isolated trees, whereas *King Lear* is a marvellous forest. . . . By the side of *King Lear*, the longest of Greek tragedies are hardly more than plays in one act. . . . *King Lear* remains the youngest of the great tragic works, the only one which time has not touched. It needs an effort of our good will, a forgetting of our place and of our present certainties, for us to be sincerely and wholly stirred by the spectacle of *Hamlet*, *Macbeth* or *Oedipus*. . . . The youngest, the most unchangeable of tragedies is also the most organically lyrical dramatic poem that was ever realised, the only one in the world in which the magnificence of the language does not once injure the probability, the naturalness of the dialogue.

M. MAETERLINCK, 'King Lear in Paris', trans. by A. T. de
Mattos, *Fortnightly Review*, 1905

Plot and Structure

OF the secondary plot of this tragedy—the story of Gloucester and his sons—Schlegel has explained one chief significance: 'Were Lear alone to suffer from his daughters, the impression would be limited to the powerful compassion felt by us for his private misfortune. But two such unheard-of examples taking place at the same time have the appearance of a great commotion in the moral world; the picture becomes gigantic, and fills us with such alarm as we should entertain at the idea that the heavenly bodies might one day fall from their appointed orbits.' The treachery of Edmund, and the torture to which Gloucester is subjected, are out of the course of familiar experience; but they are commonplace and prosaic in comparison with the inhumanity of the sisters, and the agony of Lear. When we have climbed the steep ascent of Gloucester's mount of passion, we see still above us another *via dolorosa* leading to that

> Wall of eagle-baffling mountain,
> Black, wintry, dead, unmeasured,

to which Lear is chained. Thus the one story of horror serves as a means of approach to the other, and helps us to conceive its magnitude. The two, as Schlegel observes, produce the impression of a great commotion in the moral world. The thunder which breaks over our head does not suddenly cease to resound, but is reduplicated, multipled, and magnified, and rolls away with long reverberation.

E. DOWDEN, *Shakspere, His Mind and Art*, 1875

THE plot, thus conceived less in terms of common realism than as an extension of the poetry, becomes in effect itself an expanded image, the 'symbolic' reflection of an experience which the poet, following the promptings of his creative impulse, is concerned to mould into a finished artistic form.

The story of *King Lear*, in some way the most complex and deliberately constructed of all Shakespeare's great tragedies, is precisely of this kind. There is a very real sense in which the whole action of the tragedy might be described as a projection of the conflicting issues supremely present in the mind of the central protagonist. As father, Lear produces in his daughters contrasted reactions which reflect different and contradictory facets of his own mind; as king, his wilful impulses liberate forces of social anarchy which nothing less than utter exhaustion can ultimately contain. From the conflict, whose dual aspect is thus concentrated in one mind, the various subsidiary issues of the play radiate as partial reflections of a common image, at once contributing depth and variety to the central situation and deriving from it the subsistent unity which alone can give the complete story its full meaning. In none of Shakespeare's mature plays is the correspondence between action and motive, the external event and its inner meaning, so exactly and so significantly achieved.

Both these aspects of Lear's position, the personal and the social, contribute to the unity of a tragedy whose various stages correspond, in the external action, to a closely-knit development. The first stage in this development, occupying roughly the first two acts, is concerned with the entry of uncontrolled passion as a disruptive force into Lear's mind and with the consequent overthrow of ordered balance in himself, in his family, and in the state, of whose unity he has been hitherto the royal guardian. In the second stage, which covers the central part of the play, personal disorder finds in the tempest to which the protagonists are exposed a symbol which at once reflects and transcends it; the elements at war, besides corresponding to the conflict in Lear's distraught person, act through the intense suffering which they impose upon him with the force of a self-revelation to become the necessary prelude to spiritual re-birth. That re-birth, however, although achieved in the personal order during the third and final stage, cannot affect Lear's external fortunes. His reconciliation with Cordelia in the fourth act is followed almost immediately by their final defeat and death against a background of almost unrelieved disaster; the personal and the social themes, hitherto so closely united, now separate to produce the concluding catastrophe, and the tragedy, after touching unprecedented heights in its treatment of the personal theme, is rounded off in a mood of Stoic acceptance.

D. TRAVERSI, *Scrutiny*, vol. xix, 1949

SHAKSPERE did not in this play feel that mere historical verisimilitude was of chief importance. . . . The old 'Chronicle History of King Leir' had assigned ingenious motives for the apparently improbable conduct assigned to the King. He resolves that upon Cordelia's protesting that she loves him he will say, 'Then, daughter, grant me one request,—accept the husband I have chosen for you', and thus he will take her at a vantage . . . Shakspere could, if he had chosen, by psychological fence have turned aside the weapons of those assailants who lay this charge improbability and unnaturalness. But then the keynote of the play would have been struck in another mode.

DOWDEN, op. cit.

King Lear *and* Hamlet

THE chief difference between *Hamlet* and *King Lear* is, I think, this. In *Hamlet* we see, predominantly, a mind faltering before the wickedness of men and women and before the difficulties of conduct and all its huge implications. In *King Lear* we see, chiefly, the wickedness itself. It is true enough that Lear's own mind does more than falter: it collapses. Still, I say that it is not chiefly the mind of Lear we observe and study, but the world's savagery as it overwhelms it. In *Hamlet* we see the weakened mind; in *King Lear* we see the world in its power breaking a mind. It is to be observed that in *Hamlet* we *see* little enough wickedness. . . . But if in *Hamlet* we see little enough of the fierce working of human evil, we see enough of it in *King Lear*. Goneril, Regan, Edmund, Cornwall, Oswald we see in their lusts of cruelty and anger. Therefore we can say that *Hamlet* shows us the reception of an ascertained evil by a mind; *King Lear* shows us the evil, continuing and terrible, in its actual and physical onset upon a mind. Hamlet's is a soul in which wickedness is imaged with all its consequences for thought and feeling; Lear's is a soul which will not receive that image. It rejects it, incredulously; but the wickedness falls upon it, not as an image, but as a succession of shattering blows. . . . Still, we may fairly remark that Hamlet was treated more gently than Lear; Lear's suffering, when all is said and done, was far greater than Hamlet's. We may allow that Lear was more the originator of his troubles than Hamlet of his; but it remains true, and beyond question, I think, that Lear evokes from us more pity than Hamlet. Hamlet has, at the end of the play, to win our pity by more than a touch of self-pity; Lear wins our pity because he has gone through a fire which has purged him of what, earlier in the play, had indeed been a disposition to feel pity for himself. Hamlet excuses himself, and we are willing enough for him to do so; Lear only asks to be forgiven.

It is, I think, in some such way or ways, that we see the difference between *Hamlet* and *King Lear*. *Hamlet* explores a mind arrested in dubiety before the awful problem of life; *King Lear* explores life itself. In *Hamlet* life itself is shifted off into some distance; it is misted o'er with the pale cast of thought; it loses its sting, its demand, its peremptoriness; it is arrested as far as possible in order to give play to the arrest in Hamlet's mind. But in *King Lear* it is not so. Shakespeare has turned from the torturing image to the masterful, brutal reality; and what, when he does so, does he chiefly see, and what is its prevailing pattern?

D. G. JAMES, *The Dream of Learning*, 1951

The Actability of King Lear

THE sublime images, the poetry alone, is that which is present to our minds in the reading.

So to see Lear acted,—to see an old man tottering about the stage with a walking-stick, turned out of doors by his daughters in a rainy night, has nothing in it but what is painful and disgusting. We want to take him into shelter and relieve him. That is all the feeling which the acting of Lear ever produced in me. But the Lear of Shakespeare cannot be acted. The contemptible machinery by which they mimic the storm which he goes out in, is not more inadequate to represent the horrors of the real elements, than any actor can be to represent Lear: they might more easily propose to personate the Satan of Milton upon a stage, or one of Michael Angelo's terrible figures. The greatness of Lear is not in corporal dimension, but in intellectual: the explosions of his passion are terrible as a volcano: they are storms turning up and disclosing to the bottom that sea, his mind, with all its vast riches. It is his mind which is laid bare. This case of flesh and blood seems too insignificant to be thought on; even as he himself neglects it. On the stage we see nothing but corporal infirmities and weakness, the impotence of rage; while we read it, we see not Lear, but we are Lear,—we are in his mind, we are sustained by a grandeur which baffles the malice of daughters and storms; in the aberrations of his reason, we discover a mighty irregular power of reasoning, immethodized from the ordinary purposes of life, but exerting its powers, as the wind blows where it listeth, at will upon the corruptions and abuses of mankind. What have looks, or tones, to do with that sublime identification of his age with that of the *heavens themselves*, when in his reproaches to them for conniving at the injustice of his children, he reminds them that 'they themselves are old'. What gesture shall we appropriate to this? What has the voice or the eye to do with such things? But the play is beyond all art, as the tamperings with it shew: it is too hard and stony; it must have love-scenes, and a happy ending. It is not enough that Cordelia is a daughter, she must shine as a lover too. Tate has put his hook in the nostrils of this Leviathan, for Garrick and his followers, the showmen of the scene, to draw the mighty beast about more easily. A happy ending!— as if the living martyrdom that Lear had gone through,—the flaying of his feelings alive, did not make a fair dismissal from the stage of life the only decorous thing for him. If he is to live and be happy after, if he could sustain this world's burden after, why all this pudder and preparation,—why torment us with all this unnecessary sympathy? As if the childish pleasure of getting his gilt robes and sceptre again could tempt him to act over again his misused station,—as if at his years, and with his experience, any thing was left but to die.

LAMB, *On The Tragedies of Shakespeare*, 1811

THE stage is the test of strictly dramatic quality, and *King Lear* is too huge for the stage. Of course, I am not denying that it is a great stage-play. It has scenes immensely effective in the theatre; three of them—the two between Lear and Goneril and between Lear, Goneril and Regan, and the ineffably beautiful scene in the Fourth Act between Lear and Cordelia—lose in the theatre very little of the spell they have for the imagination; and the gradual interweaving of the two plots is almost as masterly as in *Much Ado*. But (not to speak of defects due to mere carelessness) that which makes the *peculiar* greatness of *King Lear*,—the immense scope of the work; the mass and variety of intense experience which it contains; the interpene-tration of sublime imagination, piercing pathos, and humour almost as moving as the pathos; the vastness of the convulsion both of nature and of human passion; the vagueness of the scene where the action takes place, and of the movements of the figures which cross this scene; the strange atmosphere, cold and dark, which strikes on us as we enter this scene, enfolding these figures and magnifying their dim outlines like a winter mist; the half-realised suggestions of vast universal powers working in the world of individual fates and passions,—all this interferes with dramatic clearness even when the play is read, and in the theatre not only refuses to reveal itself fully through the senses but seems to be almost in contradiction with their reports. . . .

The truth is that all through these Acts Shakespeare has too vast a material to use with complete dramatic effectiveness, however essential this very vastness was for effects of another kind. . . .

The influence of all this on imagination as we read *King Lear* is very great; and it combines with other influences to convey to us, not in the form of distinct ideas but in the manner proper to poetry, the wider or universal significance of the spectacle presented to the inward eye. But the effect of theatrical exhibition is precisely the reverse. There the poetic atmosphere is dissipated; the meaning of the very words which create it passes half-realised; in obedience to the tyranny of the eye we conceive the characters as mere particular men and women; and all that mass of vague suggestion, if it enters the mind at all, appears in the shape of an allegory which we immediately reject. A similar conflict between imagination and sense will be found if we consider the dramatic centre of the whole tragedy,

the Storm-scenes. The temptation of Othello and the scene of
Duncan's murder may lose upon the stage, but they do not lose
their essence, and they gain as well as lose. The Storm-scenes
in *King Lear* gain nothing and their very essence is destroyed.
It is comparatively a small thing that the theatrical storm, not
to drown the dialogue, must be silent whenever a human being
wishes to speak, and is wretchedly inferior to many a storm we
have witnessed. Nor is it simply that, as Lamb observed, the
corporal presence of Lear, 'an old man tottering about the
stage with a walking-stick,' disturbs and depresses that sense
of the greatness of his mind which fills the imagination. There
is a further reason, which is not expressed, but still emerges, in
these words of Lamb's: 'the explosions of his passion are terrible
as a volcano: they are storms turning up and disclosing to the
bottom that sea, his mind, with all its vast riches.' Yes, 'they
are *storms*.' For imagination, that is to say, the explosions of
Lear's passion, and the bursts of rain and thunder, are not,
what for the senses they must be, two things, but manifestations
of one thing. It is the powers of the tormented soul that we hear
and see in the 'groans of roaring wind and rain' and the 'sheets
of fire'; and they that, at intervals almost more overwhelming,
sink back into darkness and silence. Nor yet is even this all;
but, as those incessant references to wolf and tiger made us see
humanity 'reeling back into the beast' and ravening against
itself, so in the storm we seem to see Nature herself convulsed
by the same horrible passions; the 'common mother,'

> Whose womb immeasurable and infinite breast
> Teems and feeds all,

turning on her children, to complete the ruin they have wrought
upon themselves. Surely something not less, but much more,
than these helpless words convey, is what comes to us in these
astounding scenes; and if, translated thus into the language of
prose, it becomes confused and inconsistent, the reason is simply
that it itself is poetry, and such poetry as cannot be transferred
to the space behind the foot-lights, but has its being only in the
imagination. Here then is Shakespeare at his very greatest,
but not the mere dramatist Shakespeare.

A. C. BRADLEY, *Shakespearean Tragedy*, 1904

DR. BRADLEY seems to assume that every sort of play, when acted, ought in a single performance to make a clear, complete and final effect on the spectator. But this is surely not so. We need no more expect to receive—lapses of performance and attention apart—the full value of a great drama at a first hearing than we expect it of a complex piece of music.

King Lear was meant to be acted. Inadequate and misdirected acting of it there may be, by which we must not judge it ; and no perfect performance of any play by imperfect human beings can there ever be. Shakespeare may have been wrong to make a play of it. Nor, if he did strain his medium of expression beyond endurance, would he be the first great artist to do so. But he put his purpose to the proof ; and so should we—to every proof, before we ignore this for the sake of disparate gains beyond.

H. GRANVILLE BARKER, *Prefaces to Shakespeare* (First Series), 1927

THE scenes on the heath . . . should be imagined in relation to the opening of the play ; the contrast of visual impression, the contrast in tableau, must be concretely perceived by the eye as the contrast of rhythm and word by the ear. In the opening scene Lear is surrounded by his court: a page holds the crown on a velvet cushion, the King of France the Duke of Burgundy and a crowd of brilliantly dressed courtiers all wait upon his imperious commands. But in the heath scenes his only companions are a fool, a madman. . . . We see him reduced to relying on the lowest dregs of human nature, his mind in pieces, trying to get reality by stripping off his clothes.

T. SPENCER, *Shakespeare and the Nature of Man*, 1942

The Characters

The Contrasted Groups

STRUCTURALLY the most significant of the groups is the Goneril-Regan-Edmund trio: to Lear's reason-in-madness there is opposed their tainted reason [madness-in-reason], a self-confident, unshackled sharpness of mind, shrewd and penetrating as far as it goes, but incapable, ultimately, of detecting its own frailty and limitations, of formulating a workable pattern of existence, and of bringing to them the saving insights of men of imagination. It is these devotees of the analytical mind, finally, who—with such exception as must be made for Edmund's partial defection—are less perceptive than Edgar, less understanding than the Fool, more mad than Lear; and who, to fill out the pattern, are more deluded and less free than their victims, are less 'successful' than those who had stuck to a waning cause, to symbols apparently outmoded. It is they, too, and their followers, who do not call upon the gods, as Edgar and Albany and Kent do, and—more markedly—Gloucester and Lear, although even to these devotees the gods may appear inevitable.

R. B. HEILMAN, *This Great Stage*, 1948

Lear

IT would seem that for this massive fortress of pride which calls itself Lear, for any old man indeed of eighty and upwards, there could be no dramatic course but declension. Who would ever think of developing, of expanding, a character from such overwhelming beginnings? Yet this is what Shakespeare does, and finds a transcendent way to do. So the actor's difficulty is that he must start upon a top note, at what must be pretty well the full physical stretch of his powers, yet have in reserve the means to a greater climax of another sort altogether. It is here, however, that the almost ritual formality of the first scene will help him. The occasion itself, the general subservience to Lear's tyranny (Kent's protest and Cordelia's resolution only emphasise this), Lear's own assertion of kingship as something not far from godhead, all combine to set him so above and apart from the rest that the very isolation will seem strength if the actor takes care to sustain it.

GRANVILLE BARKER, op. cit.

A TREMENDOUS soul is, as it were, incongruously geared to a puerile intellect. . . . Lear is mentally a child, in passion a titan.

G. WILSON KNIGHT, *The Wheel of Fire*, 1930

Cordelia

LEAR's words,

> Let pride, which she calls plainness, marry her!

are monstrously unjust, but they contain one grain of truth;
and indeed it was scarcely possible that a nature so strong as
Cordelia's, and with so keen a sense of dignity, should feel here
nothing whatever of pride and resentment. This side of her
character is emphatically shown in her language to her sisters
in the first scene—language perfectly just, but little adapted to
soften their hearts towards their father—and again in the very
last words we hear her speak. She and her father are brought in,
prisoners, to the enemy's camp; but she sees only Edmund,
not those 'greater' ones on whose pleasure hangs her father's
fate and her own. For her own she is little concerned; she
knows how to meet adversity:

> For thee, oppressed king, am I cast down;
> Myself could else out-frown false fortune's frown.

Yes, that is how she would meet fortune, frowning it down,
even as Goneril would have met it; nor, if her father had been
already dead, would there have been any great improbability
in the false story that was to be told of her death, that, like
Goneril, she 'fordid herself.' Then, after those austere words
about fortune, she suddenly asks,

> Shall we not see these daughters and these sisters?

Strange last words for us to hear from a being so worshipped
and beloved; but how characteristic! Their tone is unmistak-
able. I doubt if she could have brought herself to plead with
her sisters for her father's life; and if she had attempted the
task, she would have performed it but ill.

BRADLEY, op. cit.

MIGHT not some of the understanding of and tenderness for her
father exhibited at the end have saved the situation at the
beginning? The probable answer is 'yes'. But until her experience of life had brought her the power to understand she
was powerless to exhibit the necessary tenderness.

J. S. H. BRANSOM, *The Tragedy of Lear*, 1934

Edgar

I SPOKE of his temperament. There is in Edgar, with much else that is fine, something of that buoyancy of spirit which charms us in Imogen. Nothing can subdue in him the feeling that life is sweet and must be cherished. At his worst, misconstrued, contemned, exiled, under sentence of death, 'the lowest and most dejected thing of fortune', he keeps his head erect. The inextinguishable spirit of youth and delight is in him ; he *embraces* the unsubstantial air which has blown him to the worst ; for him 'the worst returns to laughter.' 'Bear free and patient thoughts,' he says to his father. His own thoughts are more than patient, they are 'free,' even joyous, in spite of the tender sympathies which strive in vain to overwhelm him. This ability to feel and offer great sympathy with distress, without losing through the sympathy any elasticity or strength, is a noble quality, sometimes found in souls like Edgar's, naturally buoyant and also religious. It may even be characteristic of him that, when Lear is sinking down in death, he tries to rouse him and bring him back to life. 'Look up, my lord!' he cries.   BRADLEY, op. cit.

Kent

KENT possesses no vision, like that which gladdens Edgar, of a divine providence. His loyalty to right has something in it of a desperate instinct, which persists in spite of the appearances presented by the world. Shakspere would have us know that there is not any devotion to truth, to justice, to charity more intense and real than that of the man who is faithful to them, out of the sheer spirit of loyalty, unstimulated and unsupported by any faith which can be called theological. Kent, who has seen the vicissitude of things, knows of no higher power presiding over the events of the world than fortune. Therefore, all the more, Kent clings to the passionate instinct of right-doing, and to the hardy temper, the fortitude which makes evil, when it happens to come, endurable.

DOWDEN, op. cit.

KENT is, perhaps, the nearest to perfect goodness in all Shakespeare's characters, and yet the most individualised.

COLERIDGE, *Lectures on Shakespeare*, 1818

Edmund

FROM the first drawing up of the curtain Edmund has stood before us in the united strength and beauty of earliest manhood. Our eyes have been questioning him. Gifted as he is with high advantages of person, and further endowed by nature with a powerful intellect and a strong energetic will, even without any concurrence of circumstances and accident, pride will necessarily be the sin that most easily besets him. But Edmund is also the known and acknowledged son of the princely Gloster: he, therefore, has both the germ of pride, and the conditions best fitted to evolve and ripen it into a predominant feeling. Yet hitherto no reason appears why it should be other than the not unusual pride of person, talent, and birth,—a pride auxiliary, if not akin, to many virtues, and the natural ally of honourable impulses. But alas! in his own presence his own father takes shame to himself for the frank avowal that he is his father,—he has 'blushed so often to acknowledge him that he is now brazed to it!' Edmund hears the circumstances of his birth spoken of with a most degrading and licentious levity,—his mother described as a wanton by her own paramour, and the remembrance of the animal sting, the low criminal gratifications connected with her wantonness and prostituted beauty, assigned as the reason, why 'the whoreson must be acknowledged!' This, and the consciousness of its notoriety: the gnawing conviction that every show of respect is an effort of courtesy, which recalls, while it represses, a contrary feeling;—this is the ever trickling flow of wormwood and gall into the wounds of pride,—the corrosive *virus* which inoculates pride with a venom not its own, with envy, hatred, and a lust for that power which in its blaze of radiance would hide the dark spots on his disc,—with pangs of shame personally undeserved and therefore felt as wrongs, and with a blind ferment of vindictive working towards the occasions and causes, especially towards a brother, whose stainless birth and lawful honours were the constant remembrancers of his own debasement, and were ever in the way to prevent all chance of its being unknown, or overlooked and forgotten.

COLERIDGE, op. cit.

Albany

I WOULD invite notice to a point in [King Lear] of great structural and dramatic significance which has not, I think, received adequate notice. This is the part taken in it by Albany. He is generally thought of as only on the second plane of the drama, and as of little importance. Really, he is the pivot on which it all turns. He is central, inasmuch as he is the one character in the whole play who is from first to last completely sane, balanced, and normal. Sparing of words, unhurried and even slow in action, he is never either confused or hustled; and he can strike, when the time comes, with unhesitating certainty.

J. W. MACKAIL, *The Approach to Shakespeare*, 1930

The Fool

THE theatrical fool or clown (we need not distinguish them here) was a sore trial to the cultured poet and spectator in Shakespeare's day. He came down from the Morality plays, and was beloved of the groundlings. His antics, his songs, his dances, his jests, too often unclean, delighted them, and did something to make the drama, what the vulgar, poor or rich, like it to be, a variety entertainment. Even if he confined himself to what was set down for him, he often disturbed the dramatic unity of the piece; and the temptation to 'gag' was too strong for him to resist. Shakespeare makes Hamlet object to it in emphatic terms. The more learned critics and poets went further and would have abolished the fool altogether. His part declines as the drama advances, diminishing markedly at the end of the sixteenth century. Jonson and Massinger exclude him. Shakespeare used him—we know to what effect—as he used all the other popular elements of the drama; but he abstained from introducing him into the Roman plays, and there is no fool in the last of the pure tragedies, *Macbeth*.

But the Fool is one of Shakespeare's triumphs in *King Lear*. Imagine the tragedy without him, and you hardly know it. To remove him would spoil its harmony, as the harmony of a picture would be spoiled if one of the colours were extracted. One can almost imagine that Shakespeare, going home from an evening at the Mermaid, where he had listened to Jonson fulminating against fools in general and perhaps criticising the Clown in *Twelfth Night* in particular, had said to himself: 'Come, my friends, I will show you once for all that the mischief is in you, and not in the fool or the audience. I will have a fool in the most tragic of my tragedies. He shall not play a little part. He shall keep from first to last the company in which you most object to see him, the company of a king. Instead of amusing the king's idle hours, he shall stand by him in the very tempest and whirlwind of passion. Before I have done you shall confess, between laughter and tears, that he is of the very essence of life, that you have known him all your days though you never recognised him till now, and that you would as soon go without Hamlet as miss him.'   BRADLEY, op. cit.

IT has often seemed to me that the Fool was a constant reminder to all, especially to kings, of their subjection to Truth. Pomp and ceremony, the deference that hedges a position, cannot protect men ultimately from what is the fact, from the truth about themselves and the nature of life. Nothing in Shakespeare is more marvellous than the way in which the truth both of head and heart is brought home to Lear, through the medium of this despised and rejected among men. . . . Almost as much as the storm, the Fool breaks down the self-centred unconcern of Lear for his subjects, and teaches him by his very helplessness something of humility and humanity. . . .

It must be clear that function of the Fool, however useful he is in the theatrical way, is closely related to the spiritual process and meaning of the play. He can be the popular entertainer, but he also plays the part of the confidant of the hero of tragedy, to whom the hero turns for comment, advice, and companionship. It is the Fool's business to goad Lear, to stir his conscience, to make him realize the situation he is in. 'A

pestilent gall to me,' is his master's comment on one of his
gibes. Lear walks in a world of illusions; the Fool walks beside
him like a reflection of the truth. His speech, full of homely,
vivid figures, heightens the attractiveness of his part, makes it
more credible, yet softens the irritation of his persistent goading.
He could not reach the king with argument, but he can by a
homely image. When Lear is absent—and it is to be noted that
nearly all the Fool's talk in the play is with Lear, so that he is
quite literally *Lear's* Fool, nobody else's—when Lear is absent,
it is to Kent that the Fool urges prudence, and that in his own
despite, for it is not the kind that he himself can practise. . . .

Prudence, it is given to the Fool to see, is a virtue of the
calculating head, not of the impulsive heart. It belongs to the
orderly system which the mind creates out of the chaos of
experience, a system or order which is as necessary to our
thinking as classification is to the natural sciences, an order
which we have to trust, but which is always suspected by us,
since we know that the instrument with which we make it is
imperfect, and that the experience with which we work is far
from complete. Truth and wisdom and love, the Fool knows
and Lear is to discover, are by-products of living, not objectives
to be reached by calculation, or possessions to be used to serve
other ends. The Fool's appearance on the scene with wisdom
of the kind not provided for in our categories, and collected by
unorthodox means, is greatly satisfying to us. It is comforting
to think that there is more wisdom, and deeper, somewhere, than
we have been able to acquire, with all our directed cerebration.

J. M. LOTHIAN, *King Lear, A tragic reading of life*, 1949

THE producer to-day faces another difficulty. He finds a Fool
all etherealised by the higher criticism. His first care, in the
part's embodying, must be to see restored as much as may be
of its lost aboriginal strength. Its actor must sing like a lark,
juggle his words so that the mere skill delights us, and tumble
around with all the grace in the world. Satisfy these simpler
demands, and the subtleties will have their effect; neglect them,
and you might as well try to play tunes on a punctured organ
stop.   GRANVILLE BARKER, op. cit.

[The Fool's part was removed from the play in Nahum Tate's
    acting version of 1681 and is said not to have been put
    back on the stage till 1838.]

Imagery in King Lear

IN this play we are conscious all through of the atmosphere
of buffeting, strain and strife, and, at moments, of bodily tension
to the point of agony. So naturally does this flow from the
circumstances of the drama and the mental sufferings of Lear,
that we scarcely realize how greatly this sensation in us is
increased by the general 'floating' image, kept constantly
before us, chiefly by means of the verbs used, but also in metaphor, of a human body in anguished movement, tugged,
wrenched, beaten, pierced, stung, scourged, dislocated, flayed,
gashed, scalded, tortured, and finally broken on the rack.

C. F. E. SPURGEON, *Leading Motives in the Imagery of Shakespeare's Tragedies*, 1930

THE imagery here seems to be more fully integrated into the
structure of the drama and for that reason to play a more
meaningful role than in other plays. . . . Up to now, we have
found characters speaking exclusively in imagery only in
moments of the greatest excitement. In *King Lear*, however,
this is the case throughout many scenes; imagery is for Lear his
most characteristic form of utterance. More and more Lear
loses contact with the outside world; words become for him less
a means of communication with others than a means of expressing what goes on within himself. His utterances, even when
addressed to other persons, take on, increasingly, the character
of a monologue and become less and less part of the dramatic
dialogue, although Lear (which is typical) never speaks an
actual monologue himself. . . . The characters around Lear,
too, the Fool, Edgar and Kent, speak a language rich in
imagery. If we glance, however, at the other group of characters,
Edmund, Goneril, Regan, Cornwall, we note how seldom they
employ images, how different is their whole language. In contrast to Lear and his followers, we never find that peculiar

form of 'monologic dialogue' between them. They speak rationally; they address their words to their partner, and converse in a deliberate and conscious manner. They have a goal which they seek to attain, and everything they have to say is bent upon this. Their language does not betray to us what is taking place within them—in the form of 'imaginative visions'; it reveals to us solely their aims and attitudes, and how they intend to put these into practice. Thus their language scarcely changes throughout the course of the play, whereas Lear's, Edgar's and Kent's way of speaking is constantly varied. Goneril, Regan and Edmund are the calculating, cool and unimaginative people who are incapable of 'creative' imagery. They have no relationship to nature, to the elemental powers. Their world is the world of reason; they live and speak within the narrow limits of their plans, within the limits drawn by the plot and the given moment of the action. Lear's language continually points beyond these limits. Thus the distribution of the images among the characters also gives us a hint as to their position within the play.

The middle acts of the tragedy, Acts II.–IV., are the richest in imagery. The outer action is less important here and is relegated to the background. The main emphasis does not fall upon the outer course of events, upon what Regan or Goneril are planning, or what Edmund is about, but rather upon what is passing in Lear himself. The outer drama has become an inner drama. Beneath the surface of the plot lies the deeper level of inner experience which gradually frees itself more and more from the sparse events of the action. The latter becomes a frame and an occasion in order that the former may take on living reality. . . . It is obvious that imagery is the only adequate form of expression for such an inner process. . . .

. . . The non-human nature-world enters into the play in the same measure as the human world breaks down and falls to pieces. This occurs when the father is expelled by his daughters, when the son is persecuted by the father, and madness dissolves human order; the firm bonds and laws of human society are destroyed; so now non-human powers, heavenly forces, lightning, thunder, rain and wind, animals and plants, enter in rich variety. This interrelationship is to be seen clearly in the structure of the play; the first act contains relatively little nature-imagery; in the second act it begins to grow, and it attains to its height in the third and fourth acts, which show us the forsaken Lear in his madness.

W. H. CLEMEN, *The Development of Shakespeare's Imagery*
(translated from German), 1951

Animal Imagery

THIS mode of thought is responsible, lastly, for a very striking characteristic of *King Lear*—one in which it has no parallel except *Timon*—the incessant references to the lower animals and man's likeness to them. These references are scattered broadcast through the whole play, as though Shakespeare's mind were so busy with the subject that he could hardly write a page without some allusion to it. The dog, the horse, the cow, the sheep, the hog, the lion, the bear, the wolf, the fox, the monkey, the pole-cat, the civet-cat, the pelican, the owl, the crow, the chough, the wren, the fly, the butterfly, the rat, the mouse, the frog, the tadpole, the wall-newt, the water-newt, the worm—I am sure I cannot have completed the list, and some of them are mentioned again and again. Often, of course, and especially in the talk of Edgar as the Bedlam, they have no symbolical meaning; but not seldom, even in his talk, they are expressly referred to for their typical qualities—'hog in sloth, fox in stealth, wolf in greediness, dog in madness, lion in prey,' 'The fitchew nor the soiled horse goes to 't With a more riotous appetite.' Sometimes a person in the drama is compared, openly or implicitly, with one of them. Goneril is a kite: her ingratitude has a serpent's tooth: she has struck her father most serpent-like upon the very heart: her visage is wolvish: she has tied sharp-toothed unkindness like a vulture on her father's breast: for her husband she is a gilded serpent: to Gloster her cruelty seems to have the fangs of a boar. She and Regan are dog-hearted: they are tigers, not daughters: each is an adder to the other: the flesh of each is covered with the fell of a beast. Oswald is a mongrel, and the son and heir of a mongrel: ducking to everyone in power, he is a wag-tail: white with fear, he is a goose. Gloster, for Regan, is an ingrateful fox: Albany, for his wife, has a cowish spirit and is milk-liver'd: when Edgar as the Bedlam first appeared to Lear he made him think a man a worm. As we read, the souls of all the beasts in turn seem to us to have entered the bodies of these mortals; horrible in their venom, savagery, lust, deceitfulness, sloth, cruelty, filthiness; miserable in their feebleness, nakedness, defencelessness, blindness; and man, 'consider him well,' is even what they are.

BRADLEY, op. cit.

The Scenery

THE play gives an impression of towns and villages and castles, on which the barren moor and the wild marshland are ever ready to encroach. Outside the walls lies the realm of brutishness, of animals and roots, of standing pools and naked madmen. Certain of the characters become exiles from comfort, from decent living, from politeness. Lear, in the wind and the rain and the thunder, and in the hovel is such an exile. So is Edgar in the rags of Tom o' Bedlam. So are the fool and afterwards the blind Gloucester. The beastly life is very close, near neighbour to civilised man; and man has not much to do to resume the life of the beast. . . . Brutish nature is made actual for us in the frequent mention of animals, especially those who prey upon each other. And disorder in humanity is symbolized in rank and wayward weeds which seem ever to encroach on the cultivated field.

A SEWELL, *Character and Society in Shakespeare*, 1951

Word Patterns

On 'Pray you, undo this button. Thank you, sir' (V, iii. 309)

THESE unobtrusive words extend imaginatively way beyond the bare physiological fact which at the realistic level they denote: they are a means of pulling together a whole series of lines into an embracing system of meaning. Lear makes his last royal command a very mild one, yet it takes us into the heart of the tragedy. For his words take us back to the *divest* of Act I—

when he was preparing casually for retirement, for ease before the final sleep; to the frantic *unbutton here* of Act III when he was attempting to make physical fact conform to the spiritual unprotectedness which he had brought about by his earlier disrobing; and to the *pull off my boots* of Act IV when the fiercest travel in the hard world was over; and they tell us of a final freeing from clothes that can be followed by no new agony. Lear gives up prerogative and protection, throws away clothes which have no meaning, prepares to rest after a long struggle, and finally, a consequence of all that has gone before, gives up life. The king's only safe divestment is death.

HEILMAN, op. cit.

The Reconciliation Scene

FOR the length of this scene, then, Shakespeare has succeeded in balancing the suffering of the characters of the play with an adequate harmony fulfilled in terms of external symbolism through Cordelia's prayer for 'benediction' and Lear's corresponding confession of guilt:

> I know you do not love me; for your sisters
> Have, as I do remember, done me wrong:
> You have some cause, they have not.

This is the central moment of reconciliation, full of significance for an understanding, not only of *King Lear*, but of the whole pattern of Shakespeare's last plays. The restoration of the original relationship of child to father is the resolution of the ruin originally caused by 'blood' in the unity of the family. Two features of this development are especially worthy of note. In the first place Lear, whilst still remembering his past experiences, looks back to them, as it were, across a great gap of intervening time, sees them as belonging to another world; in the second, his new state is explicitly described in terms of a spiritual rebirth. 'Thou art a soul in bliss': 'You are a spirit, I know': such phrases, added to the sense of a break in temporal continuity—

> it is danger
> To make him e'en go o'er the time he has lost—

have a double effect. They at once stress the spiritual meaning of Lear's new state by placing it outside the normal temporal process and show that it is not of this world, that in this world, indeed, it may even be cruelly interrupted. The achievement of a state which is that of 'souls in bliss' does not necessarily involve the end of exposure to suffering. If the spiritual life of Lear and his daughters is situated, from now onwards, on a level that is not that of the political action, the passions which move that action still have to work themselves out, and even annihilate the main protagonists in the last part of the tragedy. It is no accident that this scene of achieved reconciliation, towards which every incident and development since the end of the tempest has tended as its natural consummation, ends with a doubtful and sinister reference to the coming 'arbitrament' of battle with which Kent, as the loyal follower of accepted royalty, is mainly concerned.

> My point and period will be thoroughly wrought,
> Or well or ill, as this day's battle's fought.

The political action has issues of its own, spiritually relevant, which are still undecided and which the remaining action of the play will be largely concerned to resolve; the resolution may well be, as proves the case, contrary to that which we have traced to its consummation in the sphere of personal relations.

TRAVERSI, op. cit.

Final Interpretation of the Play

Pessimism

BUT in one main point it differs radically from the work and the spirit of Aeschylus. Its fatalism is of a darker and harder nature. To Prometheus the fetters of the lord and enemy of mankind were bitter; upon Orestes the hand of heaven was laid too heavily to bear; yet in the not utterly infinite or everlasting distance we see beyond them the promise of the morning on which mystery and justice shall be made one; when righteousness and omnipotence at last shall kiss each other. But on the horizon of Shakespeare's tragic fatalism we see no such twilight of atonement, such pledge of reconciliation as this. Requital, redemption, amends, equity, explanation, pity and mercy, are words without a meaning here.

> As flies to wanton boys are we to the gods;
> They kill us for their sport.

Here is no need of the Eumenides, children of Night everlasting; for here is very Night herself.

The words just cited are not casual or episodical; they strike the keynote of the whole poem, lay the keystone of the whole arch of thought. There is no contest of conflicting forces, no judgement so much as by casting of lots: far less is there any light of heavenly harmony or of heavenly wisdom, of Apollo or Athene from above. We have heard much and often from theologians of the light of revelation: and some such thing indeed we find in Aeschylus; but the darkness of revelation is here.

SWINBURNE, A Study of Shakespeare, 1880

THE playwright of *King Leir*, adhering to the letter of his text, left Cordelia happy with her father at the drama's ending. We shall never know what moved Shakespeare to drop that pall of darkness upon the mystery of inscrutable woe at the very moment when there dawned a brighter day for Lear united to his blameless daughter. For once, it would appear, he chose to sound the deepest depths of the world's suffering, a depth deeper than that of Aeschylean or Sophoclean tragedy, deeper than the tragedy of Othello . . ., a stony black despairing depth of voiceless and inexplicable agony.

J. A. SYMONDS, Shakespeare's Predecessors in the
English Drama, 1883

Optimism

BUT there is another aspect of Lear's story, the influence of which modifies, in a way quite different and more peculiar to this tragedy, the impressions called pessimistic, and even this impression of law. There is nothing more noble and beautiful in literature than Shakespeare's exposition of the effect of suffering in reviving the greatness and eliciting the sweetness of

Lear's nature. The occasional recurrence, during his madness, of autocratic impatience or of desire for revenge serves only to heighten this effect, and the moments when his insanity becomes merely infinitely piteous do not weaken it. The old King who in pleading with his daughters feels so intensely his own humiliation and their horrible ingratitude, and who yet, at fourscore and upward, constrains himself to practise a self-control and patience so many years disused; who out of old affection for his Fool, and in repentance for his injustice to the Fool's beloved mistress, tolerates incessant and cutting reminders of his own folly and wrong; in whom the rage of the storm awakes a power and a poetic grandeur surpassing even that of Othello's anguish; who comes in his affliction to think of others first, and to seek, in tender solicitude for his poor boy, the shelter he scorns for his own bare head; who learns to feel and to pray for the miserable and houseless poor, to discern the falseness of flattery and the brutality of authority, and to pierce below the differences of rank and raiment to the common humanity beneath; whose sight is so purged by scalding tears that it sees at last how power and place and all things in the world are vanity except love; who tastes in his last hours the extremes both of love's rapture and of its agony, but could never, if he lived on or lived again, care a jot for aught beside—there is no figure, surely, in the world of poetry at once so grand, so pathetic, and so beautiful as his. Well, but Lear owes the whole of this to those sufferings which made us doubt whether life were not simply evil, and men like the flies which wanton boys torture for their sport. Should we not be at least as near the truth if we called this poem *The Redemption of King Lear*, and declared that the business of 'the gods' with him was neither to torment him, nor to teach him a 'noble anger', but to lead him to attain through apparently hopeless failure the very end and aim of life? One can believe that Shakespeare had been tempted at times to feel misanthropy and despair, but it is quite impossible that he can have been mastered by such feelings at the time when he produced this conception. . . .

What then is this feeling, and whence does it come? I believe we shall find that it is a feeling not confined to *King Lear*, but present at the close of other tragedies; and that the reason why it has an exceptional tone or force at the close of *King Lear*, lies in that very peculiarity of the close which also—at least for the moment—excites bewilderment, dismay, or protest. The feeling I mean is the impression that the heroic being, though in one sense and outwardly he has failed, is yet in another sense superior to the world in which he appears; is, in some way which we do not seek to define, untouched by the doom that overtakes him; and is rather set free from life than deprived of it. Some such feeling as this—some feeling which, from this description of it, may be recognised as their own even by those who would dissent from the description—we surely have in various degrees at the deaths of Hamlet and Othello and Lear, and of Antony and Cleopatra and Coriolanus. It accompanies the more prominent tragic impressions, and, regarded alone, could hardly be called tragic. For it seems to imply (though we are probably quite unconscious of the implication) an idea which, if developed, would transform the tragic view of things. It implies that the tragic world, if taken as it is presented, with all its error, guilt, failure, woe and waste, is no final reality, but only a part of reality taken for the whole, and, when so taken, illusive; and that if we could see the whole, and the tragic facts in their true place in it, we should find them, not abolished, of course, but so transmuted that they had ceased to be strictly tragic,—find, perhaps, the suffering and death counting for little or nothing, the greatness of the soul for much or all, and the heroic spirit, in spite of failure, nearer to the heart of things than the smaller, more circumspect, and perhaps even 'better' beings who survived the catastrophe. The feeling which I have tried to describe, as accompanying the more obvious tragic emotions at the deaths of heroes, corresponds with some such idea as this.   BRADLEY, op. cit.

SHAKSPERE opposes the presence and the influence of evil not by any transcendental denial of evil, but by the presence of human virtue, fidelity, and self-sacrificial love.

DOWDEN, op. cit.

PESSIMISM is sometimes regarded as a tough and realistic attitude. Shakespeare's *total* view of human life in the play has a toughness and actuality that makes most pessimism look like sentimentality. . . .

L. C. KNIGHTS in the *Pelican Guide to English Literature*,
vol. 2, 1955

SHAKESPEARE found the story of Lear buried deep in popular legend, but a folk-story is not necessarily a fairy-tale. A folk-story may be fabulous, but it need not be confined to fantasy. A fairy-story will also have its human side, but it generally points a moral and suggests a Utopia. There is of course, a profound teaching in *Lear*, but it is the teaching of a terrible experience. More simply and exactly, it is the teaching of the Cross. Nor does it deny Utopia. But Utopia is not preached by a garrulous *raisonneur*, like old Gonzalo in *The Tempest*; it is not round the corner; it is only the tremulous articulation of a desperate and persisting hope. . . . *Lear* is not Shakespeare's last word, but it is the overture to his last act.

R. SPEAIGHT, *Nature and Shakespearean Tragedy*, 1955

As we draw near to the awful close of *King Lear* or of *Othello*, and feel the fibres of our being almost torn asunder, the comfort that comes to us when quiet falls on the desolate scene is the comfort of the sure knowledge that Shakespeare is with us; that he who saw these things felt them as we do, and found in the splendours of courage and love a remedy for despair.

RALEIGH, *Shakespeare*, 1901

APPENDIX I

THE SOURCES OF *KING LEAR*

(cf. Introduction, pp. 14–18)

A. HOLINSHED: *The Historie of Britain*, Book II, Ch. 5 (2nd edition, 1587)

Leir the sonne of Baldud was admitted ruler over the Britaines in the yeare of the world 3105, at what time Joas reigned in Juda. This Leir was a prince of right noble demeanor, governing his land and subiects in great wealth. He made the towne of Caerleir now called Leicester, which standeth upon the river of Sore. It is written that he had by his wife three daughters without other issue, whose names were Gonorilla, Regan, and Cordeilla, which daughters he greatly loved, but specially Cordeilla the yoongest farre above the two elder. When this Leir therefore was come to great yeres, and began to waxe unweldie through age, he thought to understand the affections of his daughters towards him, and preferre hir whome he best loved, to the succession over the kingdome. Wherupon he first asked Gonorilla the eldest, how well she loved him: who calling hir gods to record, protested that she loved him more than hir owne life, which by right and reason should be most deere unto hir. With which answer the father being well pleased, turned to the second, and demanded of hir how well she loved him: who answered (confirming hir saiengs with great othes) that she loved him more than toong could expresse, and farre above all other creatures of the world.

Then called he his yoongest daughter Cordeilla before him, and asked of hir what account she made of him, unto whome she made this answer as followeth: 'Knowing the great love and fatherlie zeale that you have alwaies borne towards me (for the which I maie not answere you otherwise than I thinke, and as my conscience leadeth me) I protest unto you, that I have loved you ever, and shall continuallie (while I live) love you as my naturall father. And if you would more understand of the love that I beare you, assertaine your selfe, that so much as you have, so much you are worth, and so much I love you, and no more.' The father being nothing content with this answere, married his two eldest daughters, the one unto Henninus the duke of Cornewall, and the other unto Maglanus the duke of Albania, betwixt whome he willed and ordeined that his land should be devided after his death, and the one halfe thereof immediatelie should be assigned to them in hand: but for the third daughter Cordeilla he reserved nothing.

Nevertheless it fortuned that one of the princes of Gallia (which now is called France) whose name was Aganippus, hearing of the beautie, womanhood, and good conditions of the said Cordeilla, desired to have hir in mariage, and sent over to hir father, requiring that he might have hir to wife: to whome answer was made, that he might have his daughter, but as for anie dower he could have none, for all was promised and assured to hir other sisters already. Aganippus notwithstanding this answer of deniall to receive anie thing by way of dower with Cordeilla, tooke hir to wife, onlie moved thereto (I saie) for respect of hir person and amiable vertues. This Aganippus was one of the twelve kings that ruled Gallia in those daies, as in the British historie it is recorded. But to proceed.

After that Leir was fallen into age, the two dukes that had married his two eldest daughters, thinking it long yer the government of the land did come to their hands, arose against him in armour, and reft from him the governance of the land, upon conditions to be continued for terme of life: by the which he was put to his portion, that is, to live after a rate assigned to him for the maintenance of his estate, which in processe of time was diminished as well by Maglanus as by Henninus. But the greatest griefe that Leir tooke, was to see the unkindnesse of his daughters, which seemed to thinke that all was too much which their father had, the same being never so little: in so muche that going from the one to the other, he was brought to that miserie, that scarslie they would allow him one servaunt to wait upon him.

In the end, such was the unkindnesse, or (as I maie saie) the unnaturalnesse which he found in his two daughters, notwithstanding their faire and pleasant words uttered in time past, that being constreined of necessitie, he fled the land, & sailed into Gallia, there to seeke some comfort of his yongest daughter Cordeilla, whom before time he hated. The ladie Cordeilla hearing that he was arrived in poore estate, she first sent to him privilie a certeine summe of monie to apparell himselfe withall, and to reteine a certeine number of servants that might attend upon him in honorable wise, as apperteined to the estate which he had borne: and then so accompanied, she appointed him to come to the court, which he did, and was so ioifullie, honorablie, and lovinglie received, both by his sonne in law Aganippus, and also by his daughter Cordeilla, that his hart was greatlie comforted: for he was no lesse honored, than if he had beene king of the whole countrie himselfe.

Now when he had informed his sonne in law and his daughter in what sort he had beene used by his other daughters, Aganippus caused a mightie armie to be put in a readinesse, and likewise a great navie of ships to be rigged, to passe over into Britaine with Leir his father in law, to see him againe restored to his kingdome. It was accorded, that Cordeilla should also go with him to take possession of the land, the which he promised to leave unto hir, as the rightfull inheritour after his decesse, notwithstanding any former grant made to hir sisters or to their husbands in anie maner of wise.

Hereupon, when this armie and navie of ships were readie, Leir and his daughter Cordeilla with hir husband tooke the sea, and arriving in Britaine, fought with their enimies, and discomfited them in battell, in the which Maglanus and Henninus were slaine: and then was Leir restored to his kingdome, which he ruled after this by the space of two yeeres, and then died, fortie yeeres after he first began to reigne. His bodie was buried at Leicester in a vaut under the chanell of the river of Sore beneath the towne.

The Sixt Chapter.—Cordeilla the yoongest daughter of Leir was admitted Q. and supreme governesse of Britaine in the yeere of the world 3155, before the bylding of Rome 54; Uzia was then reigning in Juda, and Jeroboam over Israell. This Cordeilla after hir fathers deceasse ruled the land of Britaine right worthilie during the space of five yeeres, in which meane time hir husband died, and then about the end of those five yeeres, hir two nephewes Margan and Cunedag, sonnes to hir aforesaid sisters, disdaining to be under the government of a woman, levied warre against hir, and destroied a great part of the land, and finallie tooke hir prisoner, and laid hir fast in ward, wherewith she tooke suche griefe, being a woman of a manlie courage, and despairing to recover libertie, there she slue hirselfe, when she had reigned (as before is mentioned) the tearme of five yeeres.

B. SIDNEY: *Arcadia*, Book II, Ch. 10 (1590)

IT was in the kingdome of *Galacia*, the season being (as in the depth of winter) very cold, and as then sodainely growne to so extreame and foule a storme, that never any winter (I thinke) brought foorth a fowler child: so that the Princes were even compelled by the haile, that the pride of the winde blew into their faces, to seeke some shrowding place within a certaine hollow rocke offering it unto them, they made it their shield against the tempests furie. And so staying there, till the violence therof was passed, they heard the speach of a couple, who not perceiving them (being hidde within that rude canapy) helde a straunge and pitifull disputation which made them steppe out; yet in such sort, as they might see unseene. There they perceaued an aged man, and a young, scarcely come to the age of a man, both poorely arayed, extreamely weather-beaten; the olde man blinde, the young man leading him: and yet through all those miseries, in both these seemed to appeare a kind of noblenesse, not sutable to that affliction. But the first words they heard, were these of the old man. Well *Leonatus* (said he) since I cannot perswade thee to lead me to that which should end my griefe, & thy trouble, let me now entreat thee to leaue me: feare not, my miserie cannot be greater then it is, & nothing doth become me but miserie; feare not the danger of my blind steps, I cannot fall worse then I am. And doo not I pray thee, doo not obstinately continue to infect thee with my wretchednes. But flie, flie from this region, onely worthy of me. Deare father (answered he) doo not take away from me the onely remnant of my happinesse: while I have power to doo you service, I am not wholly miserable. Ah my sonne (said he, and with that he groned, as if sorrow strave to breake his hearte)

how evill fits it me to have such a sonne, and how much doth
thy kindnesse upbraide my wickednesse? These dolefull
speeches, and some others to like purpose (well shewing they had
not bene borne to the fortune they were in,) moved the Princes
to goe out unto them, and aske the younger what they were?
Sirs (answered he, with a good grace, and made the more agre-
able by a certaine noble kinde of pitiousnes) I see well you are
straungers, that know not our miserie so well here knowne, that
no man dare know, but that we must be miserable. In deede
our state is such, as though nothing is so needfull unto us as
pittie, yet nothing is more daungerous unto us, then to make our
selves so knowne as may stirre pittie. But your presence
promiseth, that cruelty shall not over-runne hate. And if it
did, in truth our state is soncke below the degree of feare.

This old man (whom I leade) was lately rightfull Prince of this
countrie of *Paphlagonia*, by the hard-hearted ungratefulnes of a
sonne of his, deprived, not onely of his kingdome (wherof no
forraine forces were ever able to spoyle him) but of his sight,
the riches which Nature graunts to the poorest creatures.
Whereby, & by other his unnaturall dealings, he hath bin driven
to such griefe, as even now he would have had me to have led
him to the toppe of this rocke, thence to cast himselfe headlong
to death: and so would have made me (who received my life of
him) to be the worker of his destruction. But noble Gentlemen (said he) if either of you have a father, and feele what
duetifull affection is engraffed in a sonnes hart, let me intreate
you to convey this afflicted Prince to some place of rest &
securitie. Amongst your worthie actes it shall be none of the
least, that a King, of such might and fame, and so uniustly
oppressed, is in any sort by you relieved.

But before they could make him answere, his father began to
speake. Ah my sonne (said he) how evill an Historian are you,
that leave out the chiefe knotte of all the discourse? my
wickednes, my wickednes. And if thou doest it to spare my
eares, (the onely sense nowe left me proper for knowledge) assure
thy selfe thou dost mistake me. And I take witnesse of that
Sunne which you see (with that he cast up his blinde eyes, as if
he would hunt for light,) and wish my selfe in worse case then
I do wish my selfe, which is as evill as may be, if I speake

untruly; that nothing is so welcome to my thoughts, as the publishing of my shame. Therefore know you Gentlemen (to whom from my harte I wish that it may not prove ominous foretoken of misfortune to have mette with such a miser as I am) that whatsoever my sonne (ô God, that trueth binds me to reproch him with the name of my sonne) hath said, is true. But besides those truthes, this also is true, that having had in lawful mariage, of a mother fitte to beare royall children, this sonne (such one as partly you see, and better shall knowe by my shorte declaration) and so enioyed the expectations in the world of him, till he was growen to iustifie their expectations (so as I needed envie no father for the chief comfort of mortalitie, to leave an other ones-selfe after me) I was caried by a bastarde sonne of mine (if at least I be bounde to beleeve the words of that base woman my concubine, his mother) first to mislike, then to hate, lastly to destroy, to doo my best to destroy, this sonne (I thinke you thinke) undeserving destruction. What waies he used to bring me to it, if I should tell you, I should tediously trouble you with as much poysonous hypocrisie, desperate fraude, smoothe malice, hidden ambition, & smiling envie, as in anie living person could be harbored. But I list it not, no remembrance, (no, of naughtines) delights me, but mine own; & me thinks, the accusing his traines might in some manner excuse my fault, which certainly I loth to doo. But the conclusion is, that I gave order to some servants of mine, whom I thought as apte for such charities as my selfe, to leade him out into a forrest, & there to kill him.

But those theeves (better natured to my sonne then my selfe) spared his life, letting him goe, to learne to live poorely: which he did, giving himselfe to be a private souldier, in a countrie here by. But as he was redy to be greatly advanced for some noble peeces of service which he did, he hearde newes of me: who (dronke in my affection to that unlawfull and un-naturall sonne of mine) suffered my self so to be governed by him, that all favours and punishments passed by him, all offices, and places of importance, distributed to his favorites; so that ere I was aware, I had left my self nothing but the name of a King: which he shortly wearie of too, with many indignities (if any thing may be called an indignity, which was laid upon me) threw me out of my seat, and put out my eies; and then (proud in his tyrannie) let me goe, nether imprisoning, nor killing me: but rather delighting to make me feele my miserie; miserie indeed, if ever there were any; full of wretchednes, fuller of disgrace, and fullest of guiltines. And as he came to the crowne by so uniust meanes, as uniustlie he kept it, by force of stranger souldiers in *Cittadels*, the nestes of tyranny, & murderers of libertie; disarming all his own countrimen, that no man durst shew himself a wel-willer of mine: to say the trueth (I think) few of them being so (considering my cruell follie to my good sonne, and foolish kindnes to my unkinde bastard:) but if there were any who fell to pitie of so great a fall, and had yet any sparkes of unstained duety lefte in them towardes me, yet durst they not shewe it, scarcely with giving me almes at their doores; which yet was the onelie sustenance of my distressed life, no bodie daring to shewe so much charitie, as to lende me a hande to guide my darke steppes: Till this sonne of mine (God knowes, woorthie of a more vertuous, and more fortunate father) forgetting my abhominable wrongs, not recking daunger, & neglecting the present good way he was in doing himselfe good, came hether to doo this kind office you see him performe towards me, to my unspeakable griefe; not onely because his kindnes is a glasse even to my blind eyes, of my naughtines, but that above all griefes, it greeves me he should desperately adventure the losse of his soul-deserving life for mine, that yet owe more to fortune for my deserts, as if he would cary mudde in a chest of christall. For well I know, he that now raigneth, how much soever (and with good reason) he despiseth me, of all men despised; yet he will not let slippe any advantage to make away him, whose iust title (ennobled by courage and goodnes) may one day shake the seate of a never secure tyrannie. And for this cause I craved of him to leade me to the toppe of this rocke, indeede I must confesse, with meaning to free him from so serpentine a companion as I am. But he finding what I purposed, onely therein since he was borne, shewed himselfe disobedient unto me. And now Gentlemen, you have the true storie, which I pray you publish to the world, that my mischievous proceedings may be the glorie of his filiall pietie, the onely reward now left for so great a merite.

And if it may be, let me obtaine that of you, which my sonne
denies me: for never was there more pity in saving any, then in
ending me; both because therein my agonies shall ende, and so
shall you preserve this excellent young man, who els wilfully
folowes his owne ruine.

C. Extracts from *King Leir and his Three Daughters* (1605)

Enter GONORILL *and* SKALLIGER

Gonorill. I prithy, Skalliger, tell me what thou thinkst:
Could any woman of our dignity
Endure such quips and peremptory taunts,
As I do daily from my doting father?
Doth't not suffice that I him keepe of almes,
Who is not able for to keepe himselfe?
But as if he were our better, he should thinke
To check and snap me up at every word.
I cannot make me a new fashioned gowne,
And set it forth with more then common cost;
But his old doting doltish withered wit,
Is sure to give a sencelesse check for it.
I cannot make a banquet extraordinary,
To grace myselfe, and spread my name abroad,
But he, old foole, is captious by and by
And faith, the cost would well suffice for twice.
Judge then, I pray, what reason is't, that I
Should stand alone charg'd with his vaine expence,
And that my sister Ragan should go free,
To whome he gave as much, as unto me?
I prithy, Skalliger, tell me, if thou know,
By any meanes to rid me of this woe.
Skalliger. Your many favours still bestowde on me,
Binde me in duty to advise your grace,
How you may soonest remedy this ill.
The large allowance which he hath from you,
Is that which makes him so forget himselfe:
Therefore abbridge it halfe, and you shall see,
That having lesse, he will more thankful be:
For why, abundance maketh us forget

The fountaines whence the benefits do spring.

Gonorill. Well, Skalliger, for thy kind advice herein,
I will not be ungrateful, if I live:
I have restrained halfe his portion already,
And I will presently restraine the other,
That having no meanes to releeve himselfe,
He may go seeke elsewhere for better helpe.   [*Exit.*

Skalliger. Go, viperous woman, shame to all thy sexe:
The heavens, no doubt, will punish thee for this:
And me a villaine, that to curry favour,
Have given the daughter consel 'gainst the father.
But us the world doth this experience give,
That he that cannot flatter, cannot live.   [*Exit.*

Enter the Gallian king and queene, and MUMFORD *with a basket,
disguised like countrey folke.*

King. This tedious journey all on foot, sweet love,
Cannot be pleasing to your tender joints,
Which ne're were used to these toilesome walks.

Cordella. I never in my life tooke more delight
In any journey, then I do in this:
It did me good, when as we hapt to light
Amongst the merry crue of country folke,
To see what industry and paines they tooke,
To win them commendations 'mongst their friends.
Lord, how they labour to bestir themselves,
And in their quirks to go beyond the moone,
And so take on them with such antike fits,
That one would think they were beside their wits!
Come away, Roger, with your basket.

Mumford. Soft, dame, here comes a couple of old youthes,
I must needs make myselfe fat with jesting at them.

Enter LEIR *and* PERILLUS *very faintly.*

Cordella. Nay, prithy do not, they do seeme to be
Men much o'regone with griefe and misery.
Let's stand aside, and harken what they say.

Leir. Ah, my Perillus, now I see we both

Shall end our dayes in this unfruitful soile,
Oh, I do faint for want of sustenance:
And thou, I know, in little better case.
No gentle tree affords one taste of fruit,
To comfort us, until we meet with men:
No lucky path conducts our lucklesse steps
Unto a place where any comfort dwels.
Sweet rest betide unto our happy soules;
For here I see our bodies must have end.

Perillus. Ah, my deare lord, how doth my heart lament,
To see you brought to this extremity!
O, if you love me, as you do professe,
Or ever thought well of me in my life: [*He strips up his arme.*
Feed on this flesh, whose veines are not so dry,
But there is vertue left to comfort you.
O, feed on this, if this will do you good,
Ile smile for joy, to see you suck my bloud.

Leir. I am no Caniball, that I should delight
To slake my hungry jawes with humane flesh:
I am no devil, or ten times worse then so,
To suck the bloud of such a peerelesse friend.
O, do not think that I respect my life
So dearely, as I do thy loyal love.
Ah, Brittayne, I shall never see thee more,
That hast unkindly banished thy king:
And yet not thou dost make me to complaine,
But they which were more neere to me then thou.

Cordella. What do I heare? this lamentable voice,
Me thinks, ere now I oftentimes have heard.

Leir. Ah, Gonorill, was halfe my kingdome's gift
The cause that thou didst seeke to have my life
Ah, cruel Ragan, did I give thee all,
And all could not suffice without my bloud?

Ah, poore Cordella, did I give thee nought,
Nor never shall be able for to give?
O, let me warne all ages that insueth,
How they trust flattery, and reject the trueth.
Well, unkind girles, I here forgive you both,
Yet the just heavens will hardly do the like;

And onely crave forgivenesse at the end
Of good Cordella, and of thee, my friend;
Of God, whose majesty I have offended,
By my transgression many thousand wayes:
Of her, deare heart, whom I for no occasion
Turn'd out of all, through flatterers perswasion:
Of thee, kind friend, who but for me, I know,
Hadst never come unto this place of wo.

Cordella. Alack, that ever I should live to see
My noble father in this misery.

King. Sweet love, reveale not what thou art as yet,
Until we know the ground of all this ill.

Cordella. O, but some meat, some meat: do you not see,
How neere they are to death for want of food?

Perillus. Lord, which didst help they servants at their need,
Or now or never send us helpe with speed.
Oh, comfort, comfort! Yonder is a banquet,
And men and women, my lord: be of good cheare:
For I see comfort comming very neere,
O my lord, a banquet and men and women!

Leir. O, let kind pity mollify their hearts,
That they may helpe us in our great extreames.

Perillus. God, save you, friends; and if this blessed banquet
Affordeth any food or sustenance,
Even for his sake that saved us all from death,
Vouchsafe to save us from the gripe of famine.

> [*She bringeth him to the table.*

Cordella. Here, father, sit and eat; here sit and drink
And would it were far better for your sakes!

> [PERILLUS *takes* LEIR *by the hand to the table.*

Perillus. Ile give you thanks anon: my friend doth faint,
And needeth present comfort.   [LEIR *drinks.*

Mumford. I warrant, he ne're stayes to say a grace:
O, there's no sauce to a good stomake.

Perillus. The blessed God of heaven hath thought upon us.

Leir. The thanks be his, and these kind courteous folke,
By whose humanity we are preserved.

> [*They eat hungerly;* LEIR *drinks.*

Cordella. And may that draught be unto him, as was

That which old Eson dranke, which did renue
His withered age, and made him young againe.
And may that meat be unto him, as was
That which Elias ate, in strength whereof
He walked fourty dayes, and never fainted.
Shall I conceale me longer from my father?
Or shall I manifest myselfe to him?

King. Forbeare a while, until his strength returne,
Lest being over-joyed with seeing thee,
His poore weake sences should forsake their office,
And so our cause of joy be turn'd to sorrow.

Perillus. What chere, my lord? how do you feele yourselfe?

Leir. Me thinks, I never ate such savory meat:
It is as pleasant as the blessed manna,
That rain'd from heaven amongst the Israelites:
It hath recall'd my spirits home againe,
And made me fresh, as earst I was before.
But how shall we congratulate their kindnesse?

Perillus. In faith, I know not how sufficiently;
But the best meane that I can think on, is this:
Ile offer them my dublet in requital;
For we have nothing else to spare.

Leir. Nay, stay, Perillus, for they shall have mine.

Perillus. Pardon, my lord, I sweare they shall have mine.

[PERILLUS *proffers his dublet: they will not take it.*

Leir. Ah, who would think such kindnes should remaine
Among such strange and unacquainted men;
And that such hate should harbour in the brest
Of those, which have occasion to be best?

Cordella. Ah, good old father, tell to me thy griefe,
Ile sorrow with thee, if not adde reliefe.

Leir. Ah, good young daughter, I may call thee so;
For thou art like a daughter I did owe.

Cordella. Do you not owe her still? what, is she dead?

Leir. No, God forbid: but all my interest's gone,
By shewing my selfe too much unnatural:
So have I lost the title of a father,
And may be call'd a stranger to her rather.

Cordella. Your title's good still: for tis alwayes knowne,

A man may do as him list with his owne.
But have you but one daughter then in all?

  Leir. Yes, I have more by two, then would I had.

  Cordella. O, say not so, but rather see the end;
They that are bad, may have the grace to mend:
But how have they offended you so much?

  Leir. If from the first I should relate the cause,
'Twould make a heart of adamant to weepe;
And thou, poore soule, kind-hearted as thou art,
Dost weepe already, ere I do begin.

  Cordella. For Gods love tell it; and when you have done,
Ile tell the reason why I weepe so soone.

  Leir. Then know this first, I am a Brittaine borne,
And had three daughters by one loving wife:
And though I say it, of beauty they were sped;
Especially the youngest of the three,
For her perfections hardly matcht could be:
On these I doted with a jelous love,
And thought to try which of them lov'd me best,
By asking them, which would do most for me?
The first and second flattred me with words,
And vowd they lov'd me better then their lives:
The youngest said, she loved me as a child
Might do: her answere I esteem'd most vild,
And presently in an outragious mood,
I turnd her from me to go sinke or swim:
And all I had, even to the very clothes,
I gave in dowry with the other two:
And she that best deserv'd the greatest share,
I gave her nothing, but disgrace and care.
Now mark the sequel: when I had done thus,
I sojournd in my eldest daughters house,
Where for a time I was intreated well,
And liv'd in state sufficing my content:
But every day her kindnesse did grow cold,
Which I with patience put up well ynough,
And seemed not to see the things I saw:
But at the last she grew so far incenst
With moody fury, and with causelesse hate,

That in most vild and contumelious termes,
She bade me pack, and harbour somewhere else.
Then was I faine for refuge to repaire
Unto my other daughter for reliefe;
Who gave me pleasing and most courteous words;
But in her actions shewed her selfe so sore,
As never any daughter did before:
She prayd me in a morning out betime,
To go to a thicket two miles from the court,
Pointing that there she would come talke with me:
There she had set a shag haird murdring wretch,
To massacre my honest friend and me.
Then judge your selfe, although my tale be briefe,
If ever man had greater cause of griefe.

   King. Nor never like impiety was done,
Since the creation of the world begun.

   Leir. And now I am constrained to seeke reliefe
Of her, to whom I have bin so unkind;
Whose censure, if it do award me death,
I must confesse she payes me but my due:
But if she shew a loving daughters part,
It comes of God and her, not my desert.

   Cordella. No doubt she will, I dare be sworne she will.

   Leir. How know you that, not knowing what she is?

   Cordella. Myselfe a father have a great way hence,
Usde me as ill as ever you did her;
Yet, that his reverend age I once might see,
Ide creepe along, to meet him on my knee.

   Leir. O, no mens children are unkind but mine.

   Cordella. Condemne not all, because of others crime;
But looke, deare father, looke, behold and see
Thy loving daughter speaketh unto thee.   [*She kneeles.*

   Leir. O, stand thou up, it is my part to kneele,
And aske forgivenesse for my former faults.   [*He kneeles.*

   Cordella. O, if you wish I should injoy my breath,
Deare father rise, or I receive my death.   [*He riseth.*

   Leir. Then I will rise, to satisfy your mind,
But kneele againe, til pardon be resigned.   [*He kneeles.*

   Cordella. I pardon you: the word beseemes not me:

But I do say so, for to ease your knee;
You gave me life, you were the cause that I
Am what I am, who else had never bin.

Leir. But you gave life to me and to my friend,
Whose dayes had else had an untimely end.

Cordella. You brought me up, when as I was but young,
And far unable for to helpe myselfe.

Leir. I cast thee forth, when as thou wast but young,
And far unable for to helpe thyselfe.

Cordella. God, world, and nature, say I do you wrong,
That can indure to see you kneele so long.

King. Let me breake off this loving controversy,
Which doth rejoice my very soule to see.
Good father, rise, she is your loving daughter,   [*He riseth.*
And honours you with as respective duty,
As if you were the monarch of the world.

Cordella. But I will never rise from off my knee,   [*She kneeles.*
Until I have your blessing, and your pardon
Of all my faults committed any way,
From my first birth unto this present day.

Leir. The blessing, which the God of Abraham gave
Unto the tribe of Juda, light on thee,
And multiply thy dayes, that thou mayst see
Thy childrens children prosper after thee.
Thy faults, which are just none that I do know,
God pardon on high, and I forgive below.   [*She riseth.*

Cordella. Now is my heart at quiet, and doth leape
Within my brest, for joy of this good hap:
And now (deare father) welcome to our court,
And welcome (kind Perillus) unto me,
Mirrour of vertue and true honestly.

Leir. O, he hath bin the kindest friend to me,
That ever man had in adversity.

Perillus. My toung doth faile, to say what heart doth think,
I am so ravisht with exceeding joy.

King. All you have spoke: now let me speak my mind,
And in few words much matter here conclude: [*He kneeles.*
If ere my heart do harbour any joy,
Or true content repose within my brest,

Till I have rooted out this viperous sect,
And repossest my father of his crowne,
Let me be counted for the perjurdst man,
That ever spake word since the world began.   [*Rises.*

  Mumford. Let me pray to, that never pray'd before;
                           [*Mumford kneeles.*
If ere I resalute the Brittish earth,
(As (ere't be long) I do presume I shall)
And do returne from thence without my wench,
Let me be gelded for my recompence.   [*Rises.*

  King. Come, let's to armes for to redresse this wrong:
Till I am there, me thinks the time seemes long.   [*Exeunt.*

APPENDIX II

KING LEAR ON THE ELIZABETHAN STAGE

MOST students of *King Lear* will have studied previously other plays of Shakespeare, and will probably be acquainted to some degree with the nature of the Elizabethan theatre. It is therefore not proposed to repeat here such a short description as has been given in other volumes of the *New Clarendon Shakespeare*. Nor is *Lear* a play which young actors would be well advised to choose for presentation. Nevertheless, some readers may care to visualize the play in terms of the stage on which it was first acted rather than to see it in the theatre of the mind. An elaborate study of the staging of Lear appeared in *The J.Q. Adams Memorial Volume*, published in the U.S.A. in 1948. But, as the book is expensive and only accessible in the larger libraries in this country, a summary will be given here of the views of the author, Mr. J. C. Adams, on the probable staging of this play, based on the most recent knowledge of the Globe Theatre at which it was first produced (cf. W. C. Hodges, *The Globe Restored*, from which the drawing on p. 6 is taken).

The terms Platform, Study, and Chamber now replace what has usually been called Outer, Inner, and Upper, or Front, Rear, and Upper Stages (as in the older drawing of the Fortune Theatre reproduced in most volumes of this series). Of the twenty-six scenes in Lear six were played in the Chamber, two of them concerned with the two sons of Gloucester. The rest were played on one or other, or more often both, of the ground-floor spaces, often beginning on the Platform and finishing in the Study, so that the curtains of this could be drawn, leaving (for example), Kent in the Stocks there.

In Act I, scene i would use combined Platform and Study, the latter only for the last talk of the sisters. In scene ii the Chamber represents a room on the second floor of Gloucester's castle. Scene iii is the Study with a different set from scene i; scene iv Study and Platform, the last thirty-five lines being Study only; and scene v the Platform (out-of-doors).

In Act II, scene i is in the Chamber (and the 'descend' to Edgar is still valid as the Globe had three floors); scene ii on Study and Platform, representing the forecourt of Gloucester's castle and the parklands leading to it, scene iii on the Platform, and scene iv in the Study and Platform, till Cornwall's 'Let us withdraw' signifies the Study alone, and the curtains are drawn at the end ('Shut up your doors').

In Act III, scenes i and ii are Platform scenes, iii a night scene in the Chamber, iv a Platform scene (outdoors), v another Chamber scene, vi a Study scene, and vii a Study scene (the blinding).

Act IV opens on the Platform, moves to the Study for ii (which need not be placed out-of-doors, in spite of 'within' (l. 3)), back to the Platform for iii and iv, while v gives us the last Chamber scene, this time for Regan and Oswald instead of either of the brothers. In IV, vi, Gloucester imagines he falls off Dover cliff on the Platform, perhaps with the help of the 'moss(y) bank', a well-known moveable property, while Lear enters on the Study. The last scene of the act Mr. Adams would put on the Platform, abolishing the 'Tent' of editors' stage directions.

The final act passes entirely on the main stage, and in scene ii line i the tree would be one of the pillars supporting the roof over the platform (cf. illustration).